# D<sup>T H E</sup>REAMER'S

# DICTIONARY

## Translations in the Universal Language of Mind

by
### Barbara Condron
D.M., D.D., B.J.

SOM Publishing
Windyville, Missouri 65783

# The Dreamer's Dictionary

© December, 1994
by the School of Metaphysics No. 100151

Cover Design by Dave Lappin

ISBN: 0-944386-16-4

Library of Congress Catalogue Number pending

PRINTED IN THE UNITED STATES OF AMERICA

> If you desire to learn more about the research and teachings in this book, write to School of Metaphysics, National Headquarters, Windyville, Missouri 65783. Or call 417-345-8411.

# Contents

# *Foreword*

When I was about six years old, I remember I was in the basement of a house with my father. He was working in this unfinished, dank setting. This place was filled with cobwebs, a rather frightening place for a six year old, but I felt relatively secure and confident because my dad was there.

Dad was trying to fix some pipes, retrieving a wrench from a tool box. To a six year old it looked huge and somewhat ominous. He was striving to release a bolt, and I could tell he was having a hard time for it was very rusty. As he yanked the wrench toward his body, it hit him in the mouth causing him to bleed. I was very scared. I didn't know what he had done to himself.

I began to run all through the house looking for my mother. In searching for her I lost contact with Dad and where he was. I couldn't find my mother no matter where I went, so I went outside the front door of the house. I followed the sidewalk path to look down the street. It was totally quiet and still with the hush of midnight. No one was there.

I turned around, starting up the sidewalk to the house. As I did, Dad appeared in the doorway. In place of his head was a mole-like creature.

At that moment I awoke. I was crying and hyperventilating. I'd had the first nightmare that I could remember, in fact still do remember very vividly to this day. I ran to my parents' bedroom. As most children are aware, I knew which side of the bed my mother and father favored for sleeping. I knew which side to run to, because you didn't wake Dad up in the middle of the night with such matters. I ran to my mother, who immediately woke up, hugging and cradling her inconsolable daughter.

Her first question was "Honey are you okay? Are you sick?" I couldn't talk. I was so overwhelmed by emotion, reacting to this dream, that I was heaving and sobbing. All I could do was shake my head.

When she found out I wasn't sick, she asked, "Did you have a bad dream?" I started violently nodding my head so she would know this was what had occurred. She comforted me saying, "It's okay. It's over, it's all over. It was just a dream. It wasn't real, it's over." And I began to calm as she held me in her loving embrace. Verbalizing still escaped me, but I can remember screaming in my head, "But it was real. It *was* real!" She continued to reassure me in the way she knew how and soon I returned to my bed, and later fell asleep.

For many children, it is common to experience dreams that frighten them. It is also common for them to seek the advice and comfort of their parents, who often know as little about the phenomena of dreaming as they do. When left unexplained and misunderstood, these dreams become known as nightmares. For the innocent, uneducated mind the best way to cope becomes forgetting, following the youthful logic that if you cover your head with a blanket the bogeyman you fear will not see you.

Such was not to be the answer for me. I remembered this nightmare. This dream became a remembered stimulus to respond to a consistent inner urge to know; an urge toward understanding and enlightenment that did not fade with the passage of time but rather became more acutely motivating.

Throughout my life, I went through periods of seeking answers to the significance of dreams because as I aged I experienced more dreams. And I had more questions. I discovered that other people dream; this was not just a personal phenomenon. My parents and my friends also experienced these nighttime occurrences.

I remember learning about dreams in Christian Sunday School when we were studying the *Old Testament* of the Bible. If you are familiar with this Holy Work, you know there are stories in the *Old Testament* about a man named Joseph. Having been sold into slavery by his brothers, Joseph found himself a prisoner in Egypt. The way that he secured his release from the Pharaoh was to interpret the ruler's dreams. I was fascinated by that story. Here was a man who was not only interested in dreams, but who could also decipher their meaning!

The minister of our church was someone whom I absolutely adored. I loved and respected him a great deal. Upon learning about Joseph, the dream interpreter, I went to my minister for further guidance. In my childlike innocence I figured since he was a man of God, the head of our church, and very knowledgeable, he would surely have answers. If Joseph knew about dreams, then my minister must also know about dreams. I felt sure he would be my salvation for understanding the meaning of these nighttime experiences.

I asked him point blank, with the open honesty of childhood, "Can you interpret dreams?" He looked at me and smiled. I can even remember his face as he compassionately replied, "Barbara, I don't know how. I don't know what dreams mean."

Unwilling to accept this as an answer, I pleaded, "But Joseph does! It says so in the Bible! He knows what dreams mean, why don't you know what dreams mean?"

He was not affronted by my childlike demands. He had children of his own and worked with many others, and he understood the belief children often held that if one adult knew something, every adult should know it, and some should know even more. Gently he replied, "Barbara, I don't know how to explain it. I know that God gives certain people special abilities, and that was an ability he gave to Joseph." I could accept his answer at the time for I believed in God-given talents, but I still remembered my dreams and my questions were still waiting for answers.

As I grew older, the experiences and questions multiplied. The next time I can remember verbalizing those questions was when we studied the works of Shakespeare in high school. If you are familiar with Shakespeare you are aware that he uses a great deal of imagery, often referring to dreams. We were studying *Hamlet,* and my curiosity about dreams again reared its head.

I had an excellent teacher, Uriel Haw, whom I greatly admired. She was very well-read having spent her sixty plus years in literary education, and I thought she might know something about dreams. After class one day I stayed to talk with her and broached the question about the meaning of dreams. She told me she had never really been that concerned with dreams, but she recognized my sincerity and need to understand. Knowing I was going to college, she suggested that I take as many psychology courses as I could because she believed I might find my answers there.

I took her advice. Although my major area of concentration was in journalism, I took many hours of undergrad psychology courses. I learned a great deal of information centering upon how people respond and react to each other on a physical, conscious level to improve our lives. But I didn't find any instructor who interpreted dreams. I made it a point to pursue the subject with several of my instructors. I would ask what they knew about dreams, could they interpret dreams, did they know any good books on dreams that might offer me some guidance. Sometimes they would recommend books. I can remember reading many of them, becoming more and more frustrated.

By this time I had learned not only that I dream, but my parents dream, my friends dream, and even Biblical figures dreamed. All the people I knew, no matter what their age, where they were from, or what their background was, every one of them seemed to dream. I had read a great deal of literature from all over the world and I knew that it didn't matter what country you lived in, it didn't matter what physical language you spoke, it didn't matter what your educational level was, everyone experiences dreaming. In my independent research as well as in research gleaned through reading the works of others, I came to a conclusion shared by many great thinkers throughout history. *Dreams are universal.* My own idea had transcended the limits of personal experience and belief. It had entered the realm of Universal Truth which applies to anyone, at anytime, anywhere.

However in most of the books on dreams I was reading, the dream content didn't seem to matter. There appeared to be an ignoring of this universal flavor in the dream experience which I had already recognized as universally true. Most authors described dreams as individual experiences only, resulting in an attitude of "Whatever you think your dreams mean, that's what they mean! If you find your dreams personally relevant that's to your advantage." This did not assuage my curiosity for I knew there were universalities in the dream experience and I really wanted to understand their meaning.

I did find some insights in the works of Carl Jung, a Swiss psychiatrist who lived from 1875 to 1961. His research into the nature of man had led him to conceive concepts of man's duality. He surmised that there was a feminine expression in every male which he called the anima and a masculine expression in every female called the animus. These ideas, not readily applicable, would make more sense to me in my future research. His ideas of archetypes, symbols embodying universal qualities or characteristics, gave much more food for thought in producing the answers I had been seeking. Yet they did not seem readily connected with personal dream experience. I felt I had made some progress in finding my answers, but as often occurs the acquisition of answers birthed more queries.

I was very surprised when I, as a favor to a friend, came to a class at the School of Metaphysics in Columbia, Missouri. What impressed me the most the first evening and what kept me returning to class in the early weeks of my study, was the fact that about two hours into that first class my teacher, who was about a year or two older than I at the time, sat in front of the class and said, "I want to talk a little about dreams."

Immediately, she had my full and undivided attention. She began talking about dreams, the research conducted by the School of Metaphysics thus far, and what discoveries had been made concerning the meaning of dream experiences to our lives. Then she made a profoundly significant offer I had been waiting years to hear, "Do you have any dreams you would like me to interpret?"

Never in my life had I ever heard anyone say "Tell me a dream and I'll try to help you understand it, I'll try to interpret what it means."

I was open minded. I was skeptical. I listened to what she had to say. Some of it made immediate sense, some of it I wasn't sure of, but I knew there was something to this School of Metaphysics and what they knew about dreams. And I wanted to know what it was because I had twenty-two years of dreaming experience which had spawned thousands of questions.

I wanted to know.

In almost forty years of research and study, faculty members of the School of Metaphysics have delved into the phenomena of dreams making significant discoveries in the universal nature of dreaming and how dream messages are personally relevant. The research has produced great insights that are both universal and individual. It has been my pleasure and indeed a privilege to be one of the many during the past two decades dedicated to furthering this research. This book chronicles some of the discoveries and revelations throughout these years.

*The Dreamer's Dictionary* is presented in a way easily understandable to and applicable for anyone. It answers many of the questions in every dreamer's mind. Questions about purpose, meaning, significance, remembering, and precognition, common to any thinker, are addressed. But more importantly, this book teaches the basic foundation necessary for learning to communicate in the oldest language known to man. It is designed to aid the reader in understanding the language the inner mind uses for communication. It is my hope that learning to speak and hear this language will enhance the quality of your physical life as it fosters new awarenesses of the unlimited possibilities available to you. I trust it will expand your consciousness to use more of your potential, and will enrich both your inner relationship with Self and your outer relations with others.

I know how learning to understand your dreams liberates individual consciousness. And I have complete faith that as this is realized by more and more individuals, the way we communicate with each other as a society, a country, a world will accelerate mankind's consciousness toward Enlightenment. It is indeed time to live the third millennium of man's existence with fluency in the Universal Language of Mind, the common language for all of mankind.

# The Dreamer's Dictionary
# Section I

*"The mind is like an iceberg --
it floats with only one-seventh
of its bulk above water."*

Sigmund Freud (1856-1939)
*NY Times Obituary Sept. 24, 1939*

## The Oldest Language Known to Man

For thousands of years mankind has been captivated and perplexed by memories of experiences arising when his physical consciousness is at rest. Sometimes vague, sometimes vivid, these memories have become an integral part of every culture on this planet. Historical records and literature are filled with accounts of dreaming, and in every case man has searched for a reason for these phenomena. Common to them all is the recognition that nighttime dreams are a form of communication.

An investigation of dreams shows that the phenomenon of dreaming is as old as mankind. Since the dawning of sentience, the ability to be Self aware, man has experienced and remembered these nighttime communications seeking their meaning. Three thousand years ago the authors of the Upanishads, a holy text of the Hindu, described dreaming as a higher state of consciousness than the waking state. Throughout the Orient, it is a widespread belief that dreams are communications from the Creator. This idea is parallel to many Western concepts found in more recent spiritual ideals held by the Jewish and Christian religions. Adherents and leaders of these faiths believe dreams are a message from God given either as a personal revelation or as one to be given to the masses. The American Indian has used dreams in religious rites as a means to perceive and cooperate with nature. Even today, many begin their day by sharing dreams with family members. The family encourages the dreamer to seek purpose in life and receive guidance through dreams.

The Greeks thought that dreams were a means to be receptive to thought, a way to be telepathic. They also believed that dreams were a means for communicating with spirits or ghosts. Around 350 B.C., the Greek philosopher Aristotle determined that dreams came from within the Self. This was a revolutionary idea because until that time it was widely believed that dreams came from outside of Self rather than welling up from within. Aristotle's work spanned the nature of consciousness beyond the physical and for his incredible insight historical accounts have remembered him as the father of metaphysics. Plato, a contemporary and student of Aristotle, took these ideas a bit farther. Plato identified dreams as a communication from the *soul* of man.

Two thousand years transpired before an Austrian named Sigmund Freud, the father of modern psychoanalysis, determined that dreams were *about* the dreamer. He called dreams *"the royal road to Self knowledge."* Maligned by his contemporaries, and too often by modern fame filled with clichés, Freud's revelations are often misconstrued and falsely conveyed. Society's current fascination with external blame is a prime example. In reality, a study of his discoveries reveals that individual accountability and understanding became cornerstones of Freud's later research. Freud's life was dedicated to the constant pursuit of answering the question *"Why?"* and many of the answers he discovered elevated mankind's awareness of personal responsibility originating with and emanating from Self.

Freud's insight into man's capabilities and Self determination caused his contemporaries to consider that man was more than a plaything of God or of physical science. His significant advances in moving the control of consciousness from external people or factors to the internal motivations and desires of the individual were outstanding and laid the foundation for Self autonomy. Freud realized that dreams were an important part of unlocking the considerable potential of each individual. He realized that dreams held symbolic keys to the nature of the dreamer's consciousness. What Freud did not live long enough to discover was the Rosetta stone for understanding the language the inner mind speaks — the Universal Language of Mind.

Decades of research conducted by faculty at the School of Metaphysics in this century confirms and advances the realizations of history's great thinkers. It reveals bold and innovative insights into the nature and usefulness of this communication. Our studies show that dreams are dual in nature, being both universally understandable and personally relevant to the dreamer. Investigations reveal two principles which universally hold true in understanding dreams:

1] The first principle, recalling the theories of Aristotle and Freud, is that *every dream is about the dreamer* for it originates in the inner subconscious part of man. In spiritual literature, this inner, subconscious mind is referred to as the soul.

2] The second principle also builds upon previous observations by recognizing that *everyone and everything in the dream is the dreamer.* The dream's theme, characters, and action comprise a message for and about the dreamer when interpreted in the native language of the soul, what we have termed the Universal Language of Mind.

The discovery of this language is the most profound revelation of our research. It is innovative because it differs from what is commonly accepted about dreams and therefore in the awareness of the average person.

Dreams are communicated by using a language beyond the languages of our physical life; beyond English or Chinese or Latin. This language is a universal language of images or pictures, distinctly separate from man-made representations of thoughts known as words. Images in the Universal Language of Mind symbolize specific functions of mind and qualities of consciousness. All classical and spiritual literature of the world is penned, at least in part, by drawing upon this universal language. Fables, myths, and Holy scriptures offer insightful stories of the lives of others. Underlying the facts depicted through the written word are Universal Truths that every person on the planet can benefit from understanding and using in their lives. When read, the words conjure images in the mind defining a productive action or way of thinking such as courage, integrity, or compassion. The universality of the writings assures the literature's longevity for the truths revealed transcend the moment; they are applicable to anyone, anywhere, anytime.

An individual's dreams, originating from the soul and communicated in the universal language, are sources of truth as well. The outer mind learns a physical language for physical communication between Self and others. In order to facilitate communication within Self, the outer mind must learn the native language of the inner levels of consciousness. Just as there are dictionaries to understand physical languages, there must be a dictionary to aid in learning the Universal Language of Mind. Thus the dictionary portion of this book seeks to identify and discern the meaning of images in the oldest language known to mankind.

## *Conscious Thinking and Subconscious Thinking There is a Difference*

You are probably well aware of the clichés arising from Freudian interpretations of dreams. Ideas that if you dream you want to kill your mother this signifies some deep-seated unconscious yearning to actually be rid of her presence, do not make good common sense. If someone really wants to kill his or her mother, they will contemplate this action while awake. They do not have to go to sleep in order to think about it. Every dreamer knows that dreams occur when the conscious mind is inactive, having been disconnected from the senses of the body and therefore what is happening in the outer environment. Whereas during the waking state associated thoughts arise from this outer contact, they do not occur when the conscious mind is disconnected. The telephone may ring, a neighborhood dog may bark, your spouse may come to bed, all without your knowledge because you are sleeping. During sleep, we are also in effect disconnected from thinking as it is created and occurs in the conscious mind. Lacking awareness, conscious thoughts of whether or not to answer the phone do not arise and we slumber peacefully.

The idea that all thoughts are the same whether awake or asleep inadvertently places the origin and the experience of dreaming on the same level as conscious thought. The result is a misconception based upon a lack of knowledge of the nature and function of man's consciousness. This breeds one of today's most widespread misconceptions about dreams: dreams mean whatever you think they mean. This idea ends up confusing daydreaming with night dreaming because the source of each is not identified or understood. Daydreaming arises in the conscious, waking mind while night dreaming originates in the inner, subconscious mind.

Research into the difference between these dream states has revealed the capabilities and duties of the outer, conscious mind and those of the inner, subconscious mind. These two divisions of mind — conscious and subconscious — are distinctly different, each having their own function to perform and purpose to fulfill. For each individual, the conscious mind's function is to create experiences for the purpose of gaining understanding. The subconscious mind's function is to reproduce the conscious mind's desires for the purpose of permanently storing the understandings gained. Autonomous and equally important in their own right, these two parts of mind together form a whole unit necessary for the fulfillment of your desires and the advancement of your progression as a soul. By coordinating their efforts and causing cooperation between them, you can accelerate your growth in Self awareness. Your dreams are messages *from* your subconscious mind *to* your conscious mind concerning the state of your awareness. They have inherent meaning and it is up to the conscious mind to learn the basics of the inner language for discernment of that meaning.

Experiencing while sleeping is different from experiencing while awake. We spend approximately a third of our lives sleeping. When you arrive at the physical age of sixty, you have spent approximately twenty of those years sleeping. You have probably invested over 175,000 hours in sleeping, 87,000 of which were spent in the activity of dreaming. Your sleeping time is very important to you. For most people it is a time of passive access to the inner, *subconscious* part of Self. Sleeping is passive access because most people do not have knowledge or expertise in drawing upon inner subconscious abilities, thus in terms of awareness they are *unconscious* of what is occurring in the inner levels of consciousness within themselves. In short, they forget any inkling of what transpired during sleep.

While your conscious mind sleeps, your subconscious mind is free to communicate uninterruptedly. When something in the message captures your conscious attention, upon awakening you will say, *"I had a dream."* Such memories enable you to draw upon information that has been given to you by your subconscious mind. They are a means to become aware of your own subconscious thinking. An example of this is the experience of author Mary Shelley. She had a dream. When she awoke the images were so vivid and alive in her conscious mind that she took the information that came from her own subconscious mind and she consciously created a wonderful novel that has become a volume of classical literature. The novel is Frankenstein; a mind expanding volume posing questions of man's ability to be God-like excelling by far that which you might have seen in the horror of modern cinema.

Your ability to consciously create and bring forth creative genius is directly linked to how much attention you give to your dreams. The subconscious mind is a part of you, an inner part of you, that stores truth gleaned from experience. When you know how to draw upon your subconscious mind, you can use its wisdom in your everyday life to produce wonderful works of creativity that benefit not only you but all of mankind. When Nobel Prize winner Albert Einstein was stretching his conscious thinking to consider ideas that would eventually become known as the theory of relativity he reached a point of limitation. He went to sleep, in effect turning over the conscious problem to the workings of his subconscious mind. Upon awakening he found the piece he had been missing by remembering a dream experience. Using the information received and recalled, he fashioned his theory which served as a breakthrough in the scientific community. On accepting his Nobel Prize, Niels Bohr declared his dreams had shown him the structure of the atom.

Abilities of the subconscious mind are also illustrated in the life of Abraham Lincoln. Before Lincoln became president of the United States, he had a recurring dream that he was convinced showed that his death would be untimely, coming at an early age. He told others about this dream. As we are now aware, Lincoln's dream came true. In fact, two weeks before his death, Lincoln dreamed that he entered the East Room of the White House and found a body laid out in state. A general told him that the President had been assassinated. This type of dream is known as a precognitive dream, illustrating the subconscious mind's ability for clairvoyance. Clairvoyance is a French word meaning in English, *clear seeing*. Clairvoyance is your subconscious ability to perceive — beyond the limits of the five physical senses of the body — the past, the present, and the *probabilities* of the future.

Clairvoyance is only one of the capabilities inherent in subconscious thinking. These intuitive abilities can and do become active when you are consciously asleep and in a dream state. Telepathy is another example. Over a decade ago, I had a memory of a dream experience. This dream included my grandmother who rarely appeared in my dreams. We were in a very beautiful place filled with flowers and woods. She came to me and we communed, sharing ideas through thoughts rather than words. It was a mental communication where she could project certain thoughts to me and I would hear them, responding in like fashion. We had the deepest conversation about the nature of life and death, subjects we had never spoken of when we were together physically. When I awoke from that experience I remembered its uniqueness. It was so different from anything my grandmother and I had ever shared. Two days later my dad called informing me that my grandmother had died the night before in her sleep. Immediately upon hearing this I realized the import of the dream experience two nights before. I knew it had been a way my grandmother and I could communicate because she was preparing to withdraw from the physical, or die.

Intuitive abilities unique to the subconscious mind are often active during the sleep state, and we consciously recall them as dreams. Remembering dreams gives you access to your soul and its capabilities. Understanding the language your soul "speaks" enables you to receive the full meaning of its communication. Interpreting those messages brings timeless wisdom and newfound awareness to your waking mind, relieving fears and promoting growth and well-being. In this way you learn the difference between conscious thinking and subconscious thinking. The more familiar you become, the more respect you build for the amazing workings of the human mind. The more you understand these two parts of mind, the more freedom you have to tap and develop your full potential.

If, as our research indicates, it is universally true that every dream is about the dreamer and that everyone and everything in the dream is the dreamer, then it becomes important to be able to decode dreams. If dreams are indeed dual in nature, if they are universal in construction and personally relevant in content, then there must be a way that we can understand dreams that is simultaneously universal in nature and respectful of the unique, individual significances. As we accept these principles, the messages the inner Self is conveying to the outer self can become a part of our waking consciousness, aiding us toward peace and fulfillment in our lives.

## *What Happens While We Sleep*

The idea that dreams are a form of communication beyond the physical existence is not new. As long as man has been able to reason he has experienced the phenomena of dreaming, seeking to understand its significance. Every culture in each time period on earth has developed insight into what dreaming is and why it exists.

Mankind is now on the threshold of profound evolution and spiritual revelation. With the rapidly approaching dawn of Spiritual or Intuitive Man, humanity is turning the tide of public opinion that once shunned the exploration and understanding of dreams into a determined and valuable study of our nighttime experiences. Understanding your dreams is now becoming "socially acceptable".

The interpretation of dreams, once the territory of spiritual leaders only, is becoming the individual's domain as each person reaches into his own spiritual nature, seeking the cause for what he experiences; the source of his existence. The ability to understand the messages received in dreams is quickly being recognized as the link between the physically visible and invisible universes of man. The commonality of the dream experience reaches all ages, races, and nationalities. Just as each nation has its physical language for the communication of ideas and perceptions, so dreams are conveyed in the language spoken by a group of minds. The Universal Language of Mind is this language.

We are preparing for the next stage in mankind's enlightenment. This is characterized by growing acceptance of the idea that what is communicated during the dream state is a message from the inner Self or subconscious mind to the outer Self or conscious, waking part of mind. As we discussed before, dreams, once interpreted, will always tell you the state of your conscious awareness. Dreams put us in touch with a greater Self. They can be healing or entertainingly adventurous. Dreams will tell the dreamer about his health: mentally, emotionally, physically, and spiritually. Dreams aid us in problem solving and promote creativity. They entertain us with different perspectives of ourselves and how we see our world. They can offer glimpses of our probable futures. Dreams stimulate conscious awareness of what is beyond the physical and give us glimpses into the many worlds inside ourselves. They remind us of a common ancestry; an inkling that somewhere, somehow we come from a common source and share a common language. Dreams are an integral part of the curriculum offered in our own individual night school courses.

Produced by the inner Self in response to how we consciously use our life experiences, the communication received by our conscious mind will consistently be truthful. Since our subconscious mind only holds our past *understood* experiences, it only knows those things that will produce maturity of the inner thinker. Its power, intuition, is the direct grasp of Truth. Therefore, it is up to us to cause our conscious mind to be honest in the evaluation of the communication received. Awareness in the conscious mind must expand to accommodate messages received and given by the inner Self, just as desire for elocution spurs expansion of vocabulary enhancing the level of communication possible in our physical lives.

It is true that our dreams will always be presented in Truth. It is also true that there is an inner urge inherent to the subconscious mind which motivates its communication. This inner urge is toward soul progression. As we learn to care for the growth of our inner Self at least as much as we care for the growth of the physical parts of Self, we begin to consciously direct our thinking toward those people, places and things that will aid us in adding more understandings to our *whole* Self. This type of conscious action speeds our evolution and fosters the maturity displayed in wisdom. It is to the advantage of our whole Self that our subconscious mind be able to communicate this perspective to our outer consciousness. As the inner messages are heeded and acted upon, every part of our Self evolves toward peace and contentment, prosperity and wisdom. Our depth of perception is magnified and we advance in enlightenment of the consciousness available to mankind at this stage of evolution.

When you awake from a dream, keep in mind two important concepts that will universally hold true. This dream is telling you about *you*. In the language of mind, this dream is a message from your inner, subconscious mind to your outer, conscious mind about the present state of your conscious awareness. It is a perspective of Truth concerning the way you are using the power of your mind to work toward or against gaining what you most desire. The dream will also inform you of your next step to be taken toward manifesting what you want.

Second, realize *everyone* and *everything* appearing in the dream is *you*. Your mother, father, brother, sister, spouse, best friend and your pet cat that you've had for ten years, may all appear in your dream. They may all be sitting down to a delicious and rich meal in your boss's office. All of this, in the language of mind, is telling you a story about *you*. The images in your dream are a parable conveyed by your subconscious mind concerning your conscious awareness. As with all parables, you will use reasoning to discern the import or moral in the message for it reveals a personal lesson that will advance your learning.

How does this work? Several things have occurred before you consciously awake and begin to record what you have dreamed. First, you achieved a state of relaxation of the physical body and released your conscious attention into what is known as sleep. During this period, somewhere between methodical choice and total exhaustion, you systematically removed life force from the five physical senses. You prepared for bed, going through your own routine. Perhaps you took a bath, brushed your teeth, put on nightclothes, checked to make sure outside doors were locked, and the house lights out. Then settling into bed, you might have set your alarm clock, made sure your paper and pencil were ready for the next morning, and turned out the light on your bedstand. Lying in bed, you now prepare yourself for sleep by closing your eyes, turning off the registering of the clock ticking, and moving into your favorite going to sleep position in bed. You have systematically turned off the five senses.

Perhaps at this point you are aware of thoughts going through your mind. Events of the day or plans for the next day might flow through your consciousness. As you put these in their proper place you cause your conscious mind to settle down into what we call sleep. You have accomplished the first step necessary that will culminate in remembering a dream.

Throughout the sleeping period your subconscious mind is now free to perform its duties. Although it is within your grasp to learn how to take control of your breathing, heartbeat and other bodily functions, most people take these pertinent actions of physical life for granted. Such people depend on the subconscious mind to direct these functions. During sleep, your subconscious mind stays alert to perpetuate and monitor these physical actions. This is accomplished by a stream of consciousness that remains attached to your body until the time of withdrawal from the physical, or what is commonly referred to as physical death.

Your subconscious mind also uses your sleeping time to go into each of its inner levels of consciousness to energize and replenish what has been expended during your the previous day. Each time you create a desire during your waking state, each time you promote fearful thinking, each time you experience something you have wanted but become frustrated because things don't seem to be happening, energy from your subconscious mind has been used. Since most people do not know how to consciously return this used energy back into mind, they rely upon the subconscious mind to accomplish this while the conscious mind is asleep. This re-energization is important to the health of the body as well as the mind. Recent studies at the San Diego Veterans Hospital show even missing three hours of sleep decreases the immune systems by as much as fifty percent. This type of change makes the physical body more susceptible to viral diseases.

Through the sleep research performed at universities throughout the world, an interesting fact has once again gained the attention of reasoning man. When the average man is prohibited from sleeping for extended periods of time, there are marked effects which take place in his ability to function during the waking state. Initially, emotions flare more easily, the individual becomes irritable and angers readily. If the sleep deprivation continues past several sleep cycles, concentration abilities are lost, coordination decreases, bodily systems become impaired and eventually the person experiences stages of what would culminate in physical death. This is what occurs when the mind's energy is continually used and not returned or replenished. Your subconscious mind performs a vital function in maintaining your ability to continue to experience physical life while your conscious mind sleeps.

While you consciously sleep, your subconscious mind experiences the freedom to go into the past, present, and probable future. It is during this activity that you can capture and remember a dream. Because your subconscious mind recreates what your conscious mind desires, at any given time there are many thoughts being formed in the inner levels of your subconsciousness. Your dreams will be messages informing you of how you have used your conscious, waking state to create. In this way, your subconscious mind can offer valuable insight into how you can consciously cause your soul progression. Researchers seek physical indications of dreaming, the most common evidence being rapid eye movement (REM) sleep. Dream messages occur during this phenomena alternating with other sleep phases at ninety minute intervals throughout a sleeping period. You are most likely to remember a dream when you awaken directly after a dream phase. A lack of sleep interferes with dream cycles. Drugs that act upon the central nervous system will also interfere with dreaming, as noted by a suppression in REM sleep.

To convey its insight, the subconscious mind will use the images already stored in the brain so your conscious mind can readily register and remember the subconscious message. As your subconscious mind forms the thoughts that will comprise this special communication pertinent to you right now, intelligence causes energy to be used to create form in mind substance. So that we can relate to this in the physical level of consciousness, the subconscious mind uses the hypothalamus in the brain as a receiving station. The energy moves from the hypothalamus to the pituitary gland in an action similar to an echo moving across a canyon. Moving through time and space causes the energy to dissipate similarly to how an echo begins to fade until it is no longer heard. For this reason, it is to our advantage to record our dreams when we first become consciously aware of them. To procrastinate means we progressively lose the essence of the message.

As the vibration or energy is received by the pituitary gland a magical happening occurs. The pituitary gland is the interpreter of energies. In our waking state, vibration that is received through the physical senses is impressed upon the sensory nerves receptors. The vibration then becomes electrical impulses traveling through nerves to the pituitary. The pituitary, having received this energy for interpretation, then reaches into the brain for information that has already been stored to aid the conscious mind in understanding the experience at hand. This arrangement of information becomes the images you remember as a dream.

Have you ever met someone on the street and could swear in court that you had seen the person before? This rapid thinking process in the conscious mind is in part a product of the function of the pituitary gland. "Seeing" the person on the street is the reception of a reflected light image of what is before you. You do not take that person into your brain. What is impressed through your sense of sight upon the retina of the eye is all the light that is reflected from the object you are seeing. The light absorbed by the object or person viewed is not what you see, you see the *light* that is reflected from them. Thus when we experience an absence of physical light, we say we cannot "see".

Once the reflected light image is impressed on the retina, the vibration we have received is transmitted as energy through the optic nerve to the pituitary. The pituitary functioning under the command of the conscious mind interprets this energy by reaching into the brain for information -- this person is male, tall, blond, dressed in a business suit, about 40 years old. Our conscious mind begins to put all this information together to reach a conclusion: *"He looks like..."*

The physical brain of man is the most advanced receptacle for knowledge that exists in the physical world today. Computers are fashioned along the same principles which are exhibited by the brain. In fact, the brain can be considered by far the most evolved computer system. If the computer is a metaphor for the brain, the computer programmer is an analogy for the conscious mind, for it is the intelligence in the conscious mind which exhibits the desire and will necessary for determining how the brain will be made useful. When we know the right computer commands we can cause the memory to work perfectly. In this way we determine the name of the person the man looks like or where we have seen him before, accessing this information from the brain's storehouse. When we fumble for the correct computer button, we are left with *"Haven't I seen you somewhere before?"*

Our brains are like computers. Just as a computer is an intricate machine, so are the physical brain and body. The hardware, maintenance, and creative use of a computer is dependent upon the intelligent direction it receives from man. The same is true for our own personal computer, the brain.

Have you been amazed by what others can cause a computer to do? So have I. I am also continually in awe of the mastery we can attain in using our "personal computers". This mastery is produced as you strengthen the power in the conscious mind. This power is the ability to reason: the command of recalling information already stored and available which is memory, the command of the only sense of the mind known as attention which is the will, and the command of the faculty for imaging which is visualization. By gaining mastery in your use of reasoning, you will produce intuition.

By this time in your life, you have millions of pieces of information that you have stored in your brain. These are the images that your subconscious mind will use to communicate to your conscious mind the state of its awareness of the whole Self. You can take more information into your awareness from your environment by using your five senses, and you can also receive information from your inner environment by using the sense of the mind, attention.

While the conscious mind sleeps, the inner subconscious mind sends thought, in the form of vibration, to the physical receiving station known as the hypothalamus. The hypothalamus receives the vibration transferring it to the master gland of the endocrine system, the pituitary, causing a chemical reaction. The pituitary gland then reaches into the brain in order to interpret the energies presented to it. That is why your mother, sister, and your pet cat appear in your dream, rather than your father, brother, and pet dog. These energies, originating in the subconscious mind, are being used to represent the many different aspects of you and tell you, the conscious mind, a story about how you are using these aspects. The interpreted energies are the symbols that make up your dream.

The Positron Emission Scan (PET) gives scientists a means to see and study the effects of dreaming on the brain. The scan measures how much of a special artificial sugar the brain burns and translates the activity into a color image. The hotter the shade, the greater the activity. What is most outstanding is the similarity of patterns in the dreaming brain and the awake brain. These almost identical patterns show the brain is being used in like fashion whether the consciousness of the individual is awake and alert or asleep and passive. This physically illustrates the thinking process used in consciously storing information in the brain and the thinking process used in subconsciously accessing the information as has been described.

Scientists also note two predominantly active brain centers during dreaming: the temporal lobe, the brain's verbal center, and the gyrus of the cerebral cortex, seat of consciousness, memory, and intellect, which connect so-called emotional centers of the brain. Scientists see this in a linear sense as evidence that dreams are emotional storytelling. The metaphysician knows it as the natural process of pulling the dream out of the inner levels, through the emotional level of consciousness to the physical waking mind for conscious description. One of the most fascinating realizations is that no matter how much research is conducted on the physical effects of dreaming and inner level experiences the research remains just that — a record of effects. The research may answer questions and verify theories such as those in this book, but it does not directly explore the cause and origin.

One of the most frequent questions about dreams concerns their origins: *"Where did these symbols come from?"* Of all languages you will learn or any that man will invent, the language of mind is the oldest and was created by humanity as a whole. By the choices reasoning man has made in his physical existence from the point of entrapment forward, man has created by his evolvement and progression the symbols that appear in our dreams. If human man still lived in caves, the cave rather than a house would be the dream symbol representing mind. The meaning of symbols is determined not by one person, including the dreamer, or a group of experts, but rather by *how* the symbol is used by mankind. The *function* of the cave or the house is an abode, a place to live, thus in the Universal Language of Mind the cave or house represents where the individual lives, his mind. As Dr. Daniel R. Condron revealed in his book, The Universal Language of Mind: The Book of Matthew Interpreted, *"the language of the conscious mind is the language of form and structure. The language of the subconscious mind is the language of function."*


## Fifteen Wasted Years
## Why Dreaming is Important to You

Years ago when I was a guest on a talk show discussing dreams, a lady called in to ask for my analysis of a dream. In the dream, she was traveling alone along an ocean side highway. As she drove down the mountainside the car began gaining speed. Suddenly, the road sharply veered. She tried to slow the car but the brakes failed. Unable to safely negotiate the curve, the car continued its forward motion going over a cliff and crashing on the rocks below. She said she was so frightened when she awoke that she hadn't been able to drive since having the dream. In fact, she hadn't even been able to be in a car. Her fear revolved around the belief that this dream might be warning her of a future physical occurrence.

I asked her if this was a recent dream and she replied, "No, it was fifteen years ago."

Fifteen years!

Immediately what flew through my mind was all the ways that her life must have changed in fifteen years. The little things that you and I take for granted, hopping into a car and going to the grocery store. Or being free to see relatives. The places she might have wanted to travel to but did not. How she must have become dependent upon others to accomplish the simplest errands we take for granted — going to the grocery store or to the dentist. The arts, or sports events, or classes she might have participated in previously, now removed from her life. Far from a mere inconvenience, her decision to stop driving because of one frightening dream experience, had indeed affected the type and quality of this woman's life-style for the previous fifteen years. She had robbed herself of free will. Her desire to understand the dream had been colored by conscious fears of the dream "coming true", so her conscious waking experiences had been seriously affected.

To think that someone would have a dream, be scared of it because they didn't understand what it was saying, and would change their physical life to suit their fear was disheartening to me. And yet it made me realize that this is how the vast majority of the world exists, having dreams with little inkling of their raison d'étre or meaning. Most people still wrestle with unanswered questions, just as I had for two decades, not knowing what their dreams mean or their value to the waking mind. This woman and her misinterpreted dream added to my resolve to share the benefits of research so that she and others have a readily available means to understand and use the Universal Language of Mind.

What did the dream mean? Her dream was indicating her need to slow down in her assimilation of the challenges she had met in her life at the time the dream occurred. Her dream was not telling her she should not drive. This dream was telling her about her physical health as symbolized by the *dream-car* being out of control. The crashing indicated an impending difficulty resulting from the construction of her attitudes at the time she remembered the dream. When asked, she did not remember what was occurring in her life at that time. Not only did she miss the import of the message at the time, but the fears she harbored in her lack of knowledge produced limiting handicaps in how she lived fifteen years of her life.

When I began explaining what the dream had been telling her in the language of mind, her fears were dispelled and the desire to drive again was rekindled which she verbalized. One of the benefits of learning to communicate in the language the inner minds speak is knowing how energy and substance functions in each of the levels of consciousness. I responded to her desire to drive again by suggesting she become familiar with controlling a car just as she had when she first learned to drive; to take the learning steps over again in order to have the freedom she wanted to regain. This woman was once again on her way to controlling her life.

The crashing of the car in the dream made this message a warning signal of disorders manifesting in her physical body, rather than a stimulus for a fear that the dream was a foreboding preview of coming events in her physical life. Even if the dream had been precognitive, it would still signify what was happening within her consciousness during the time of the dream. The woman had lived in Kansas City all her life, far from the ocean and mountainsides, so the probability that this was a precognitive dream was almost nonexistent. If she had found herself living out the dream, just as it had been revealed to her, she could use the memory of her dream experience to consciously cause a different outcome in her physical life. In this way a precognitive dream experience would serve as a signal to be more alert when she was driving so she could change the probable dream-outcome of crashing to a physical-outcome of safely controlling the automobile. Had this woman understood this she would have been free of fear, realizing the dream experience whether precognitive or merely symbolic in nature existed to offer her greater insight and thus more understanding of her Self and her life.

Some dreams are considered health dreams because they concern the health and well-being of the physical body, symbolized by the working order of any small vehicle such as a car, small plane or boat. I've had people tell me about dreams where they walk outside to find four flat tires on their car or a car that won't start. I had a dream one time where the water pump on my car was broken. I'd been studying and using dreams for years by then so upon awakening I knew it was a message about my physical health. I tried to figure out what a water pump on a car does so I could find the correspondence with my physical body, respond to the impending condition, and therefore assure my good health. I didn't figure it out quickly enough because about three days later I was experiencing a terrible cold virus that set me back for several days.

For most people, however, a health dream will usually occur about three months before physical symptoms become apparent. This is because what is being reported in the dream is occurring in the inner levels of consciousness and are some distance-time away from being apparent in the physical body. The attitudes held in the inner levels go through a process which ultimately results in physical manifestation. While this process is carried on, physical time transpires. Because most people scatter the mind's energies, the timing of the process is elongated. One of the benefits I've discovered in performing mental and spiritual disciplines is that the degree of distance between the time you think of something and when it actually happens decreases rapidly proportionate to the increase in your awareness. Thus how the mind reproduces desires is accelerated according to how the mind is utilized.

During another call-in show in Des Moines, Iowa, a gentleman called in with a dream that had caused considerable upheaval in his life. He explained he was plagued by a dream of having an affair with a coworker who was not his wife. The man was deeply troubled. He loved his wife and had no desire to be unfaithful to her. He described himself as a born-again Christian who devoutly believed in fidelity as part of the marriage vows he had taken. Secure in his own intention of faithfulness and believing it might stop the unwanted dreams, he had discussed the dream with his wife, assuring her that his conscious thoughts were not the same as those appearing in the dream. She was very understanding but still the man's dream would recur.

Since his conscious thinking and dream experience did not seem related at all, he wanted some guidance on why he was having this kind of dream. I began by explaining that the dream was about him, and that everything and everyone who appeared in his dream was symbolic to him. The dream was not addressing this "other woman" he knew in his everyday physical life or his physical relationship with her. A sigh of relief was heard as he realized the dream was talking about his relationship inside Self rather than any deep, dark desire for a relationship outside his physical marriage. He could identify the woman as representative of his inner, subconscious ability for assertiveness, for this is the quality he most associated with the woman. The sexual activity in the dream indicated a harmonizing of the outer, conscious Self with the aspect of assertiveness as symbolized by the woman. He could readily recognize the meaning of the dream because he had been actively drawing upon inner resolve to ask for a promotion at work. He had yet to garner the courage to approach his boss and so the dream was repeated because the same message was pertinent. Some time later, the man wrote to inform me he had indeed procured the desired position and since that time the dream had not recurred.

I had heard this type of dream many times. Sometimes it would be related after the conscious fears and guilts had manifested in the ending of what was otherwise a beautiful and fulfilling marriage. I had seen far too many relationships end because a spouse had misinterpreted "sleep talking" as a bonafide indication of adultery. The repercussions of these destroyed relationships often resulted in financial problems, divided possessions, tug-of-war games with children, as well as the mental and emotional difficulties left unresolved in the individuals themselves. Dreams misinterpreted often change others' lives as well as our own.

Dreams often re-occur in our lives. As we become knowledgeable in the language of mind they reveal insights into lessons to be learned and understandings to be gained which enrich our souls as well as our daily lives. One middle-aged dreamer had a recurring dream of being back in college. In his dream he awoke to find he was late to class. In rushing around he would forget his books and upon arriving in the classroom discover that a test was being given that he had not studied for. The man stated he had repeatedly had this dream over more than ten years. It would seem to come and go. Sometimes he would remember having it several times over the period of a few months, then it would not recur for a couple of years. When interpreted, this dream indicated the man's tendency to remain removed from the potential learning in his life. The many opportunities for mental and spiritual advancement available to him were being wasted because he was engrossed in mulling over past opportunities which were no longer relevant in his life. Rather than using the information he was receiving to better himself and his life, he would dwell upon what was no longer relevant thus missing present opportunities. His subconscious mind was bringing to his awareness his need to cease pondering the import of his experiences and begin to reach points of resolve and understanding. When the man could learn to use memory to promote the fulfillment of desires in the present, the dream would not recur for that message would no longer be pertinent to the changes in his conscious state of awareness.

The subconscious mind will repeat the same message whenever necessary. When the conscious mind fails to remember or does not act upon the message, the inner Self will repeat itself much like someone who repeatedly gives you instructions when you didn't receive and understand them the first, second, or third time. Whatever you are trying to achieve with the instructions remains important to accomplish, so the person knowledgeable in the endeavor will repeat himself however many times it takes for the job at hand. Or like a parent instructing a child in how to use dinnerware or how to dress. The guidance is lovingly provided over and over until the child understands and masters the skill. Your subconscious mind also provides loving guidance and valuable instruction, and is willing to offer these time and again until the conscious mind either understands and acts with awareness upon the message received or merely makes changes with virtually no understanding of how the message relates to the life. Either way, a recurring dream ceases when conscious action is taken that changes the awareness in the conscious mind.

A nightmare is often the result of recurring dreams that have been ignored. Earlier messages, less shocking to the conscious mind, are forgotten so the subconscious mind begins to communicate by using appropriate images more pointedly vivid to the conscious mind. Like a parent who quietly and gently instructs a child to stay in the yard and not play in the street, the messages are at first benign. If the child continues to disregard the teaching, the parent becomes louder and more disciplinary. If the potentially offensive behavior continues, the parent uses whatever measures it requires to keep the child safe and off the street. A nightmare is the subconscious mind using whatever measures it requires to gain your conscious mind's attention. Giving attention to your dreams is the best way to end nightmares -- forever.

Developing the skill of communicating in the language of mind brings new awarenesses and understandings that can be used to enrich your life and your relationships with others. Translating your dreams produces an inward thrill of Self discovery. Dreams are no longer a waste of time because you realize they have meaning and you are educated in discerning that meaning. Responding to your dream messages brings you closer to your subconscious mind. You are actively building a rapport with your own soul. Too many people believe in the soul only as a concept; an idea that will someday be important but with little relevance to their present experiences. Nothing is further from the truth. You are a soul having a temporary physical experience. Utilizing your dreams teaches you the truth about your soul.

## A Stranger in a Foreign Land

Xtsoi bsksiutye snrigkksue jisginr gpt kidy s opqrmy.

Confused? Imagine if everything looked like gibberish to you. You would feel lost, isolated, and lonely.

In a 1993 survey by *USA Today* the biggest worry of international travelers was the inability to communicate. This worry or fear motivated most global travelers to become at least rudimentarily familiar with the language native to the land they visited. Learning the basics gave them confidence and security, opening the door for understanding and being understood.

Most dreamers never consider that feelings of being lost, isolated, or lonely arise from a lack of Self knowledge, a deficiency that can be easily remedied by understanding dreams. Even though the dream arises from within themselves, they too often feel powerless to comprehend the images they remember. It is as if they are visiting a foreign land each time they sleep. Rather than being motivated to learn the language of this foreign land, they quickly forget their nighttime journeys. Their confusion, worry, fear, or forgetfulness can be easily remedied by learning not a physical language but the language of the soul; the language used by the inner Self in dream communication. Once the basics are learned, the door is open for understanding these nightly messages from the Self, about the Self, and for the Self.

Each one of us was taught and has learned English. Otherwise writing and reading this book would be very difficult if not impossible. If this book was penned in a language foreign to you, you would see strings of letters and symbols unfamiliar to you -- characters without meaning. You wouldn't identify them as words so you wouldn't be able to assess any meaning to them. Communication would not occur. This is often what happens with our dream states. Communication does not break down, rather it does not occur because the outer mind and the inner mind do not speak a language common to both of them.

Yet, because of curiosity and our drive to understand, we consciously try to assess meaning to our dreams without the benefit of education. We erroneously believe the inner mind speaks the same physical language we are accustomed to using in our everyday physical life, leading to the misconceptions about dreams held by most people today. We try to make dreaming a phenomenon of the waking, conscious mind — a daydream — instead of respecting its integrity as images arising from another part of ourselves without conscious provocation. Dreams originate in the subconscious mind. They are communicated in the language the inner mind speaks which is not a language you have chosen to learn and use with your conscious mind in your everyday life. As long as we remain uneducated in the nature of the whole Self, we are like strangers in a foreign land.

If you are native to the United States, you are fluent in the language of your homeland: English. If you plan to visit a foreign country where English is not spoken, it would be wise to learn the new language to facilitate communication while in the foreign land. When you do, you will find great freedom in expression and in understanding those who speak another language. With practice, the previously foreign language will no longer seem strange to you. Rather it will be very familiar. In order to understand the messages being conveyed by your subconscious mind you must be willing to learn *its* language, just as you are willing to learn the language of the foreign country you plan to visit.

As with physical languages, there are basic components and principles in the Universal Language of Mind that you can learn in order to facili-

tate interpreting and understanding your dream messages.  These principles
and components are the universal part of the duality of dreaming.  By learning
this language you can identify the symbols or images appearing in a dream
and assess meaning to them thus bring understanding of the communication
from the inner levels of your mind into your conscious mind.

The images comprising your dream are chosen by your subconscious
mind, not by somebody else but by your own inner Self.  They appear in order
to convey a message to you.  The message will always pertain to your conscious state of awareness.  This is universally true.  Your dreams are for you,
about you.  They will tell you where you are, where you are going, where you
have been.  Sometimes they will commend you when you are using your potential wisely, sometimes they will reprimand you when you are procrastinat-
ing and lazy.  They will always offer a truthful assessment of who you are
right now.  This is the beauty of dream interpretation.  When you learn to
translate the images in your dreams, you can establish a rapport with your
soul.  You have the best in you coming forward and saying, "This is what I
think about who you are and what you are doing.  This is how we can progress
and move forward.  This is how we can meet the challenges in life."

Just as you were taught and learned to communicate in English, you
can be taught and learn to communicate in the language of mind.  Remember
as a child you received your first book.  At that time you didn't know how to
read, you were only captivated by the pretty pictures and those little marks on
the page didn't mean anything to you until someone who was knowledgeable
cared and took the time to teach you, "This is an '*a*' and when you see it by
itself it represents a singular unit, meaning one thing."  Then that someone
taught you what a *"b"* was, and a *"c"* and a *"d"*.  Then they taught you how
to make different combinations of these symbols-letters to represent something.  L-o-v-e took on  meaning.  You learned the combinations of letters
*represented* meaning.  As you progressed in using language, you learned you
could write poetry or essays communicating your thoughts through the written word and sharing those thoughts with others.  You also learned to wield
language as a means to convey your desires to others and acknowledge their
desires by receiving words with meaning.

This is very similar to what your inner, subconscious mind does when
it gives you a message in a dream.  The inner mind uses images similar to the
pictures which captivated your attention before you learned a physical language.  The images your subconscious mind chooses to use are drawn from
information stored in your brain.  For this reason, our dreams tend to be comprised of people, places, and things we have experienced sometime, somewhere.  Sometimes we don't know the people in our dreams, but we do recog-

nize them as people. The subconscious mind draws on the brain's memory to form the images for communication. This might include what a male looks like, his hair coloring, the type of clothing, and even a previously stored bit of information that would lead us to assess this male as intelligent. Your subconscious mind uses what is stored in your brain as memory to create the images that will correspond to the message it wants to give to the conscious mind. When you learn what those *dream-people*, *dream-places*, and *dream-things* indicate you can understand what the message is conveying just as you learned physical words and their meaning.

When people appear in dreams they represent aspects of the dreamer. An easy way to identify aspects of ourselves is to realize how we change our expression according to who is in our environment. I have found that no matter how many years I live, when I am around my parents as far as they are concerned I am still their six-year-old daughter. The stories they tell and often how they communicate with me based upon this old image serves to stimulate thoughts deeply imbedded in my consciousness that have been accepted as a part of me for years. It constantly raises the choice in my mind between reverting to that six-year-old or revealing the person I have become. The aspect of six-year-old Barbara has a certain way of expressing.

At work, you may have a capable and efficient persona that you bring forth. You are dedicated in your work and are very skilled in the activities you perform. When you are the parent or interact with a child, perhaps you become a little lighter, a bit more open and friendly. When you are in the company of someone you feel doesn't like you, perhaps you feel threatened and you close off trying to protect yourself. If you're with a best friend maybe you're very communicative, you feel relaxed and you talk about anything. These are aspects of you.

To communicate its message, your subconscious mind chooses a male or a female, depending upon your physical sex, who exhibits a particular quality. That specific person will appear in your dream to tell you about *your* efficiency or friendliness, or protectiveness, or talkativeness. If your subconscious mind is trying to tell you that you should talk more, you should express yourself more and let people know what you have on your mind, your subconscious mind will choose someone of the same sex who is familiar to you and who exhibits qualities of gregariousness. Maybe it will be somebody who always talks to the point that you find them annoying when you are with them. This *dream-person* will illustrate the quality and attitudes of gregarity in you. People of the same sex universally represent conscious waking aspects of the dreamer.

People of the opposite sex, when they appear in a dream, will represent an aspect of the dreamer's subconscious mind. You can interpret the quality of those aspects in the same way you would a conscious aspect appearing in the dream as a person of the same sex.

Learning how to identify the aspects and what they mean can prove a challenge for some people. If this seems difficult or elusive to you, think of it in this way. If you were to describe the person who has appeared in your dream to me, a stranger, what would you want me to know about them? What descriptive quality would come to your mind? You might be tempted to describe physical qualities such as they are pretty, dress well, or make a lot of money. These descriptions are relevant to certain qualities of thought that are the point of origin for what is experienced in the outer physical world. If they are pretty, perhaps they are a very gentle person, very loving; this would identify the aspect being revealed in your dream communication. If they dress well maybe they possess high esteem or a healthy Self respect which displays itself in personal hygiene and care in the clothing they wear. If they make a lot of money perhaps they are hardworking, ambitious, or successful. *However you assess that person is the reason your subconscious mind chose this image from all available in your brain to communicate its message.* Your subconscious mind placed Ann or Mary or John or Peter in your dream to tell you about a specific quality in you.

This is the blending of what is universal in dreams and what is personally relevant. No matter who you are *dream-people* represent aspects of Self. For everyone, people of the same sex signify conscious aspects and people of the opposite sex signify subconscious aspects. These concepts are universally true for anyone, anywhere, anytime. The specific people who appear in your dream will tell you of specific qualities unique to you. They will be personally relevant for your subconscious mind uses the information you have stored in your memory for dream communication.

For instance, two sisters dream. One of the characters in both dreams is Susan, a woman they both know. One sister thinks that Susan is the most trustworthy person she has ever met. The other sister thinks Susan is the biggest liar she has ever met. This illustrates differences in perception arising from individual experiences. The woman in both dreams represents a conscious aspect of the dreamer. But for the first sister Susan represents a conscious aspect of loyalty and for the second sister Susan signifies a conscious aspect of deceit. The meaning of the dream message will be entirely different for each sister. Remember, dreams will commend or reprimand depending upon the state of your conscious awareness and therefore your own individual needs for growth.

Honesty in your conscious mind is very important in evaluating your dreams. Your subconscious mind will present truth, letting you know exactly where you stand. This is a true advantage to learning the language your inner mind speaks. This dictionary is intended to be a resource for the meaning of images in the Universal Language of Mind, thus it will define the universally true elements of anyone's dream. How and why the symbols appear in your dream depends solely upon your subconscious mind's intended message. As with any dictionary, this one can only translate the image's meaning. It is up to you to place that meaning in the context of your dream message. By understanding dream messages, you access your own subconscious perception that will aid you in developing your mental, emotional, physical, and spiritual powers.

There is another kind of person who will appear in your dreams which signifies an even deeper part of you which is termed the superconscious mind. When people of authority appear in your dreams, they will represent your superconscious mind. Your parents, your boss, the president of your country, or your minister, are examples of images representing your divinty, an inner authority. The superconscious mind is the part of mind closest to the Creator who brought you into existence as a spiritual being. The spark of life from that Creator expresses first in the superconscious mind. Authority figures are the symbol used in the dream language to illustrate your awareness of your own spirituality and sense of divine presence. When these *dream-people* appear, they will indicate your spiritual progress, how you are learning and responding to spiritual maturity.

In the commonly cited Freudian dream of wanting to kill your mother, the subconscious mind would be indicating something you want to do with your superconscious mind. The something would be causing death. Death in a dream indicates *change*. Therefore, if in a dream you are killing your mother, the message revolves around a change in your spirituality that you are forcing to transpire. When the message is understood, the dreamer is free to apply this new information in his or her everyday life. Perhaps the subconscious mind is commenting on the fact that although you attend a church or temple regularly you are missing the spirit of your faith because it is lacking in your everyday life. Another possible interpretation of the dream might be indicating that although you are knowledgeable about meditation and stilling the mind, you haven't been using this skill to promote peace in your life. Or maybe you have been trying to force spiritual awareness artificially through drugs or hypnosis. Maybe you are being selfish, refusing to share the wisdom you possess with others and in that way denying your own inner authority. These are all possible individual interpretations of the same dream. It is up to the dreamer to place the translated message into his or her life for greater Self awareness. There really is no one else who can do that for you. Nor is there anyone else who will be able to apply the insight and wisdom relayed by your subconscious mind to you in the form of your dream. You are the final authority on what your dreams mean to you.

How the dream applies to the dreamer is as rich and varied as the dreamers are. Once the dream is understood you, the dreamer, must determine the significance of the dream message to your life. Knowing how to read words in a physical language gives you a means to acquire new knowledge. If you read without comprehending the intended meaning, you lose the import of what is being communicated. You will find the same is true in using the Universal Language of Mind. Use this dictionary as a resource to acquire new knowledge, then seek to comprehend how the knowledge is personally relevant. In this way the significance of your dreams will become apparent and immediately useful to you.

## The Rosetta Stone to the Soul

Throughout my childhood I can remember dreams where I would be standing in a field. I would lift my arms and be able to float above houses, trees, power lines, and people. To change directions, all I would need to do is change the position of my arms or turn my hands. During the dream and after I would awake, what impressed me the most about these types of dreams was the incredible sense of freedom moving at will brought to me.

This same incredible sense of freedom is produced when human man begins to identify with the soul. Until this happens, man is mostly a creature of habit, a prisoner of his own limited thinking. Instead of the five physical senses -- sight, hearing, smelling, tasting, and feeling -- being used as the means to experience physical life, they become the end in themselves. In this way, human man convinces himself that if you can't see it, hear it, taste it, smell it and feel it with the bodily senses then it cannot, must not, should not, and therefore surely is not "real". When we accept this limitation in our thinking, we become a slave to our senses denying any awareness of our existence as spiritual beings being the physical existence.

As we begin to consciously understand the purpose of function of the physical body and senses, we discover there is much more to us. This "more" lies in the expansive new worlds of our mind.

The structure of mind for human man is complete and whole. The way it is designed to function is universal, much like the human body is universal in its functional design. Just as there are all shapes, sizes, colors, and appearances of physical bodies, there are the unique qualities that each of us display as thinkers. These differences as thinkers are determined by how we have used mind in the past, how we are using mind today, and how we intend to use mind in our futures.

To drive an automobile, most of us get in a car, turn the key in the ignition, and go. We don't think much about what makes that automobile work.

Imagine that you are driving late at night down a lonely stretch of highway. All of a sudden, you hear an unfamiliar noise and the engine of your car begins to die. You pull your car to the shoulder of the road, try to start it again, and nothing happens. You are stranded.

Imagine what your reactions might be: anger, *"I just had a tune-up"*; blame, *"It was working fine until so-and-so drove it"*; fear, *"What if someone comes along and takes advantage of me!"*; self-pity, *"I have no idea what's wrong, what am I going to do?"*; condemnation, *"I knew I should have taken the time to get this checked."*

Now, imagine that you are a mechanic. You have spent many hours learning and using what you've learned about the inner workings of an automobile. You are driving late at night down a lonely stretch of highway. All of a sudden you hear a noise and the engine in your car dies. You would be able to identify the probable source of the noise since you have refined the sense of hearing for this purpose many times in your work. You could use what you know from experience to diagnose the point of difficulty. You would follow-up on your suspicion, adjust the difficulty and be on your way. Perhaps you would entertain a few quick reactions but your attention would be directed toward using what you know to correct the problem and be on your way.

Most of us invest little time in understanding how an automobile performs its function. We expect the vehicle to take us to our destination, and if it doesn't we employ an expert to diagnose and correct the problem. We don't spend much time thinking about what makes the car work. In fact, we take the inner workings for granted until something goes wrong. Then our reactions are usually similar to those mentioned leaving us in the same ignorance that produced our unpleasant experience. Sometimes a fleeting thought of *"I really should take that mechanics course at the adult education department"* might enter into our thinking. Fewer times do we act on such thoughts.

When human man identifies with being a creature of habit, he is a prisoner of his own limited thinking. Too many times we take the workings of our minds for granted just like we do with an automobile. We wait for a breakdown to occur before we are stimulated to take action. It is common for human man to wait for an ill before finding a cure. Human man often waits for disease before exploring health, for death before discovering life, for failure before pursuing success, or for a weird or strange nightmare before studying the nature of dreams.

Learning to interpret your dreams teaches you the inner workings of your mind. Each dream you have is a message from a part of your inner self to your outer, conscious self. The message, once decoded, will give you valuable information concerning the conscious state of your awareness. In our physical everyday life we communicate with words that form what we call a language. When we learn the language our inner minds "speak" we can decode the messages we gain while asleep.

Stretch your memory recapturing the awareness of a child. When we were very young, we were exposed to all kinds of leather bound papers with ink on them. At one time we would look at the pages of a book and only see straight and curved lines. To someone educated in the meaning of these symbols new worlds could be opened. To us at that time they were meaningless.

As months passed in our early lives, someone around us began to instruct us in the alphabet. We learned that certain shapes made with pen and paper represented something. Then we were taught how to put these shapes together to form words. Words could then be up together to create sentences, and sentences placed together to form paragraphs. In this way we learned in our early years how to use a language to communicate our ideas, to give thoughts to and receive ideas from others who speak the same language.

How often do we take this beautiful ability of physical communication for granted? Imagine being close to someone, wanting to express your ideas of closeness, desiring to let them know how much you respect and appreciate knowing them, yet you never learned the words that would communicate your ideas. Imagine experiencing love with no means of communicating it in the physical. How limited and empty our experiences would be.

Learning the language of mind is similar to learning a physical language like English or French or Chinese. Comprehending the individual characters whether they are letters of the alphabet or symbols in a dream gives you the ability to identify at will what is being communicated. By developing your foundation, you can form words, sentences, and paragraphs in the language of mind. At this point you will be able to interpret energy as it moves through the inner levels of your consciousness into the physical.

Throughout the years, I have met many people who flatly declare, *"I do not dream."* When we explore this statement further we usually arrive at some point in that individual's life where dreams were remembered. For some it might be a few years ago, for others twenty or thirty years ago. Eventually there is a remembrance of several dreams which reaffirms their ability to dream.

When I first began teaching people how to interpret dreams, some felt they had to take my word for it that dreaming occurs each time man is consciously asleep. In those ensuing years, many studies of brain activity have been done at colleges and universities in the United States and the world which substantiate the fact that each of us do indeed dream nightly. Although these studies serve a valuable purpose for many because they offer physical support of our common mental experience, they do not address the questions of the origin of our dreams, why they exist and what they mean. This is the realm of the meta-physicists, those who explore what is beyond and behind those physical effects in our brain, body, and environment.

For the individual who states they do not dream, the first step is to realize that the short-circuit is not in the dreaming ability. Rather, it exists in the control of recalling the dream experience. Those who forget their dreams are often the same people who have difficulty remembering in their daily life. Rather than direct their full attention toward the experience before them, they scatter their mind's energies receiving information in a piecemeal manner. Later, when they desire to recall the information it comes to them in the same scattered form it was stored and they can recall faces but not the names or events but not the demarcation of time.

Being able to recall your dreams is the first step in learning the Universal Language of Mind. To enhance your recall begin developing conscious control of your attention during your daily activities. Endeavor to direct your mental will so you can receive through the five sensory receptors the full experience. Take nothing for granted and do not ignore what is occurring from boredom or because you find the experience unpleasant. Through exercising your will in this manner, you will develop skill in wielding your attention, honing your ability to systematically store information in the brain for later recall. You will be able to draw upon this enhanced skill to remember the details of your dream experiences.

Nurturing a sincere desire to use the communication received in your dreams is another important factor for dream recall. In order for your will to be productively active, desire must be present. You must want to receive information from your daily experiences otherwise you remain ignorant, *ignoring* what is presented to you. People who claim they do not dream perpetuate the lack of knowledge available to them because they ignore the messages being relayed from their inner Self to their waking Self. Develop a keen interest in what your dreams are saying. Build your desire for clear and prolonged inner communication by wanting to discover what your subconscious mind has to say about you and the way you are leading your life.

To aid in dream recall, place a stenographer's pad and a pen next to your bed. Before you go to sleep, make your last conscious thought and action be that of writing down the next day's date. This will serve as a signal to your subconscious mind that you consciously expect to remember your dream. Immediately when you consciously awake the next morning, write down what you recall. Even if it's only *red car, mountain,* or *mother and a dog.* This is the beginning of mastering your dream state. The *red car* is a letter in the language of mind's alphabet that you will need in order to read great mental novels.

You may be familiar with this suggestion from other articles, books, or discussions about dreaming. This is because following these instructions does work. What you may be unaware of is how and why these directions produce the desired results. As we accept the probability of enhancing our soul's progression by interpreting our dreams and become serious in our efforts, our subconscious mind registers the intent of our conscious mind. Since the subconscious mind has a duty to fulfill all our conscious desires when allowed, it will go to extreme lengths to performs its duty. Giving conscious thought to building our desire to remember our dreams and acting on that desire (writing the next day's date on our writing tablet) cause that desire to be planted like a seed in the inner levels of the subconscious mind. The subconscious mind then begins to respond by fulfilling that desire. Thus with this mental action we are causing our conscious and subconscious minds to begin working together toward a common goal.

Learning the language the inner mind speaks is the key to your storehouse. By becoming fluent, you are no longer a stranger in a foreign land. You have the means to communicate, comprehending the messages given to you and responding with your directives. You become bilingual for you are knowledgeable in a language spoken in the physical world, such as English, Latin, or Chinese, and in the language of images spoken in the metaphysical world. This skill abundantly increases your awareness of the power of the subconscious mind which is intuition. The efforts you make to remember, interpret, and understand the meaning of your dreams give you access to inner wisdom.

## How to Use the Dreamer's Dictionary

As we gain greater Self awareness, we realize that to understand our Self and our world is to know the parts that together create a whole. Using your dreams gives you the advantage of identifying the elements of Self that, when operating as a single unit, compose your whole functioning Self.

The people, places, things, and action in your dreams individually are important elements in comprehending the message your subconscious mind is giving to your conscious mind. *Dream-people* will signify aspects of your Self and will indicate the qualities you are using in each division of mind whether conscious, subconscious, or superconscious. *Dream-places* -- a house, a hospital, a church, your hometown, another planet -- tell us the level of consciousness where those aspects are expressing and often are indicative of a combination of thoughts which comprise an attitude. The *things* that are present in our dreams -- the food, the telephone, the car, the clothing -- will describe what each aspect is using to express itself. The *dream-action* will reveal the point of the dream. It will present to you a type of allegory that is specifically intended for you, about you.

After recording your dream, you can use the dictionary as a reference for identifying the universal meaning of the images appearing in your dream. It will serve as a reference book giving for words of one language, English, equivalents in another, the language of mind. From *abbey* to *zoo*, you will find the universal meaning of the most common symbols that are used in dreaming. For instance, an *apple* in your dream signifies knowledge, a *baby* represents a new idea, and a *house* represents your mind.

The dictionary also includes information on how the symbols might be used which will assist you in interpreting the dream message. This gives insight into the meaning of the action in the dream or assists in combining the meaning of several symbols for accurate interpretation. An example of the first, an action in a dream, would be *eating an apple,* symbolizing knowledge that you have received and are assimilating. An example of the second, is a *male infant* which would signify in which part of mind the new idea has arisen.

This dictionary gives clues to the origin and development of the language used in the inner levels of consciousness: the Universal Language of Mind. Every physical word we use has a history, and in almost every case it is a story of action, a story of something happening. Word-forming activity has been going on for thousands of years in response to man's need to communicate his ideas to others. The English language is a melting pot of previous languages used by man, whether the origin is French, Greek, or Sanskrit. Each word, regardless of its physical language, describes an image or picture. In reality, the thought or image is the point of origin for communication. Physical language came later as a response to man's desire to be understood. This dictionary defines the thought beyond the physical word. It reveals the universal essence of the action or happening that is being outwardly described. This universal essence is the nature of the inner mind's communication to the outer, waking mind in what we call dreams. The language of mind is the language used by the inner, subconscious mind for communication.

The extensive dictionary provided here will aid you in translating from the language of mind into the English language. As with dictionaries of any language, it contains alphabetically arranged terms important to a particular subject or activity along with discussion of their meanings and applications. In many cases it will offer explanations of the reason behind the interpretation of the symbol.

Each entry in the dictionary gives the following information: *1) the word/symbol and its meaning in the Universal Language of Mind, 2) more in-depth meaning in the language of mind and possible contexts of the symbol, 3) the physical derivation of the word, 4) thoughts to consider.* You will find this information valuable in learning the universal meaning of dream-images and in understanding the significance of your personal dream-messages.

Upon awakening, immediately record what you remember about the dream. You will find a stenographer's pad, which has a vertical center line, will be quite useful as a dream journal. Write your dream on the left side of the center line, leaving the right side blank. The more details you recall, the more images or dream symbols you will be able to reference. When you have written down everything you remember about your dream, review it, underlining or circling the specific images that appear. These will be the symbols to reference in the dictionary. The images that arise during the dream state are listed alphabetically in the dictionary. You will find that the word describing the image will also describe a part of the action of the dream. For example, the people participating in the dream action may be listed as *brother, minister, servant,* or *teacher.*

To find each symbol's meaning in the Universal Language of Mind, look up the word describing the image. On the right side of the paper next to the text of your dream, record each symbol's meaning in the language of mind. You may find the index at the end of this book useful for referencing related symbols that will assist you in defining meaning. For instance, if you dream you are at a *banquet,* you might want to research related symbols appearing in the scene: *food, table, flowers, candles.* Each part of the image exists purposefully and, when understood in the Language of Mind and perceived as a whole, the image describes the dreamer's state of awareness. When this is completed you will have the translation of the symbols in your dream.

Learning the language of mind is the first step toward command of inner communication. As with any physical language, fluency will arise from consistent use of the language. As you become proficient in deciphering dream symbols you are prepared to understand the import of the action in your dream.

Identifying symbols and looking them up in the dictionary is only the first step to becoming an interpreter of your dreams. You must be able to connect the symbols' meanings in order to perceive the thought-sentences being conveyed by your subconscious mind. The dream action explains the means of expression for the many aspects of Self, revealing an inner train of thought in response to your conscious way of thinking. For example, if you dream your boss is drowning in a pool of jello, this will indicate your sense of authority (*boss*) is being overwhelmed (*drowning*) by insignificant knowledge (*jello*, which is a food poor in nutrition). If you dream the bus you're riding is going the wrong way on a one-way street and crashes, your subconscious mind is telling you that the organization (*bus*) that you are a member of (*riding*) is no longer moving toward its stated goals (*traveling on street*), thus eroding the organization (*crash* or *wreck*).

To combine the translated thought-words into thought-sentences, you will find the next dictionary entry helpful. Here you will find an explanation of the word's meaning in the language of mind, often giving examples of combinations of symbols and their meanings. For instance the extended explanation of the image *hair* is:

> *"Hair in a dream represents the dreamer's conscious, waking thoughts. How hair appears in the dream will indicate the quality of the thoughts, thus giving the dreamer insight into the way s/he is thinking and what alterations can be made to enhance thinking. For instance, if hair is being cut this will symbolize the dreamer's current tendency to reorganize thoughts; baldness will indicate a need to exercise conscious thinking particularly relevant to the aspect of Self that appears in the dream. A hairy dream-creature will indicate an unknown part of Self consumed by conscious thoughts."*

This entry category will assist you through a more in-depth explanation of the symbol's meaning. Many times it will also give examples of how the symbols may appear in a dream. When interpreted, the message from your subconscious mind will become clearer.

The "Derivative Meaning" category gives information concerning the physical origin of the word and its common meaning. This category will become more important to you as you become fluent in the language of mind. In most instances, word origin is more closely aligned with the thought it seeks to describe. Thus the derivative meaning more accurately describes the intent of the word. For instance, you will find the origin of the word *father* is the Sanskrit *pa* meaning "to feed". This aptly describes the duty of the superconscious mind which is to energize the outer mind, in essence "to feed" the subconscious mind thus insuring its continued existence. This category will assist you in discerning the depth of your dream message.

Having translated the symbols of your dream, now it is time to interpret the message -- to determine the significance of the dream in your life. The final dictionary entry is designed to assist you in this process through thought-provoking questions or examples of how the language is used. For instance, "Thoughts to Consider" associated with the dream image of the *sea* are:

> *"Note the way in which the sea appears in your dream. Is it tumultuous and threatening, or peaceful and awe-inspiring? The activity occurring and your response to it will give you feedback concerning how you are leading your life or running away from it. Realize your experiences are your own. No two people perceive the same experience exactly the same owing to the differences in temporary and permanent memory. However, in any experience there are facts. Seek to identify the facts in your experience, free from bias or ego motivation, then draw upon your intuitive understanding to gain the most from life experiences."*

The entry in the same category for *books* is:

> *"Am I learning from my experiences? Learning is a step-by-step process beginning with the reception of information. Note the kind and subject matter of the books in the dream to discern the type of information being addressed in your dream. A library of books will indicate a wide range of information available to you. If they remain unread, you need to use information for the considerable resource for learning they afford you."*

Drawing upon this section will stimulate new ways of thinking that will help you apply the dream message to your life. Answering the questions posed will lead to deeper contemplation of the dream's meaning and significance in your life.

This dictionary will give you the basic information needed to begin to interpret your dreams in the language of mind. It will open doors to the wisdom of your inner Self. With practice of these new skills, hopefully you will be stimulated into responsive action, acting on the wisdom offered to you from your soul.

Following the Universal Language of Mind dictionary, you will find a closing section devoted to the art of interpreting dreams and the benefits of rapport with your own inner mind. This will assist you in realizing the magnitude of the wisdom your dreams afford. You will learn how the many different images that appear in a dream are unified in content and meaning when they are interpreted in the language of mind. Every dream tells a story about the dreamer, often teaching a lesson to be discerned and applied by the dreamer. The lesson is learned when it is applied in the dreamer's life. As you begin to study your own dreams, recording, researching, and understanding their meaning, you can expect to become more fluent in the Universal Language of Mind.

# The Dreamer's Dictionary
# Section II

*"Dreams
are the true interpreters of our inclinations;
but there is art required
to sort and understand them."*

Michel de Montaigne (1533-1592)
*Essays 1580-88*

| Symbol | Meaning in Universal Language of Mind |
|---|---|

A

**Abbey**
*represents*
*spiritual*
*qualities.*

The spiritual quality of the dreamer's mind is an important part of the message when a religious place appears in a dream. These spiritual qualities range from awareness to mercy, truthfulness to discipline, forgiveness to devotion. Each can be employed by the mind in the physical life. Because of its secluded nature, an abbey in a dream will symbolize the dreamer's spiritual qualities that have yet to be fully used or integrated into the life.

**Abortion**
*is the cessation*
*of creative*
*thought.*

A baby in the dream symbolizes a new idea. Physically conception occurs from the cooperative effort of a male sperm and a female egg. For human beings, this uniting naturally progresses under the direction of DNA codes resulting in a newborn physical body within nine months. Symbolically, this is the uniting of the aggressive and receptive principles that give rise to new thoughts. When abortion occurs in a dream it represents a cessation of this creative process.

**Acupuncture**
*symbolizes a*
*purposeful*
*movement in*
*thought*
*patterns to*
*produce well-*
*being.*

Knowing where the acupuncture is being received and what correspondence this has to organs will help you identify the specific attitudes that are being healed. If the dream acupuncture is performed on the meridian where the kidney functions, the dream will be addressing a transformation of self-condemnation into Self appreciation because the attitude producing kidney disorders is self-condemnation or guilt. For more information on the mental attitudes promoting health or disease in the body, use the reference book Permanent Healing by Dr. Daniel R. Condron.

**Acting**
*indicates the*
*dreamer's use*
*of imagination.*

The ability to imagine is what sets man apart from all other animals. Imagination is one of three components needed for reasoning to occur. When acting occurs in a dream, the message will revolve around your imaging ability and how it is being used to create your life experiences.

| *Derivative Meaning* | *Thoughts to Consider* |
|---|---|
| *Dict. A monastery or monastic establishment of the highest rank; a society of persons of either sex, secluded from the world and devoted to religion and celibacy.* | Are my spiritual ideas practical? Do they influence my everyday thinking and actions, or are they isolated from my physical life? Endeavor to bring your spiritual ideals into physical reality by acting upon your ideals — courageously speak the truth as you know it, display compassion for what you at first do not understand. |
| *Dict. The act of miscarrying, or producing young before the natural time or before the fetus is perfectly formed.* | Have I recently been considering new ideas, but given up on them before they had a chance to manifest? Have I been rejecting ideas offered by others? Have I been forcing myself to remain the same rather than pursue new ways of thinking or new ways of life that I find stimulating and desirable? Learn to identify your own thinking processes. Developing concentration skills will empower you to hold your attention on your desires long enough for them to manifest in your life. |
| *Dict. A healing art performed for thousands of years in China and ancient Persia; a physical practice designed to stimulate energy flows in the body thus releasing blockages, and their resulting pain, and restoring proper function.* | What have I recently released in my way of thinking? Which old patterns of thinking that were holding me back have I actively been seeking to change? How can I build upon my newfound understanding to promote wholistic health in spirit, mind and body? Becoming aware of self-defeating patterns of thinking is the first step to unlocking your potential for wholeness. Completing what you begin frees the energy and substance in the mind, making it available for the fulfillment of your desires today. |
| *Dict. Performing duty, service, or functions; doing the real work of an office for nominal or honorary holder of the post; representing a character through acts in a play.* | Am I initiating new ways of thinking and acting, or just living life by rote? Begin asking yourself "what if...". This will stimulate the use of your imagination, guiding the mind toward envisioning a different kind of life thereby expanding your imaging capability. Choose the "what if" that is in alignment with your desires, then begin living it. |

| Symbol | Meaning in Universal Language of Mind |
|---|---|
| *Actors* *identify specific aspects of Self involved in the use of imagination.* | When the actor is the same sex as the dreamer, s/he represents the imaging ability in the conscious mind. When the actor is the opposite sex, s/he signifies the reproducing ability in the subconscious mind. Visualization is a cooperative effort between the conscious and subconscious minds. The conscious mind produces the mental image of what is desired and subconscious mind re-produces that image so it can manifest in physical form. If the actors in a dream are known to the dreamer, the dream message becomes even clearer once the dreamer identifies the outstanding quality s/he attributes to the actor. |
| *Adults* *symbolize productive aspects of Self.* | There are four stages of man: infancy, adolescence, adulthood, and old age. These descriptions of physical maturation are guided by metaphysical stages in the growth of spirit. Spiritual maturity begins by absorbing information and receiving guidance (infancy). This leads to a time of experimentation (adolescence), which produces experience and knowledge of what is productive and non-productive in thought and action. The application of productive action (adulthood) produces leadership and response-ability adding understanding to the Self. The dissemination of understanding (old age) completes the cycle through the sharing of wisdom. |
| *Advertisement* *is communication occurring within Self.* | Since most ads are involving money, the communication will revolve around the dreamer's value. What is being advertised will convey the kind and quality of the communication. If a house for sale is being advertised, this will symbolize the willingness of the dreamer to communicate the value of his mind. If it is a want ad notifying people of potential employment, it will signify learning opportunities available that could bring awareness of the value the dreamer has to offer. |
| *Air* *signifies motion.* | One of the four primary elements, air in a dream will signify movement. |

| *Derivative Meaning* | *Thoughts to Consider* |
|---|---|
| *Dict. One who acts or performs representing a character in a play.* | Do I know the actor? If so, how would I describe him to someone who has never seen him before? This will be the aspect of your Self that is using imagination. If you do not know the actor, he is an aspect of Self which is unfamiliar to your waking consciousness. Determine if the dream is addressing your imaginative skill in the conscious mind or the subconscious mind. When active in the conscious mind, determine how this quality can be built upon and more fully used in creating your desires. When active in the subconscious mind, use the dream message as insight for greater cooperation with your inner Self by preparing to receive the manifestations of desires previously set into motion. |
| *Dict. Having arrived at mature years; a person grown to full size and strength.* | How am I using my spiritual maturity to gain understanding of my experiences? Am I responding to opportunities for learning and growth to the best of my ability or expecting others to provide leadership in my life? It is true that every experience is an opportunity to learn something. Look beyond this, gaining greater understanding of Self and life. Instead of asking, "What am I supposed to be learning", ask "How can I use my understandings to better this situation." |
| *Dict. A written or printed notice intended to make something known to the public.* | What do I consider important in life? What thoughts and activities do I hold in high regard? Your dreams will aid you to deepen your sense of value and encourage you to reevaluate your value when it will accelerate your soul progression. Endeavor to uphold those principles and truths in life you know are valuable and communicate these in your waking thoughts and actions. If you value trust, be trustworthy; if you value truth, be honest; if you value time, be productive in your experiences; if you value spirituality, pursue spiritual disciplines. |
| *Dict. A heterogeneous mixture of tasteless, odorless, colorless, and invisible gases sur-* | Look for why the air is important in the dream, is it a turbulent windstorm or a soft breeze across a lake? By identifying the other universal symbols in the dream you will be able to determine the |

| Symbol | Meaning in Universal Language of Mind |
|--------|----------------------------------------|
| *Airplane represents the physical body.* | Small airplanes are vehicles of conveyance, enabling one to travel quickly from one place to another. What enables the thinker to travel from one place to another is the physical body. If in a dream the airplane is in jeopardy or broken, this will indicate a potential disorder in the physical body. |
| *Airport is a condition of mind concerning the diversity of Self expression.* | Populated by large and small planes, cars and busses, and many people, airports symbolize how you express Self individually and in a group. |
| *Alcohol signifies an interference with the conscious will.* | The physical intake of alcohol into the body affects the nervous system impairing brain function thus decreasing conscious volition. Examples of the interference with the will range from a lack of control of motor functions such as walking to becoming involved in activities contrary to the nature of the person and his best judgement such as unbridled displays of anger or giddiness. When alcohol appears in a dream it will symbolize an interference in the conscious mind's ability to employ will. |
| *Algebra represents the form of reasoning.* | Reasoning is produced by employing three conscious mind skills: memory, attention, and imagination. Mathematical equations in a dream represent the use of reasoning, applied in systematic fashion, to understand cause and effect in the life. |

| *Derivative Meaning* | *Thoughts to Consider* |
|---|---|
| rounding the earth; that which we breathe and which is essential to all plant and animal life. | kind of motion and what it is producing. |
| Dict. Any one of different kinds of flying machines, heavier than air, and supported in the air by planes or wings. | Have I been attentive to the needs of my physical body? Am I giving it the nutrition, exercise and rest it requires to remain strong and viable? |
| Dict. A field, with a hangar or hangars, for the landing, taking-off, and servicing of aircraft. | After determining the meaning of the action in the dream, examine what it is telling you about the way you express Self. Are you the same person at all times, in all situations, with all people or are your ideas and expression determined by your environment? Do the people with whom you associate share your ideals and goals, thus bringing out your best? Direct Self toward being the best you can be and choose avenues of Self expression that will accelerate and support your desire. |
| Dict. A liquid forming the intoxicating principle of all vinous and spirituous liquors, obtained by distillation. | Am I pursuing ways to build my will power or looking for excuses for mental laziness? Do I direct my will toward the fulfillment of my ideals and accomplishment of my goals? Am I becoming distracted, procrastinating and perpetuating dissatisfaction in my life? Replace your habit of escaping from life's experiences by developing a reason to live. This reason gives your will something productive to act upon. |
| Dict. That branch of mathematical analysis in which signs are employed to denote arithmetical operation and letters are used to represent numbers and quantities. | What am I seeking to understand in my life? Am I utilizing the full power available to me in my conscious mind? Do my desires "equal" my experiences? Realize your need for balance in your life arises from an inner desire to understand cause and effect. By becoming aware of thought as cause you will take greater care in how thinking occurs and begin mastering the power in your conscious mind. |

| Symbol | Meaning in Universal Language of Mind |
|---|---|
| **Alien** *is an unknown aspect of Self.* | Aliens are unfamiliar life forms not indigenous to our planet. In a dream these unidentified aspects of Self will appear in a form unfamiliar to the conscious mind and be described by the conscious, waking mind as an alien *(see God, devil)*. An alien signifies an aspect of Self foreign to the image of Self held by the dreamer. |
| **Alley** *signifies an abbreviated means to a goal.* | Alleys are short cuts to a destination. In a dream they signify a way to accomplish something in a short amount of time. The question is will the abbreviated outcome be equal to one where no short cuts are made. |
| **Altar** *is directing your attention inwardly.* | Attention is the ability to focus the mind, inwardly on a particular concept or idea, or outwardly on an object. A physical altar is a structure or place on which sacrifices are offered or incense is burned in worship. When an altar appears in a dream it will represent a reverent and complete direction of attention inward toward wholeness. |
| **Ancient** *symbolizes a longstanding condition.* | Further interpretation can be gained by identifying the meaning of what is being described as ancient, for instance, an ancient monument or an ancient culture. |
| **Angel** *is a thought form from the superconscious mind.* | The superconscious mind is the part of Self closest to the spiritual origin. It houses the complete plan or blueprint for maturity as an offspring of the Creator. Since angels are a concept rather than an occurrence in the physical existence, when the dreamer identifies a symbol as an angel it signifies the conscious ability to make the superconscious inner urge known. |
| **Animals** *represent habits.* | Animals function from instinct, a reaction to pleasure or pain. Having differing degrees of memory and the ability for attention, animals do not possess the evolutionary development including a sufficient brain capacity for imagination. Most animals in a dream will represent the dreamer's habits. There are four animals which represent specific types of habits. A *Horse* or other beast of burden |

| *Derivative Meaning* | *Thoughts to Consider* |
|---|---|
| *Dict. Not belonging to the same country, land, or government; foreign.* | Have I been thinking and acting in a way foreign to my nature? Realize being unique and different does not necessitate separation or "alienation" from Self or others. Develop a pioneering attitude; explore this aspect of Self. Determine how it can become useful to your growth making what was previously unknown, known. |
| *Dict. A narrow passage or way in a town.* | Am I taking short cuts in my life? Are there unnecessary risks in how I pursue my goals? By the action in your dream, determine if you are accelerating the achievement of a goal or becoming distracted from a goal. |
| *Dict. An elevated place on which sacrifices were offered or incense burned to a deity.* | How does my concept of spirituality affect the thoughts and actions of my daily life? Am I living my spiritual ideals becoming closer to my Creator? Learn to give freely and completely to the highest ideals you can imagine. Realize you are a soul inhabiting a physical body for the purpose of spiritual growth. |
| *Dict. That happened or existed in former times, usually at a great distance of time, associated with or being marks of the times of long ago.* | What attitudes or thoughts have I been holding onto for years? What purpose does this longstanding condition serve in my present life? Determine if the dream is addressing an enduring understanding productive to your growth or a limiting attachment that is no longer needed. |
| *Dict. A divine messenger; a spiritual being employed in the service of God.* | How am I using my inner authority? Does my concept of God affect the way I think and how I live? Do I give credence and respect to my existence beyond the physical, everyday life? Begin to heed your inner sense of what is righteous or productive. Establish a means of strengthening this inner connection through communing with your Creator in prayer and meditation. |
| *Dict. A living being characterized by sensation and voluntary motion; an inferior or irrational being in contradistinction to man.* | What habit is being addressed? Is it a physical habit such as punctuality or eating, or a mental habit such as attentiveness or sensitivity? Does this habit ensure greater efficiency in my life or is it a compulsive distraction to the fulfillment of my desires? Realize habits are neither good nor bad; what they are and how they are used will deter- |

| Symbol | Meaning in Universal Language of Mind |
|---|---|
| | represents the will of the dreamer, a *Fish* signifies spiritual knowledge, *Birds* are subconscious thoughts, and a *Snake* represents wisdom born from creation. |
| *Antiques are longstanding ideas which have great value.* | Identifying the kind of antique and its function will aid in determining the specific idea intended in the subconscious communication. *See Furniture.* |
| *Apartment signifies the dreamer's mind.* | Apartments are living spaces owned by another individual and rented for a specific length of time as a dwelling. In a dream, an apartment will symbolize the mind; the dwelling of the thinker. An apartment can also be a building made up of individual dwelling units. When an apartment building appears in a dream, it is indicative of what is termed universal mind. |
| *Apartment Building represents universal mind.* | Universal mind describes the interconnectedness of all minds experienced in the inner levels of consciousness. The subconscious, intuitive ability for telepathy is an example of this interconnectedness which transcends physical limitations of time and space. The power of influence has its origin in the ability to send and receive thoughts through the energy and substance of universal mind. This is one of the reasons why great thinkers can reach the same inven- |

| *Derivative Meaning* | *Thoughts to Consider* |
|---|---|
| | mine the action you can take for increased Self awareness. The easily distracted puppy you love may represent a habit of being inattentive. The magnificent eagle flying above the mountains may represent your freedom and inner strength to meet challenges. The "King Kong" gorilla may represent a habit of gross exaggeration or a physical habit that is overtaking your life. The lion who scares you in a dream may be indicating your resistance to your own courage. |
| *Dict. Having existed in ancient times; having come down from antiquity.* | Most of the valuable ideas which are of enduring value are understandings which comprise the evolution of the soul. Dreaming of antiques will aid you to become aware of specific understandings, giving you the opportunity to use them more fully in your conscious life. If you dream of an antique mirror, begin respecting your ability for self-examination; an antique car, begin appreciating your ability for health and fitness. If the antique in your dream is broken, ask your Self, "What understanding am I taking for granted?" |
| *Dict. A room in a building; a division in a house separated from others by partitions.* | Whose apartment is this? Does it belong to me or someone else? Determining the ownership will aid you in understanding the dream message by identifying what aspects of Self are predominate in your patterns of thinking. If the apartment belongs to a stranger, the dream is addressing unconscious ways of using your mind. If it belongs to a competent friend, the dream is highlighting your efficient use of mind. Also, examine the composition of the apartment: how many rooms or floors. A one room apartment will indicate a marginal use of your mind's potential. A large apartment comprising several floors will represent an expansive use of your mind. |
| *Dict. A structure including many dwellings separated by partitions.* | Become more aware of your intuitive ability for thought projection and reception by developing your concentrative and visualizing skill. By knowing your own thoughts, you will be more equipped to distinguish your thoughts from those of others. You will also be able to distinguish when you are sending thoughts you have visualized and when you are receiving impressions from someone else. |

| *Symbol* | *Meaning in Universal Language of Mind* |
|---|---|
| | tive discoveries seemingly simultaneously across the globe, or why someone can have knowledge of a distant loved one's thoughts or experiences. |
| *Apparel represents the outer expression of the dreamer.* | "Clothes do not make the man" is a true statement, yet they do reflect a quality of thinking and the choices of the dreamer. Apparel in a dream indicates how the dreamer expresses Self and the influence s/he has upon others. |
| *Apple is knowledge.* | Physically, food is received for the sustaining and nourishment of the physical body. Food in a dream will represent nourishment for the mind. |
| *Apron is the outer expression of the dreamer.* | An apparel used during the act of cooking, the stylized use of an apron indicates how the dreamer's learning expresses itself. |
| *Armor is the outer expression of the dreamer.* | Apparel used to protect the body during combat, the stylized use of armor indicates the dreamer's need to preserve or defend his ideas. |
| *Arms indicate purposeful intention.* | When arms and hands are a predominant part of the dream action this will indicate your resolve to attain or achieve. |

| *Derivative Meaning* | *Thoughts to Consider* |
|---|---|
| | Command of your own mind brings awareness of the wisdom available to you in universal mind. |
| *Dict. Clothing, vesture, garments.* | Define the apparel. Is it elegant or dowdy, old or new, clean or tattered and dirty? Your judgement will indicate the essence of your dream's message informing you about how you express yourself outwardly. Ask yourself does this expression reflect who I am? Is it a truthful reflection of how I see myself? Make sure what you are expressing and how you communicate is in alignment with your ideals and Self concept. |
| *Dict. A fruit of a well-known fruit tree.* | Observe the action in your dream. Am I eating an apple or just noting its presence in the dream? The act of eating will indicate knowledge you are currently receiving in your daily life. If you are observing the fruit, you are aware of knowledge available without assimilating it. Begin appreciating the vast array of information open to you. Choose to pursue knowledge for it is the beginning of learning. |
| *Dict. A piece of cloth worn on the forepart of the body to keep the clothes clean or defend them from injury.* | How am I putting the information I receive into use in my life? Am I using it toward greater understanding of Self and others or merely "wearing" it to show others how much I know? Use the information you gain to better your Self, improving your own life and that of others. |
| *Dict. Any covering worn to protect the body in battle.* | Have I been overly sensitive lately, taking things too personally? Am I rejecting new ideas or what others offer me? A defensive attitude is often an attempt to mask insecurity. Relax! Just because you receive an idea doesn't mean you are obligated to accept it as part of your thinking. Put your ideals into practice so you can develop inner confidence in your abilities. You'll be more open to others. |
| *Dict. The limb of the human body which extends from the shoulder to the hand.* | Place the meaning in the context of your dream. If your arms are graceful, like a dancer's, this indicates a flowing ease toward your objective. If your arm is broken, you need to examine what is important to you and your willingness to pursue it. If |

| *Symbol* | *Meaning in Universal Language of Mind* |
|---|---|
| **Art** *is creativity.* | Art is skill acquired by experience, study, or observation. What is produced by using this skill is artwork. For the mind, art is the utilization of the power of creative imagery. |
| **Artillery** *signifies tools for change.* | Physically associated with war, in the language of mind artillery represents the elements contributing to inner turmoil. Dream artillery signifies forced change leading to self-destruction or caused change leading to resolve of conflict. |
| **Asleep** *signifies assimilation.* | Sleeping is a time of rest and relaxation for the mind and body. It is also the time when your inner mind can communicate uninterruptedly. When you are sleeping in a dream you are recognizing how your experiences are affecting your consciousness. |
| **Astral Projection** *represents the use of the inner levels of the subconscious mind.* | Astral projection is the ability to separate the mind and body at will. When astral projection occurs in a dream it symbolizes the dreamer's ability to identify with the inner mind, the soul. |
| **Astrology** *is conscious awareness of subconscious* | The study of astrology acquaints you with your relationship to our universe by offering insight into the Universal Law of Relativity. The universe, the placement of planets in relationship to the time/place you were born on planet |

| *Derivative Meaning* | *Thoughts to Consider* |
|---|---|
| | the arms are missing, you are unaware of the intentions behind your acts. |
| *Dict. The use or employment of things to answer some special purpose; one of the fine arts that appeal to the taste or sense of beauty such as painting, sculpture, music.* | Am I creating my desires and receiving their manifestations in my life or am I a victim of repeating the same thoughts over and over again, a creature of habit? Develop the skill of visualization to free your consciousness from compulsive patterns and become a creative thinker. |
| *Dict. Formerly offensive weapons of war in general whether large or small; now, ordnance and its equipment both in men and material.* | Determine if you are fighting change or causing change in your life. Do not wait for circumstances to dictate your awareness of the need for change in your life. Use reasoning to guide your life and the inner battles will cease to occur. |
| *Dict. In or into a state of sleep; to be in that well-known state in which there is a suspension of the voluntary exercise of the powers of the body and mind and which is periodically necessary to bodily health.* | Make Self realization your ideal in life. Be willing to review the impact of your experiences during your waking life. At the end of your day, ask yourself, "What did I learn today that will make me a better person?" Learn to wield the energy available to promote soul progression. |
| *Dict. Belonging to the stars; to throw out or forth.* | Are you pursuing spiritual development in your everyday life? If not, doing so will accelerate your conscious understanding of your whole Self. If you are, continue your practices for they are aiding you toward greater Self realization. Strengthen your awareness of the inner planes of existence through daily meditation. Bring the insights gained from meditation into your dealings with others in your everyday life. In this way the purpose of your existence will be revealed to you. |
| *Dict. The science which professes to discover effects and influences of the heavenly bodies on* | Keep in mind that astrological references in your dream reveal information concerning the purpose for your existence. Each zodiacal sign will lend insight into the nature of that purpose. The fol- |

| *Symbol* | *Meaning in Universal Language of Mind* |
|---|---|
| *purpose for existence.* | Earth, offers influences that were chosen by your soul and can be used by you as you move through your life. Zodiac signs indicate the soul's intention for learning at the onset of your lifetime. Planets influence the mode or activity that can be used to bring this learning about. The universe exists as part of creation. It does not determine; it merely exists. You, the thinker, determine how any influence will be used, whether productive or nonproductive, in your life. |
| *Attic signifies superconscious part of mind.* | Physically, an attic is the uppermost part of a house; the part of the structure closest to the sky or heavens. In a dream, the attic symbolizes the part of mind closest to your origin as spirit and farthest from your existence in the physical. The action occurring in this part of a house will revolve around how you view your own divinity. |
| *Audience represents aspects of Self united for a common purpose.* | The types of people and the reason for their gathering will indicate the individual character of the dreamer's message. An audience of younger people gathered for a rock concert will indicate attitudes of experimentation for the purpose of harmony. An audience of executives gathered for a business seminar will signify attitudes of productivity for the purpose of learning. A diverse audience with a religious figure, such as the Pope, will represent all aspects of Self unified for a spiritual purpose. |
| *Auras signify mental expressions of energy.* | An aura describes the expression of energy emanating from a life form. All life forms, be they gas, mineral, plant, animal, or human, utilize energy to sustain their existence. The energy used can be perceived with mental attention as light or waves radiating from the source. For example, the halos surrounding religious figures in classical art are representative of the artist's conception of the aura of the subject. |

| *Derivative Meaning* | *Thoughts to Consider* |
|---|---|
| *human and mundane affairs.* | lowing key words for each sign indicates the inner soul urge inherent in the expression of each sign: *Aries - I become; Taurus - I value; Gemini - I express; Cancer - I sense; Leo - I aspire; Virgo - I discriminate; Libra - I integrate; Scorpio - I create; Sagittarius - I perceive; Capricorn - I serve; Aquarius - I understand; Pisces - I transcend.* When these references appear in a dream, they will reflect an inner drive toward greater Self awareness in the specific area cited.

When planets of our universe appear in your dream, they will indicate the activity being taken or needing to be taken to produce greater Self awareness. The following key words for each planet indicates the nature of the action: Sun origination; Mercury expression; Venus reception; Earth reflection; Mars initiation; Jupiter expansion; Saturn contraction; Uranus transformation; Neptune perception; Pluto generation. |
| *Dict. A room under the roof of a house where the ceiling follows the line of the roof.* | How do I understand my own divinity? Am I consciously aware of an inner authority far beyond the physical position or accomplishment in my everyday life? Daily meditation upon the Creator will aid you to build this awareness in your conscious mind. |
| *Dict. The act of listening; an assembly of hearers.* | Determine which aspects of Self are present in your dream by discerning their age, background, race, economic status, educational level. Then discern the purpose of their meeting. This will reveal the essence of the dream message. Are the people gathered to be entertained, to learn, to pay respects, or to participate? This will give insight into the intentions being revealed in your dream. |
| *Dict. An air; outward appearance, mien, manner of a person or thing.* | How am I influencing others? Am I consistent in my thoughts and actions or sending conflicting signals to others by thinking one thing and doing another? When auras appear in your dream, you are capable of utilizing your mind beyond the five physical senses. Pursue a scientifically based course of study in disciplining and developing your mental faculties for greater Self awareness and |

| Symbol | Meaning in Universal Language of Mind |
|--------|----------------------------------------|
| **Authority Figures** *symbolize the superconscious mind of the dreamer.* | The superconscious mind is the oldest division of mind. It is the part of mind closest to the Source or the Creator, thus holding the plan for spiritual maturity in man. Authority figures appearing in a dream relate to the superconscious mind of the dreamer. These aspects of Self, symbolized by those who hold authority in the dreamer's waking life, demonstrate the power and right to command that is reflective of the dreamer's superconscious mind. |
| **Automobiles** *represent the physical body.* | Physically, a car is a mechanical means of conveyance for transporting people and cargo from one location to another. When an automobile appears in a dream, it signifies a vehicle -- a physical body -- providing mobility for the thinker. The physical body is a temporary means of conveyance for the soul; it is used by individual consciousness from the point of birth through life to physical death. |
| **Autumn** *is the completion of creation.* | Autumn is the time of harvesting when the fruits of previous labor are gathered. In dreams, autumn signifies the fourth stage of man; the wisdom produced from previous life experiences and understandings. Autumn represents the culmination of the maturity and the preparation for a new cycle of growth. |

**B**

| | |
|--|--|
| **Baby** *is a new idea.* | In the physical world, a child is the result of the uniting of a male and female. In the language of mind this represents the cooperative use of aggressive and receptive principles to create something new. |

| *Derivative Meaning* | *Thoughts to Consider* |
|---|---|
| | enhanced understanding of your intuitive abilities. |
| *Dict. from the root* author, *from Latin* augeo *meaning "to increase" or "to produce". Power or right to command or act.* | What is my attitude in the dream toward this authority figure? Am I respectful and cooperative or disparaging and rebellious? The former will indicate a seeking for divine inner guidance that can be cultivated by daily meditation upon your Creator. The latter will indicate a rejection of inner authority characterized by attachment to the finite, physical world. |
| *Dict. A vehicle propelled by self-contained power plant used for carrying passengers over ordinary roads.* | The type of the car in your dream, be it a Rolls Royce or a Volkswagen, will give insight into the value you place upon your physical body. The condition of the car, whether it is in good or ill repair, will provide indications of your physical health state. For instance, if your *dream-car* has four flat tires or lacks an engine, you will want to pursue healthful activities to strengthen your body. |
| *Dict. A season of the year beginning at the autumnal equinox and ending at the winter solstice.* | What have I created in my life that is now reaching a point of conclusion? This will usually be a point of accomplishment: the end of a work assignment, graduating from a course of study, receiving recognition or award for efforts made, retiring or sending your children out on their own. Any of these could be relevant to your dream's message. Most importantly, realize how this creation has deepened your awareness of Self and others. This is the wisdom being highlighted in your dream message. |
| *Dict. An infant, a young child of either sex.* | Is the baby male or female? A child of the same sex as the dreamer will indicate a new idea in the conscious mind, therefore one that can be easily identifiable. A baby of the opposite sex as the dreamer signifies an idea manifesting in the inner levels of the subconscious mind. Noticing whose child this is will give you insight into the quality of the new idea. |

| Symbol | Meaning in Universal Language of Mind |
|--------|----------------------------------------|
| *Back* represents a structure for thinking. | The back of the human body revolves around the spinal column as the supporting structure for the head and appendages. In a dream, the back symbolizes that which provides structure for the mind. Examples of this structure for thinking are an ideal (which gives direction to the mind), purpose (which provides motivating energy), and activity (which brings about the desired transformation). |
| *Bald* signifies the absence of conscious thoughts. | Physically, baldness is the cessation of hair growing out of the scalp. Hair represents conscious thoughts in the language of mind. When it ceases to grow this indicates a lack of new conscious thoughts. |
| *Ballet* signifies balance in the thinking. | In a dream, ballet symbolizes the skillful employing of will to create equilibrium within the Self. |
| *Balloon* is a thought form. | Balloons represent the thoughts of Self or others. Ownership of the balloon in the dream will indicate the origin of the thought form. |
| *Bank* is a condition of mind where value is stored and exchanged. | In the Universal Language of Mind a bank will symbolize the individual's understanding of giving and receiving. The dream action will provide insight into how value is assessed and used by the dreamer. For example, saving money in a bank will indicate the accumulation of understanding which will be stored in the permanent memory of the subconscious mind. Writing a check without sufficient funds will indicate a mental attitude of taking. |

| *Derivative Meaning* | *Thoughts to Consider* |
|---|---|
| *Dict. The posterior part of the trunk; the region of the spine; the hinder part of the body in man and the upper in other animals.* | How do I use my mind to create my life? It is universally true that thought is cause. Reasoning, the power in the conscious mind, is a sequence of events in thought requiring the coordination of memory, attention (will), and imagination. Intuition, the power of the subconscious mind, is also a sequence of events in thought. |
| *Dict. Destitute of hair, particularly on the top or back of the head.* | Am I continuing to learn in my everyday life, thus stimulating new ideas and new ways of thinking? If not, do something different! Take a class, change jobs, develop new relationships. Give yourself the stimulation you need. |
| *Dict. A dance, more or less elaborate, in which several persons take part. The intricate movements of the human body executed in ballet require physical strength, dexterity, and balance.* | Are you in the ballet or just an admiring observer? As a participant you are bringing this balance into your life. If you are watching a ballet you are appreciating the balance within Self without owning how you are responsible for it. |
| *Dict. A large hollow spherical ball filled with hydrogen or any gas lighter than common air, causing it to rise and float in the atmosphere.* | Are the balloons being controlled or allowed to drift in the wind? Learn to direct your thoughts through focusing the mind in concentration. This will aid you to distinguish your thoughts from those of others, which is the beginning of developing mind-to-mind communication or telepathy. If the balloon bursts your thought has dissipated, losing its individual characteristics to more restless thoughts in your mind. This will occur when the attention has become scattered. |
| *Dict. A bank is an establishment for the deposit, custody, remittance, and issue of money.* | How do I assess value in my thinking, and therefore my life? Become more aware of the worth of your Self, your time, your activities. Be more willing to give freely and completely so you can receive in similar fashion. Realize the true value of your experiences is revealed in the increased understanding gained, not in the accumulation of possessions or acclaim. |

| Symbol | Meaning in Universal Language of Mind |
|--------|----------------------------------------|
| **Banquet** *signifies a time and place of receiving a wide variety of knowledge.* | Food in a dream symbolizes knowledge. Attending a banquet will symbolize a variety of sources and types of knowledge currently available to the dreamer. |
| **Bar** *represents a condition of mind characterized by a lack of will power.* | Relative to its primary meaning, a bar in a dream indicates a weak will arising from a lack of Self discipline. In its secondary meaning, a bar indicates the restrictions arising from a weak will and the dreamer's need to become cognizant of the importance of his will in utilizing the laws of creation. |
| **Barefoot** *signifies an open and honest spiritual foundation.* | Being barefoot in a dream indicates a recognition or willingness to express the true character of the Self which exists beyond the physical. |
| **Barn** *signifies the compulsive patterns of thinking held by the dreamer.* | From the time we are physically born, we begin to think in specific ways according to what and how we learn from our environment. In a relatively short period of time, these thought patterns create neuron pathways in the brain. What was at one time mentally challenging — walking, talking, eating — is learned and becomes easily accomplished with little thought because a pattern of thinking, or habit, has been established. Habits can produce greater efficiency and ease thereby freeing our consciousness from the basic necessities of physical life. |
| **Basement** *represents the unconscious thinking of the dreamer.* | When a thinker fails to utilize the sense of the mind — attention — he or she is no longer sentient. You are unconscious of your thoughts and actions. Mastering attention causes all experiences to become consciously acknowledged. An important distinction must be drawn here between unconscious and subconscious, for the terms are often mistakenly confused. Unconscious refers to the lack of attention given in the conscious mind. Subconscious |

| *Derivative Meaning* | *Thoughts to Consider* |
|---|---|
| *Dict. A feast.* | Note your actions in the dream. Choosing to sample many types of food will indicate a willingness to learn from many sources. If the food is available but for some reason you are not eating, this will indicate a deficiency in responding to the knowledge available to you in your life. |
| *Dict. The enclosed place of a tavern, inn or other establishment where liquor is served. Secondary meaning: a place in court where prisoners are stationed for arraignment, trial, or sentence; the profession of the law.* | If you are indulging in drugs, including alcohol, or prone to excessively long periods of sleep, cease these nonproductive activities. The first chemically alters the natural function of the body thereby interrupting the mind's ability for clear thinking. The second is an avoidance of physical experience which deprives you from gaining new awarenesses. Both are a means of escaping from life rather than facing life with strength and determination. |
| *Dict. Feet are bare, without shoes or stockings.* | Strengthen your spiritual foundation through daily meditation upon your Creator. This will deepen your awareness of your Self as a soul. If being barefoot in your dream seems inappropriate to you during the dream, this will indicate a reticence upon your part to reveal your true Self to others. Appreciate your ability to be open and honest about your spirituality, realizing this will positively influence others in your life. |
| *Dict. A covered building for securing grain, hay, or other farm produce.* | How am I being compulsive in my life? Am I using habitual ways of thinking as stepping stones for deeper thought or are they impairing my growth by distracting me from more thoughtful action and communication? The other symbols in your and the dream action will aid you to determine which of these is true. |
| *Dict. The lowest story of a building whether above or below ground.* | The activity occurring in the basement during your dream will offer insight into how you are negligent and where you need to place your attention. For instance, if you are looking for your pet cat this will indicate a habit you are presently unaware of. Discovering which habit your dream is referring to will require your attentiveness during your waking hours. If your basement is flooded, your |

| Symbol | Meaning in Universal Language of Mind |
|---|---|
| | refers to a particular division of the whole mind characterized by the function of reproducing conscious desires and by the purpose of storing understood experiences which serve as permanent memory. As an example, dreams are messages from the *subconscious* mind to the conscious mind. When you recall a dream, you are conscious (aware) of the message. When you do not remember a dream, you are *unconscious* (unaware) of its occurrence in your conscious mind. |
| *Bathing indicates a purification of thoughts.* | In a dream, bathing symbolizes the action of bringing something into the waking life experiences. Who is bathing will indicate the aspect of Self. The reason for the bathing will signify the purpose for the action; ie. for health would indicate acting on a desire for wholeness; for cleanliness would indicate acting on a desire for clarification. |
| *Bathroom is a condition of mind for purifying and cleansing. (see bathing)* | Thoughts sometimes become confused, muddled, or distorted due to insufficient, or lack of, attention. When time is made for reflection, the thinker can put his thoughts in order by reviewing their content. He can reestablish purposeful thoughts and eliminate those that are no longer wanted or needed. This type of activity purifies the consciousness, offering a refreshing point of view. This is the type of activity that will be occurring when a bathroom appears in a dream. |
| *Battle symbolizes inner turmoil.* | The greatest battles we face are those existing within our own minds. These are self-created, self-perpetuated, and eventually self-resolved. A battle in a dream will symbolize conflict or turmoil between aspects of Self. |
| *Beach represents the area of action between the conscious and subconscious parts of mind.* | The conscious and subconscious minds are connected by a level of consciousness known as the emotional level. The emotions act in the subconscious mind and react in the conscious mind. A beach in a dream symbolizes this action within mind. A peaceful beach will indicate productive use of emotion; a hurricane reaching a beach will symbolize emotional turmoil and reaction. |

| *Derivative Meaning* | *Thoughts to Consider* |
|---|---|
| | lack of attention is prevalent during all your waking hours and affecting your life experiences. |
| *Dict. To immerse in water for pleasure, health, or cleanliness.* | What or who is bathing in the dream will give you more insight into the content and quality of the thoughts. If you are bathing, this will indicate an assessment of your thoughts. If you are bathing a baby, it will symbolize a clarification of a new idea. If you are bathing a dog, this will indicate examination of a habit. |
| *Dict. A room for bathing.* | Note the people and activity occurring in your dream for this will indicate the alteration in your thinking. If the bathroom is ornate it will indicate the importance and value you give to clarifying your thoughts. If the bathroom is dirty and foul, it will signify your need to organize your thinking on a more regular basis. |
| *Dict. A fight or encounter between enemies or opposing armies.* | How and why have I been fighting my Self? Look to your motivations. Often *dream-battles* indicate dual intentions. Depending upon who is fighting in your dream, this can often reveal the dichotomy in your thoughts and your actions. Cease destroying your Self by admitting the purposes in your actions. Admitting will aid you to create a unity in your Self; a common ideal or aspiration will give a guideline for resolving inner conflicts. |
| *Dict. The part of the shore of a sea or lake which is washed by the tide and waves.* | How do I understand emotional energy? Are you aware of how your thoughts manifest within the subconscious mind and express into physical reality through the emotional level of consciousness? Becoming educated in the inner workings of mind will aid you toward greater awareness of the purpose and power of your own emotions. |

| Symbol | Meaning in Universal Language of Mind |
|---|---|
| *Beasts represent compulsive ways of thinking.* *(see animals)* | What distinguishes man from all other animals is sentient consciousness; the potential for awareness of Self and others. Beasts appear in a dream when the dreamer needs to respect his or her capability for sentience and reasoning. Beasts that are being tamed will indicate the dreamer's attempts toward taking control of compulsive ways of thinking; wild beasts attacking will symbolize compulsions that are ruling the dreamer's life. |
| *Bed signifies a mental tool, usually relaxation, necessary for assimilation.* *(see asleep)* | Mental calmness and peace is required for full assimilation of what is being learned through experiences. This state of mind begins with mental relaxation, a stilling of the thoughts through focused attention and will power. In a dream, sleeping in a bed will symbolize relaxation employed for complete learning; an unkempt bed will indicate restless thoughts which disturb peace of mind. |
| *Bells bring the dreamer's attention to harmony.* | Harmony is the result of a cooperative effort toward a common goal. Bells will symbolize the unification of energies described by the participants or action in the dream. For example, a school bell will represent the harmony resulting from the dreamer's learning; a telephone bell will indicate harmony produced by communication. |
| *Bible and any other Holy work represent information of creation, its construction and reason to exist.* | A Holy work is a text written to convey the spiritual nature of man and all of creation. What makes such a book Holy is the intention of the author(s) and its wholistic content. Holy works are penned in the Universal Language of Mind. When interpreted in this language, each reveals to man his origin, his purpose, and his destiny. |
| *Bicycle symbolizes balance.* | A bicycle is a device used for accelerated travel. Its use depends upon the coordination and balance of its rider who propels its movement. In a dream, a bicycle will indicate the dreamer's skill in utilizing the aggressive and receptive principles which cause motion to occur. A bicycle with training wheels indicates the dreamer is developing his or her skill; a broken bicycle will symbolize stagnation because no movement can transpire. |

| *Derivative Meaning* | *Thoughts to Consider* |
|---|---|
| *Dict. Any four-footed animal, as distinguished from birds, insects, fishes, and man; any irrational animal.* | Have I been utilizing the power in my conscious mind to create what I desire in life? Do I rely on memory, what has already been, rather than imagining improvements in my Self and my life? Your conscious power resides in your ability to wield reasoning. Each day imagine something new and different for your Self, then endeavor to make your dream a reality. This will increase your efforts toward greater awareness. |
| *Dict. That on or in which one sleeps, or which is specially intended to give ease to the body at night.* | What do I know about relaxation? Most people believe relaxation comes after an exertion of effort, thus confusing exhaustion with peace. You can learn to relax at will, from desire and upon command. This requires learning how to still the mind, releasing restless thoughts of distraction, and producing a mental state of peace. Mental relaxation is the cause for physical relaxation. |
| *Dict. A metallic vessel which gives forth a clear, musical, ringing sound on being struck.* | How are my waking thoughts and activities lending themselves to inner well-being? Note how you are cooperating with your own desires. Be attentive to the signs of opportunity for greater harmony within Self and your life. |
| *Dict. Sacred scriptures consisting of two parts, the Old Testament originally written in Hebrew, and the New Testament in Greek.* | What am I seeking to understand about creation? Respond to your yearning for spiritual awareness by pursuing information of a spiritual nature. Cultivate your desire for understanding by applying the learning you gain in your own thoughts and actions. Strive toward compatibility with your Creator through daily meditation and service to others. |
| *Dict. A two-wheeled velocipede propelled by the feet of the rider.* | Note your sense of timing. Are you assured in your thinking and actions, accomplishing your desires with equilibrium, or do you falter by hesitating or forcing the manifestations of what you want in life? Learning when to be aggressive and when to be receptive requires refinement of your innate mental capabilities and once mastered can greater accelerate your soul progression. |

| Symbol | Meaning in Universal Language of Mind |
|---|---|
| **Bill**<br>*represents the value of energy expended and needing to be replenished.* | Bills reflect a debt incurred from a service previously provided. In a dream, they will indicate an evaluation of the energy a specific action required therefore the amount of energy that now needs to be recycled. The recycling of mental energies transpires through a system of energy transformers known as chakras. Although a bill in a dream does not symbolize these chakras, it does indicate a need to return the energy expended in the manifesting of desires. It can also indicate the dreamer's karmic indentures. |
| **Birds**<br>*represent compulsive thoughts in the subconscious mind.* | As with other animals, birds in a dream will symbolize compulsive ways of thinking. However, physically, birds are animals capable of flight therefore they represent mind patterns in the subconscious mind of the dreamer. Examples of such patterns might include a propensity for generosity or authority or perception. These illustrate understandings previously gained by the dreamer that are now stored in the soul as a part of the individual's permanent memory. |
| **Bishop**<br>*represents the dreamer's superconscious mind.* | The superconscious mind is the part of mind closest to your origin therefore closest to your Maker. The superconscious mind is your divinity, your inner spiritual authority. A bishop, or any other physical position of religious authority, will symbolize this part of your own being. As with all other aspects of Self highlighted in a dream, the dream action will indicate your attitude toward this part of your Self. |
| **Blind**<br>*indicates a lack of perception.* | The dictionary definition of blindness describes the physical aspects of blindness and offers wisdom concerning its relevance in the Universal Language of Mind. Being blind in a dream indicates the lack of discernment. In order to discern anything, one must become aware of what exists within Self and around Self. This knowing is accomplished through the mental action of perception. To be blind in a dream is to lack this perception. |
| **Blood**<br>*represents life force.* | Blood in a dream represents the power that invigorates all life forms. The saying "You can't get blood from a turnip" may be true in physical life but it can happen in a dream. When it does it represents the life force (blood) |

| *Derivative Meaning* | *Thoughts to Consider* |
|---|---|
| *Dict. A note of charges for goods supplied, work done, or the like, with the amount due on each item.* | Am I using energy wisely or wasting it? Are the activities of my life worthy of the amount of time and effort (both types of energy) I invest in them? Endeavor to use your life fully by learning from every experience rather than merely living to satisfy your physical senses. Do you seem to repeat efforts with similar results or are your efforts producing greater benefits? Greater benefits will indicate responding to karmic indentures; you are in essence paying the debts you owe to your soul. |
| *Dict. A feathered, warm-blooded animal producing young from eggs and generally capable of flight.* | Do you exhibit a talent that no one taught you during this lifetime, an ability that you've just always seemed to have? Many people consider this a gift from God, and it is the result of your efforts toward understanding how to become God-like. Be attentive to these talents, cultivating them, so they become more a part of your conscious awareness and thereby are more readily usable in your everyday waking life. |
| *Dict. A prelate having the spiritual direction and government of a diocese, overseeing the clergy within it and with whom rests the power of ordination, confirmation, and consecration.* | How do I respond to my own inner urge toward knowing my Self as a spiritual being? Do I realize I am a spirit having a temporary physical experience, or do I define my Self by my physical body believing that I have a soul? Make efforts to mature your awareness of Self as spirit through meditation. |
| *Dict. Destitute of the sense of sight; not having the faculty of discernment; destitute of intellectual, moral or spiritual light.* | What am I taking for granted? Do I look but fail to see what is occurring in my Self and my life? Endeavor to more fully appreciate the opportunities your life affords you by admitting the facts that exist. Move beyond immediate sensory reactions into the realm of contemplative thought. Ask yourself, "What do I think about this situation? Why do I hold this view? How does my perception compare to the facts?" Learn to discern the facts thereby providing a stable and honest foundation for your perceptions. |
| *Dict. The fluid which circulates through the arteries and veins of the human body and that of* | Am I fully using the life force available to me or do I tire often? Do I easily relate to other people or find interaction mentally and physically depleting? Realize your interrelationship with others, |

| *Symbol* | *Meaning in Universal Language of Mind* |
|---|---|
| | emanating from knowledge (turnip). Everything in creation is made of energy which is termed cosmic energy. When cosmic energy enters a life form such as the human body, it becomes the energizing power that sustains life and this is the meaning of blood in a dream. |
| *Boat*<br>*is the physical*<br>*body.* | As a boat is physically a means of conveyance from one location to another, for the thinker the means of conveyance is his or her own physical body. A boat in a dream will symbolize the dreamer's body. A large ocean liner will symbolize an organization comprised of many people in the dreamer's life such as a company, a church, or a club. |
| *Body*<br>*signifies the*<br>*mental attitudes*<br>*of the dreamer.* | The human body is an organized system of substances called cells which utilize energy for their maintenance and reproduction. Every cell in the body replaces itself within a seven year period of time. The body is a vehicle for the soul of the thinker. The thinker's thoughts not only influence, but cause, the condition of his vehicle. The quality of thinking and the attitudes promoted affect the natural order and function of his body. Therefore in a dream a human body will give insight into particular attitudes held by the dreamer. [For further information on specific attitudes and their effect upon the body see <u>Permanent Healing</u> by Dr. Daniel R. Condron.] |
| *Bomb*<br>*indicates*<br>*uncontrolled*<br>*change.* | Bombs in a dream are usually used in war indicating the forced change arising from internal conflict. The nature of the physical is change. When the mind is directed with intelligence, the thinker is free to cause and adapt to change readily. When the mind is not being utilized productively, it often seems that change happens *to* the thinker or is *forced* upon him. A nuclear bomb will symbolize unknown change whereas a smoke bomb will indicate unforeseen change. |
| *Books*<br>*symbolize*<br>*information.* | Books symbolize the information available in the dreamer's life. The thinker receives information from the environment through the five physical senses. This information is then stored in the brain for future use. Information becomes knowledge when it is used by the thinker in his experiences. Thus reading a book will represent the acquir- |

| *Derivative Meaning* | *Thoughts to Consider* |
|---|---|
| *other animals, and which is essential to life and nutrition.* | endeavoring to give and receive completely. Learn to respect the power in all life forms. |
| *Dict. A small open vessel or watercraft usually moved by oars or rowing.* | Notice the action in the dream. Smooth sailing will indicate good physical health; a storm causing damage to a boat will symbolize a need to care for your physical health by directing your thoughts and emotions more productively. Keep in mind physical illness begins as mental dis-ease. Cure the attitudinal disorders to promote physical well-being. |
| *Dict. The frame or material organized substance of an animal in distinction from the soul, spirit, or vital principle.* | Note the condition of the body in the dream. Is the body healthy or diseased? Is it strong or weak? The condition will aid you to identify the attitudes being addressed in your dream. Many people find their *dream body* is free from disease or restriction impairing them physically. For instance, an individual who has lost the ability to walk in their waking life many times will experience freedom of movement in a dream, or a person who is physically deaf will hear during a dream. In the Universal Language of Mind the first example shows the volition in the thinking; the second indicates the ability to receive external stimuli. Both are capabilities of the mind described by the condition of the body in the dream. |
| *Dict. A projectile filled with explosive or flammable materials fired from a mortar or dropped from an airplane.* | What changes are occurring in my life? Are they welcomed and anticipated changes or unpleasant and unexpected? Increase your adaptability to change by creating ideals and purposes to guide your activities. This will enhance your ability to make transformations in your Self and your life. You will cease fearing change and begin to embrace it as an indication of progress. |
| *Dict. A number of sheets of paper or other material folded, stitched, and bound together on edge, blank, written, or printed.* | Am I learning from my experiences? Learning is a step-by-step process beginning with the reception of information. Note the kind and subject matter of the books in the dream to discern the type of information being addressed in your dream. A library of books will indicate a wide range of in- |

| Symbol | Meaning in Universal Language of Mind |
|--------|----------------------------------------|
| | ing of information; writing a book will symbolize using information to create what is desired. |

*Bouquet indicates subconscious existence.*

Subconscious existence describes the energy and substance of the inner part of mind known as the subconscious mind. Here previously imaged conscious thoughts are reproduced for manifestation, similar to the developing process stage of photography. Bouquets, flowers, trees, or woods, will all indicate activity occurring within the subconscious mind of the dreamer.

*Bowling symbolizes how the dreamer is approaching life.*

As with all games, bowling in a dream symbolizes an attitude held by the dreamer. This attitude is viewing life as a game, a contest of will and skill, a constant challenge of ability revealed in competition.

*Bracelets represent value. (see jewelry)*

Since bracelets are a kind of apparel used to adorn the physical body, they represent an outward expression of value in a dream.

*Braces indicate support for structure.*

A brace will usually indicate an area where the dreamer is dependent. In a dream the use of the brace will reveal the structure being supported. For instance, braces on the teeth will indicate needing help in the assimilation of knowledge; a brace or beam to support a staircase will symbolize requiring assistance in moving to and between levels of consciousness.

*Brain symbolizes use of thinking processes.*

Physically, the brain is an organ of the body utilized by the intelligence of the thinker. When the brain appears in a dream it will symbolize the capability for all forms of thinking from reasoning to intuition to transcendence. If the brain in a dream is injured this will indicate the dreamer's need to master his attention so the thinking processes can be fully utilized. If the brain is enlarged, the dreamer needs to place his thoughts in a proper perspective.

| *Derivative Meaning* | *Thoughts to Consider* |
|---|---|
| | formation available to you. If they remain unread, you need to use information for the considerable resource for learning they afford you. |
| *Dict. A bunch of flowers.* | How do I know my Self apart from my physical identity? Do I realize I exist beyond the limits of my physical body? Realize each conscious thought you create will seek to become a part of your life through the manifesting power of your own subconscious mind. Begin to strengthen your identity as a soul through contemplation and daily meditation. |
| *Dict. A game played with a ball used for rolling on a level surface.* | What motivates me? Is winning my objective in life? If so, expand your vision to realize the way you will win is to gain understanding from every experience. Although many people are motivated through competition with others, the true competition is to insure that you are better than you were yesterday and that tomorrow you will be better than today. |
| *Dict. An ornament encircling the wrist.* | How am I demonstrating my worth to others? Am I living up to my own standards or values, serving as an example? Or am I imitating values and in need of greater understanding of their worth? |
| *Dict. That which holds anything tight, tense, firm, or secure or which supports, binds, or strengthens.* | Who or what am I relying upon? Is my dependency a necessary step in learning to become Self sufficient or a line of least resistance? Build trust in your Self by making decisions and acting upon them. This creates Self reliance and independence. |
| *Dict. The soft whitish mass enclosed in the skull of man and other vertebrate animals, forming the center of the nervous system, and the seat of intellect and cognitive ability.* | How much value do I place upon my ability to think? Thinking is what separates man from all other animals and creative thought elevates man's awareness enabling him to understand his reason for existence. Realize that thought is cause. The quality of your thinking determines the calibre of your life. |

| Symbol | Meaning in Universal Language of Mind |
|---|---|
| **Bridge** *indicates a means of transition in the life.* | Bridges in a dream symbolize a way for the dreamer to move through his life. This indicates the goals the dreamer has set that enables him or her to easily and quickly accomplish objectives. If the bridge ends, this symbolizes the need for new goals to be created by the dreamer. |
| **Bridle** *is the way to control the will. (see horses)* | Attention, the only sense of the mind, is the means for directing the will. Thus when a bridle appears in a dream, it symbolizes the foundation for Self government which is focused attention. |
| **Broom** *is a tool for cleansing.* | A broom in a dream symbolizes a means for clearing the mind of clutter. It will indicate the dreamer's freedom to distinguish wanted thoughts from unwanted thoughts. |
| **Brother** *is a familiar aspect of Self. (see people)* | A brother in a dream will represent a well-known aspect of your own Self. Depending upon your physical sex, this will signify a conscious or subconscious aspect. |
| **Building** *indicates the mind, specifically the condition of the mind.* | Mind has a specific structure designed as a vehicle for individual intelligence. The condition of the mind is determined by the thinker. The state of the mind can be focused or scattered, directed or wandering, peaceful or tumultuous, stable or erratic, creative or compulsive, expansive or stagnant. The type of building will give the dreamer insight into the specific condition being addressed; the activity occurring in the building will reveal how the current state of mind is affecting the dreamer's life. |

| *Derivative Meaning* | *Thoughts to Consider* |
|---|---|
| *Dict. Any structure of wood, stone, brick, or iron raised over a river, lake, road, valley for the purpose of a convenient passage.* | Are the goals I have set for my Self taking me where I want to go? Do they reflect the person I am and want to become? Goals in life give the mind a direction and offer a place for the mind's energies to be used. Set your goals high, including the betterment of Self and others in your thinking. Make sure your present-day thoughts and actions are in alignment with your goals, thus bringing you closer to their fulfillment. |
| *Dict. The portion of gear or harness fitted to the head of a horse (or animal similarly used) and by which he is governed and restrained.* | Do I find my Self thinking one thing and doing another? Do I try to accomplish two or three things at the same time? These actions will scatter your attention and produce incomplete results. Harness your will by mastering your attention. Cause your thought and action to be in alignment by directing your attention to the task or experience at hand. |
| *Dict. A brush with a long handle for sweeping floors.* | Do I hold unproductive thoughts (doubt, fear, worry) that keep me from accomplishing my objectives? Concentration exercises are an excellent means for directing the thoughts toward what is desired and keeping desired thoughts in mind. |
| *Dict. A male born of the same father and mother.* | After identifying the specific aspect your brother represents, determine your attitude toward your brother. Do you admire and respect him with great affection or do you find him offensive and wish you weren't related? Your attitude toward your brother will reveal how you view this aspect of your Self. |
| *Dict. A frame or structure created to serve a particular function such as a house, church, employment, etc.* | Do I cause my state of mind or am I a victim of my environment, letting the world around me dictate my peace or turmoil? You have the capability for determining your frame of mind at all times, in any place. Appreciate the freedom of thought available to you. Strengthen your resolve by endeavoring to use your mind more fully. |

| Symbol | Meaning in Universal Language of Mind |
|---|---|

### C

**Cage**
*indicates*
*restraint.*

A cage in a dream symbolizes an attitude of restriction. When used to confine animals, it will signify the dreamer's attempt to control or limit a habit. When used to confine people, it will indicate a restriction of aspects of the Self.

**Camera**
*represents the*
*mechanics of*
*forming con-*
*scious desires.*

In a dream, a camera represents the conscious ability to utilize memory, attention, and imagination to produce an image of what is desired. This is the beginning of what is commonly known as visualization. Visualization describes the mental process of creation. Taking a picture with a camera in a dream will symbolize conscious imaging; a broken camera will indicate the dreamer's need to develop skill in one of the areas required in imaging.

**Campus**
*is an attitude of*
*learning.*

In a dream, a campus will indicate the dreamer's thoughts are centered on learning.

**Cancer**
*signifies*
*self-hatred.*

Cancer in a dream will indicate a predominant misunderstanding that affects the dreamer.

**Candle**
*is a means for*
*illumination.*

A candle in a dream represents the dreamer's awareness.

**Candy**
*is shallow*
*knowledge.*

Candy in a dream symbolizes knowledge that stimulates the senses but fails to promote sustained growth.

| Derivative Meaning | Thoughts to Consider |
|---|---|
| Dict. A box or enclosure consisting of latticework for confining birds or beast; a prison. | Am I holding back in my expression as a means to control my Self? Refusing to give does not bring Self control. Self control is the result of discrimination between productive and nonproductive thinking and behavior, and choosing to further that which is productive. |
| Dict. An optical instrument for facilitating the delineation of distant objects by producing a reflected picture of them upon paper by means of a glass prism suitably mounted. | Am I content with my life? Does it reflect the fulfillment of my most heart-felt desires? Commit to knowing your Self as a creator by giving greater care to how and what you think. Realize each imaged desire will seek to manifest itself in your everyday, waking life. Enjoy the kind of life you want by creating the thoughts that will produce the experiences you desire. |
| Dict. The grounds of a college or school. | How am I using my life for learning? Do my experiences increase my awareness of my whole Self? True learning is not the accumulation of information but rather the incorporation of mind-expanding ideas into your way of thinking. |
| Dict. A malignant growth. | What or who am I hating? Hatred is caused by a lack of understanding. "Putting yourself in the other's shoes" can change your perspective enabling you to release prejudices and become more compassionate. Strive for understanding, for where there is understanding there is love and growth. |
| Dict. A taper used for portable light. | Make time to acknowledge new awarenesses in your life. Note how these newfound truths affect the quality of your thoughts and the way you think. This will accelerate the illumination of your thinking. |
| Dict. A solid preparation of sugar or molasses, either alone or in combination with other substances to flavor, color, or give it the desired consistency. | Am I caught up in sensory pleasures with little regard for my soul progression? Seek knowledge that will enhance your development in the long run, beyond the present moment. Live with tomorrow in mind. |

| Symbol | Meaning in Universal Language of Mind |
|--------|----------------------------------------|
| **Carnival** *indicates a frivolous attitude.* | A carnival in a dream reflects a trifling attitude. The dreamer is dallying in life, looking to be entertained. |
| **Cartoon** *is the use of imagination.* | Cartoons in a dream signify the dreamer's ability to imagine. When directed by intelligence, the imagination becomes the creative power for the thinker. When undirected, it becomes pretense. |
| **Cash** *indicates value.* | Cash in a dream symbolizes the value assessed by the dreamer. How the cash is being used in the dream will indicate what is being valued. For instance, if cash is being used to buy food this will symbolize the value the dreamer places upon knowledge. |
| **Castle** *represents the mind.* | For a king or lord, the owner, a castle in a dream will represent the mind. For most people who do not use a castle as an abode, a castle will still symbolize the mind of the dreamer and it will further indicate a tendency toward a closed mind. |
| **Cat** *is a compulsive way of thinking.* *(see animals)* | Most cats are pets, indicating the dreamer's attachment to the habit. |
| **Cathedral** *represents the mind, specifically spirituality.* | The spiritual quality of the dreamer's mind is an important part of the message when a cathedral, church, synagogue, temple, or other religious place appears in a dream. |

| *Derivative Meaning* | *Thoughts to Consider* |
|---|---|
| *Dict. A traveling show with amusements such as merry-go-rounds.* | What is important to me? Whatever is valuable to you deserves your best. |
| *Dict. A caricature, often satirical, representing important events in politics, etc., in the comic strips or on film.* | Am I becoming the person I want to be or just pretending I am someone or something I'm not? In *As You Like It*, William Shakespeare said, "All the world's a stage, and the men and women merely players. They have their exits and their entrances, and one man in his time plays many parts." Life is the play, it is not meant to be a rehearsal. Use your imagination fully and completely to bring to your Self the maturity and wisdom you desire. |
| *Dict. Money.* | Value in a dream can relate to your own sense of Self worth or to the worth you are willing to give. The action in your dream will indicate which is appropriate. |
| *Dict. A building fortified for defense against an enemy; a house with towers often surrounded by a wall and moat.* | Am I closing my Self off from new ideas? Different ways of thinking can broaden your opportunities and sharpen your command of reasoning. Stop being afraid, and therefore defensive, of what is at first alien to you. Be willing to give thoughtful consideration to anyone or anything which enters your sphere. |
| *Dict. A name applied to certain species of carnivorous quadrupeds of the feline tribe, many varieties of which have long been tamed and kept in houses for catching mice.* | When identifying what habit is being addressed in your dream, keep in mind that habits can be mental or physical. A mental habit could be a tendency toward compulsively refusing to accept compliments or toward jumping to conclusions before gleaning the available facts. A physical habit might be overeating or interrupting others. |
| *Dict. The principle church in a diocese, that which is specially the church of the bishop.* | Note the activity taking place. Are you attending church services or merely seeing the building from afar? Your activity in the dream will indicate your investment in your own spirituality. |

| *Symbol* | *Meaning in Universal Language of Mind* |
|---|---|
| *Cave* *symbolizes* *subconscious* *mind substance.* | Consciously imaged desires are reflected into and impressed upon the substance of the subconscious mind. This begins the reproduction function of the inner mind that will bring about the manifestation of conscious desires. A cave in a dream signifies this inner mind substance. |
| *Chair* *indicates* *support for* *thinking.* | A chair provides rest and support for the body. In a dream, a chair will signify relaxation from mental exertion. |
| *Children* *are new or* *recently devel-* *oping ideas.* | Children in a dream symbolize new ideas that can develop and mature into aspects of Self. They reflect a new skill, talent, or ability that the dreamer is practicing, or a quality or characteristic that the dreamer is making a part of the Self. |
| *Choir* *represents* *aspects in* *harmony with* *each other.* | When the dreamer has an ideal he desires to accomplish many aspects of Self are called upon to manifest this goal. A choir in a dream will indicate that various aspects are cooperating toward the intended ideal. |
| *Christmas* *symbolizes the* *birth of Christ* *consciousness in* *the awareness of* *the dreamer.* | Jesus of Nazareth was a man who lived 2000 years ago. He became a Master Teacher and was given the Greek title Christ, as reflected in the gospels of the *New Testament* of the Bible. In a dream, Christmas will indicate the initial awareness of the Christ consciousness in the individual. |
| *Church* *represents the* *mind, specifi-* *cally spirituality.* | As with any building structure, a church in a dream will represent the mind of the dreamer. Because a church is used in physical life for a specific purpose, it will denote the dreamer's intention toward spirituality. This is also true of a temple, synagogue, sanctuary, or any building used for religious purposes. |

| *Derivative Meaning* | *Thoughts to Consider* |
|---|---|
| *Dict. A hollow place in the earth.* | What secret desires have I been contemplating? Many times the appearance of a cave in your dream will indicate the wants in your thinking that you have not divulged to others. If the cave is dark and your reaction in the dream is fear, become more aware of what you want and how you think. |
| *Dict. A movable seat, with a back, for one person.* | Are you acquainted with methods of relaxation? Physical relaxation begins with mental relaxation, therefore learning how to control mental energies will give you the freedom to sustain motion without tiring. |
| *Dict. A son or daughter of any age; one of immature knowledge, experience, judgement, and attainments.* | Pay attention to the child's action in the dream. This will indicate your attitude toward this newer, developing aspect of Self. The dream action will also indicate if the aspect is furthering your Self knowledge and growth or inhibiting it in some way. |
| *Dict. A collection of singers, especially in a church.* | Note the aspects that make up your *dream-choir.* Are they male or female, young or old, known by or unfamiliar to you? Answering these questions will give you insight into the specific aspects of Self uniting within Self to accomplish your endeavors. |
| *Dict. The festival of the Christian church observed annually on December 25th in memory of the birth of Jesus.* | How have I recently expanded my awareness of my own spirituality? Becoming aware of the Christhood within can be the result of unexpected and unpremeditated glimpses of the inner realms of Self but is usually the result of anticipated and pursued Self awareness. Depending upon the context Christmas appears in your dream, commence spiritual pursuits — through knowledge and disciplines — or continue those you have already initiated. This will mature your understanding of your own Christhood. |
| *Dict. A house consecrated to the worship of God among Christians.* | Note how the church appears in the dream. Is it empty or filled with worshippers? Is it a simple chapel or an elaborate cathedral? Answering these questions will give you insight into the value you place upon your own spirituality. |

| Symbol | Meaning in Universal Language of Mind |
|--------|----------------------------------------|
| *Circle* *signifies* *continuity and* *wholeness.* | A circle in the Universal Language of Mind represents wholeness and completeness. It will signify the continuity of thought. |
| *Circus* *indicates* *compulsive ways* *of thinking that* *are directed for* *the dreamer's* *pleasure.* | This symbol is derived from the many elements that comprise the circus: trainers, animals, clowns, games, and food. Combining the symbolism in these dream images produces a whole image indicating the dreamer's ability to control compulsive ways of thinking. |
| *City* *is a condition of* *mind where* *many aspects* *are connected.* | A city in a dream will indicate a particular pattern of thinking. Each physical city exists as a common living and working place for many different people. In a dream, it will give insight into a common attitude that the dreamer holds. |
| *Clock* *is a tool for* *measuring* *understandings.* | Time pieces in a dream will signify how the dreamer is gaining understandings that will become a part of permanent memory in the soul or subconscious mind. Physically time is measured horizontally, by experiences gained during the time of the rising and setting of the sun. Within the subconscious mind, time is measured vertically, by the acquiring and building of understandings. |
| *Closet* *represents a* *condition of* *mind.* | Determining the specified use of the closet gives the dreamer the further insight into the condition of the mind being addressed in the dream. For example, a clothes closet will indicate a preoccupation with how the dreamer is presenting Self to others; a room for privacy will signify an |

| *Derivative Meaning* | *Thoughts to Consider* |
|---|---|
| *Dict. A plane figure, comprehended by a single curve line, called its circumference, every part of which is equally distant from a point within it called the center.* | What thoughts do I hold concerning completeness and continuity in my life? Look for those thoughts which bring you fulfillment. Noting how the circle appears in your dream will assist you in determining the specific type of thinking that is being addressed in your dream message. |
| *Dict. A place of amusement where feats of horsemanship and acrobatic displays form the principal entertainment.* | Am I using habits for mental efficiency or as a convenience? Evaluate whether practiced ways of thinking that are second-nature to you are being used productively in your life or as blocks that inhibit your productivity. If a habit furthers your development and growth use it with intention. If it impairs your creativity, fostering laziness, begin utilizing reasoning to promote freedom from compulsion. |
| *Dict. A large and important town; an incorporated town governed by a mayor and aldermen.* | Is the city familiar to me? The city where you grew up will indicate a long-standing attitude. An unidentified city will signify a predominant attitude you have yet to consciously identify. Determine your waking attitude about the city. For instance, if you view Paris as a city of romance and Paris appears in your dream it will indicate attitudes you hold about love. |
| *Dict. A machine for measuring time, indicating the hours, minutes, and often seconds by means of hands moving over a dial plate, the motion being kept up by weights and springs, and regulated by a pendulum or a balance wheel.* | Am I using my time horizontally or vertically? To gain the most from the time you have, endeavor to increase the wealth of your understanding through each experience. Cease experiencing merely for the gratification of the senses by creating a purpose for your experiences. Interact with others for the purpose of giving and receiving, work for the purpose of learning and increasing Self knowledge, travel for the purpose of expanding your awareness. |
| *Dict. A small room or apartment for retirement; any room for privacy, a small side room or recess for* | What is the condition of mind being highlighted in the dream? Is it helpful in the fulfillment of my goals, or detrimental? Is this a frame of mind I want to maintain or can I imagine one that is different and better? |

| *Symbol* | *Meaning in Universal Language of Mind* |
|---|---|
| | introspective frame of mind conducive to meditation as referred to in the *New Testament* when Jesus instructs his disciples to "go into your closet to pray". |
| *Clothes* *signify how the dreamer is expressing Self.* | Clothes indicate the part of Self others view.  Many cultures have a way of describing the three-fold nature of Self: the person we show to others, the person we believe ourselves to be, and the person we truly are.  Clothes in a dream signify what we allow others to see. |
| *Clouds* *represent the separation between the subconscious and superconscious parts of mind.* | Within the inner levels of man's consciousness comprising the whole mind, are three specific divisions:  conscious, subconscious, and superconscious.  The conscious and subconscious minds are like two halves that together form a single unit.  The superconscious mind is a single unit unto itself.  There is a distinct separation between the superconscious mind and the outer subconscious/conscious minds.  Clouds in a dream will signify this separation, indicating the dreamer's awareness of the distinction between the innermost consciousness of the superconscious mind and the more outer consciousness of the subconscious and conscious minds.  In Hindu philosophy, this dual nature in man and all of creation is termed the pairs of opposites. |
| *Clown* *is an aspect of Self.* | As indicated in the dictionary definition, a clown in a dream will represent an aspect of Self that is lacking in grace or skill. |
| *Coffee* *is knowledge used to stimulate the thinker.* | Because of its caffeine content, coffee stimulates the nervous system of the human body.  In a dream, coffee will represent knowledge used as a stimulant. |
| *Colors* *signify where the dream is taking place.* | Black and white dreams will indicate the dream is occurring in the sixth level of consciousness, the emotional level.  Technicolor dreams are experienced in the next inner level, the lower spiritual level of mind.  Dreaming in pastels indicates the dreamer is experiencing in the fourth level of consciousness, the higher spiritual.  When the dream occurs in |

| *Derivative Meaning* | *Thoughts to Consider* |
| --- | --- |
| *storing utensils, furniture, provisions, etc.* | |
| *Dict. Garments for the human body.* | Is my outward expression conveying what I desire? Am I causing an alignment in the three-fold nature of Self, or am I thinking one way and behaving another? Endeavor to be honest, first with your Self and then with others. This will strengthen your ability to know your Self. |
| *Dict. A collection of visible vapor or watery particles suspended in the atmosphere at some altitude.* | How am I beginning to recognize the difference between the spiritual and the material, the soul and the body, the metaphysical and the physical? Realize that the purpose for your physical existence is to gain understandings that will further your soul progression. Begin to cooperate with your own inner urge toward maturity and growth by responding to the messages from your subconscious mind that come in the form of dreams and through daily meditation upon your Creator. |
| *Dict. An awkward fellow, a person without refinement; a jester or buffoon as in a theater, circus, or other place of entertainment.* | How can I become more confident? What can I do to become more at ease with my Self and others? Stop pretending you are something you are not. If you want to be different, image the difference and become that new person. |
| *Dict. A drink made from the roasted or ground seeds of a tree native to Arabia or Abyssinia but now extensively cultivated throughout tropical countries.* | Am I seeking sensory gratification in my experiences rather than knowledge that can be used for growth and increased awareness? |
| *Dict. That in respect of which bodies have a different appearance to the eye independently of their form; any tint or hue distinguished from* | Remembering the tint and shades of a dream will indicate your conscious ability for concentration. People who remember predominantly black and white or color dreams tend to direct and keep most of their attention upon their physical life. Those who remember pastel or white dreams tend toward |

| *Symbol* | *Meaning in Universal Language of Mind* |
|---|---|
| | the third level, the deepest level of the subconscious mind, everything in the dream will appear white, only forms will be distinguished. |
| **Comedian** is an aspect of Self. | A comedian in a dream will symbolize an aspect of Self reaching toward understanding of the Universal Law of Proper Perspective. Humor is one of the most common ways of gaining objectivity and perspective. |
| **Computer** represents the brain. | The most elaborate machinery of the human body is the brain. The brain is used to store information gained through mental activity. The information can be gleaned, retrieved, and reorganized upon command and at the thinker's will. A computer in a dream will represent the brain. |
| **Conception** signifies the creation of a new idea. | In a dream conception symbolizes the mental act by which an absent object of perception is brought before the mind by imagination. The dreamer is bringing about a new idea through the process of visualization that will begin manifesting in the inner levels of consciousness. |
| **Conflict** indicates disharmony between aspects of Self. | Conflict in a dream signifies the dreamer's need to become decisive. Internal conflict is the result of doubt or fear. It is resolved by applying the will toward a desired objective. The nature of the *dream-conflict*, who is involved and the issue of the discord, will lend more insight into the origin of the doubt. |

| *Derivative Meaning* | *Thoughts to Consider* |
|---|---|
| *white.* | a greater direction of their attention, thus experiencing more freedom in their life. Exercising your concentrative skill will aid you to control your mind and physical body enabling you to reach deeper states of rest during sleep and consciously recall dream experiences in deeper levels of consciousness. |
| *Dict. An actor or player in a dramatic composition of a light and amusing class, its characters being represented as in the circumstances or meeting with the incidents of ordinary life.* | Note the activity of your dream's comedian. This will give insight into your use or misuse of humor. It will tell you if you are seeking objectivity, trying to put your Self and your life in perspective, or if you are hiding behind humor, pretending things are fine when they really are not. |
| *Dict. An electrical machine used to calculate and estimate.* | Note why the computer appears in your dream. If you are the computer programmer this will indicate your ability to use your brain for reasoning. If your *dream-computer* doesn't seem to be following your commands, you need to develop your ability for undivided attention. If your computer won't turn on, you need to begin exercising your mental capabilities; strengthening your ability for recall, attention, and imagination. |
| *Dict. The act of conceiving; the first formation of the embryo of an animal. Latin conceptum meaning "what is conceived".* | Note the new ideas you have been considering recently. Your dream will give valuable insight into how you are being inventive and innovative in approaching your life. Is the *dream-fetus* a male or female? This will tell you if the idea is a conscious or subconscious conception depending upon your physical sex. |
| *Dict. A fighting or struggle for mastery.* | What has been troubling me recently? Once identified, you will be able to determine the source of your conflict. Fear and doubt stem from incomplete reasoning. Fear is caused by a misuse of either memory or imagination. You can allow unpleasant past experiences to distort current and future experiences by fearing the same outcome. You can fail to imagine what you desire, therefore fearing the unknown. Doubt is caused by a misuse of will. It arises from insecurity in your ability to |

| *Symbol* | *Meaning in Universal Language of Mind* |
|---|---|
| *Cooking* symbolizes the mental action of preparing knowledge. | Cooking in a dream indicates the dreamer is taking the necessary previous measures to receive knowledge. Since the physical preparation of food includes the use of a heat source, the expansion of consciousness is an important ingredient in making one's Self ready to receive potential learning. |
| *Copy Machine* signifies memory. | Memory provides a temporary storehouse of information, knowledge, experiences, and understandings that have transpired in the physical life of the thinker. In a dream, a copy machine, or any device which duplicates an original, will symbolize memory. |
| *Costume* represents the dreamer's outer expression. | Any clothing will signify how the dreamer expresses Self to others. The word costume describes a particular type of clothing used for a specific purpose. In a dream, it will indicate a particular attitude held in the dreamer's mind that determines how he or she appears to others. When the entire dream seems to be from another time period, with no element being anachronistic, the dreamer may be accessing the permanent memory of the subconscious mind. |
| *Counterfeit* indicates worthlessness. | When something in a dream is counterfeit, it will symbolize a way the dreamer is lying to Self about his or her own worth. |
| *Cradle* symbolizes a place of rest and rejuvena- | Infants in a dream indicate a new idea. A cradle provides a place for the re-energization of a new idea. |

| *Derivative Meaning* | *Thoughts to Consider* |
|---|---|
| | have what you desire. To resolve inner dilemmas, use this formula for success: image an ideal, establish a purpose for that ideal, and pursue the activity that will cause this ideal to manifest. |
| *Dict. To prepare for the table by boiling, roasting, baking, broiling, etc.* | Who is cooking in the dream and what are they preparing? The who will tell you the aspect of Self that is adapting to receive new knowledge. The what will indicate the kind and quality of knowledge available to you. If your gregarious best friend is baking bread this will indicate that you are adding to your awareness by learning about friendliness and happiness. If your ambitious co-worker is cooking a hat this will signify learning about how you express your Self to others in an eager or pushy way. |
| *Dict. An electrical or mechanical device used to reproduce a facsimile or imitation of the original.* | Am I repeating experiences? Are there similar situations occurring in my life that I have experienced before? The value of memory is the potential for progression and change in awareness. Use recall as a foundation for imaging rather than a trap to avoid new learning that will produce growth and maturity in Self. |
| *Dict. The style of dress peculiar to a people or nation, to a particular period, or class of people.* | What do I associate with these costumes? If they are indicative of a foreign country, this will signify a way of expressing Self that you do not readily recognize; others see you in this way but you do not identify it. If the costumes are from another time period, this will indicate a tendency toward expressing your Self in ways that may seem out-of-date to your Self or others. |
| *Dict. Made in imitation of something else with a view to pass the false copy for genuine or original.* | What makes you valuable, worthy of respect and deserving of merit? Many people judge their worth according to physical position or possession. This is short-sighted and highly limiting. Look to the inner qualities that are valuable for your true sense of worth. |
| *Dict. A small bed, crib or cot in which an infant is rocked.* | Determine which new idea your dream is addressing. Giving thought to this new idea, developing it, in essence nurturing it with attention, will provide the rejuvenation required to keep this idea |

| Symbol | Meaning in Universal Language of Mind |
|---|---|
| *tion for a new idea.* | |
| **Credit Card** *symbolizes a belief in the value of what is gained.* | Physically, credit cards were originally intended as a substitute for cash, a means of convenience for someone to purchase goods. However, for many people, they have since become an easy way to procure a loan, thus enabling the holder to purchase beyond his or her means. The use of the credit card in a dream will determine its meaning in the language of mind. In its original context, the credit card will symbolize the dreamer's belief in the value of what is gained; in the latter context it will symbolize the dreamer's dependency upon someone or something outside of the Self for the assessment of value. |
| **Cross** *is a barrier or obstacle.* | A cross in a dream will indicate what stands in the way of the dreamer achieving. |
| **Crown** *indicates Self control.* | A crown is worn as a symbol of honor, victory, or joy thus when it appears in a dream it will reflect what has been gained through Self control. |
| **Cup** *symbolizes receptivity as a tool.* | A cup in a dream highlights the dreamer's ability to readily receive and contain what is offered. |

| Derivative Meaning | Thoughts to Consider |
|---|---|
| | alive and growing until it becomes a part of your life. |
| *Dict. a means for procuring in confidence of future payment.* | Am I aware of the beliefs I hold? Are they my own perceptions based upon my own experience or do they arise from what I have heard from the experience of others? Being aware of your beliefs is an important step in Self development for believing is a prerequisite for knowing. Faith and trust are integral elements in the concepts you hold about your Self and your life. |
| *Dict. An instrument on which malefactors were anciently put to death.* | What is the greatest obstacle in my life right now? What is hindering me from achieving my most heart felt desires? Determine what this obstruction is and you will know the meaning of the cross in your dream. By admitting what is keeping you from attaining your desires, you are free to determine a course of action that will eliminate the barrier or to make it useful in the fulfillment of those desires. |
| *Dict. An ornament for the head in the form of a wreath or garland, worn by monarchs on state occasions as a badge of sovereignty or real power.* | Note who wears the crown and in what context it is being used or worn. This will give you insight into your efforts for Self control and dominion of your skills and capabilities. |
| *Dict. A vessel of small capacity used commonly to drink from.* | Realize your ability to receive, paired with your ability to give, forms the foundation for knowing your Self as a creator. Every creative act requires the use of the Universal Laws of Creation and the implementation of the principles which keep these Laws in motion. Together the principles of receptivity and aggressiveness enable you to progress and move forward in your soul progression. |

| Symbol | Meaning in Universal Language of Mind |
|---|---|

*ID*

**Dam**
*symbolizes a means to contain conscious life experience.*

Building upon the physical purpose of a dam, in the language of mind a dam signifies a means for the dreamer to contain conscious life experiences (water). This can be a means of directing the experiences by use of conscious mental skills such as concentration or mental qualities such as discrimination. It can also be a means of unconsciously limiting experiences producing restrictions, such as prejudice or stagnation, in the dreamer's conscious life experiences.

**Dance**
*indicates a coordination of aspects producing harmony in thinking.*

Dancing in a dream indicates the cooperation of aspects that work together to produce harmonious patterns of thinking. A harmonious pattern of thinking will be conducive to understanding and growth for the dreamer, and will usually indicate a desire to respond to the rhythm of creation.

**Darkness**
*indicates ignorance.*

In the Universal Language of Mind, darkness represents ignorance. Ignorance does not imply mentally insufficiency or stupidity. It implies an active state of *ignoring* what is present or available to the dreamer.

**Dawn**
*indicates the beginning of awareness.*

Dawn signifies the recognition of what is available to the dreamer. What was previously obscured can now be perceived; what was previously ignored is now becoming acknowledged by the dreamer.

**Day**
*signifies awareness.*

In the Universal Language of Mind, day will always represent awareness. Awareness is the inner urge of any thinker for it is what elevates and advances consciousness. To be aware is to bring forth realization, above and beyond the norm, through the use of mental perception.

| *Derivative Meaning* | *Thoughts to Consider* |
|---|---|
| *Dict. A bank, mound of earth, wall, or other structure, built across a current of water, to raise its levels for the purpose of driving millwheels, or for other purposes.* | Am I conscious or unconscious of the way I am living my life? Are my goals steps toward a greater desire or limits to what I can achieve? Use your imagination to go beyond today, reaching into tomorrow with purpose and foresight. |
| *Dict. To leap or move with measured steps, regulated by music.* | How have I been thinking lately? These thoughts will indicate a productive means of achieving your most heart felt desires. Note who is participating in the *dream-dance* as an indication of the parts of you invested in creation and wholeness in thought and action. Continue this pattern of thought in your daily life. |
| *Dict. The state or quality of being dark, the want of physical light; not radiating or reflecting light.* | Who or what have I been failing to acknowledge? The *dream-characters* and *dream-action* will give you specific indications of what you are ignoring in your consciousness and probably what you can do to make changes that will lead to awareness. |
| *Dict. To begin to grow light in the morning; to grow light.* | What new awarenesses have I entertained recently? Look to the people, places, and activities of your recent days to define how your consciousness has been expanded. This will give you the information you need to build upon these new awarenesses, to "grow light". |
| *Dict. That space of time during which there continues to be light; the time between the rising and setting of the sun.* | Do I recognize the importance and extent of the awareness I possess? How has this awareness affected how I see myself, others, God, and creation? Increased perception leads to greater awareness. Note what you are willing to perceive that before you wanted to ignore, and realize how this is expanding your awareness. |

| *Symbol* | *Meaning in Universal Language of Mind* |
|---|---|
| *Death* *symbolizes* *change.* | Death in a dream is frightening to most dreamers because they lack understanding of the nature of physical life and death. For the aware thinker, the physical life is known to be a temporary existence for the soul; one of many brief sojourns offering opportunity to further progression. The French philosopher Voltaire said centuries ago, "It is no more surprising to be born twice than once, everything in nature is resurrection." In the Universal Language of Mind, death signifies a change from one state of being to another. |
| *Desert* *is a lack of* *productivity in* *subconscious* *existence.* | In the Universal Language of Mind, a desert represents unused mind substance. The substance of the subconscious mind is always available to the thinker for the reproduction of conscious desires. When the dreamer is failing to image desires, the inner mind substance is fallow for it has received nothing to reproduce. |
| *Detective* *represents an* *aspect of Self.* | As with any person appearing in a dream, a detective will symbolize an aspect of Self. Because a detective is skilled in particular activities, there is more insight available. This aspect of Self will reflect the dreamer's developed ability for discovery, a necessary skill for learning. |
| *Devil* *is an unknown* *aspect of Self.* | The appearance of something in a dream that the dreamer identifies as a devil symbolizes his/her inner struggle with what is not productive or evil. Since devils do not exist in physical form, the dreamer is identifying something unknown, describing it as a devil due to its malevolent appearance or action in the dream. In the language of mind, devil will symbolize the motivating force of mind, seated in the ego, which is harmful or damaging to the Self. |
| *Dictionary* *symbolizes* *information* *about the* *language of* *mind.* | As with any book in dream, a dictionary will represent information available to the dreamer. Since a dictionary is a particular type of book, it will clarify the type of information be addressed in the dream — information concerning the language for communication within the inner levels of consciousness. A *dream-dictionary* will signify the dreamer's acquaintance with a means for non-physical communication. |

| *Derivative Meaning* | *Thoughts to Consider* |
|---|---|
| *Dict. That state of being, animal or vegetable, in which there is a total and permanent cessation of all the vital functions.* | Identify the change that has occurred in your life. This will be the heart of your dream message. Who or what has died in your dream will lend insight into the nature of the change you have experienced, and will assist in responding to this change joyfully instead of fearfully. Keep in mind the change symbolized by death in a dream can be followed by a resurrection of your consciousness. Reach for this elevated awareness. |
| *Dict. Lying waste; uncultivated and uninhabited; in the natural state and unimproved by man.* | How can I use my imagination more productively? By spending a specific length of time each day visualizing something you desire in your life, you will call upon your subconscious mind's reproductive power. This will cause productivity — consciously and subconsciously. |
| *Dict. Fitted for and skilled in discovery, finding what is concealed, hidden, or formerly unknown.* | Note the dream action. What is the sex of the detective in your dream and what are his/her activities? These answers will tell you 1] what parts of mind are active in discovery and 2] the nature of the discovery being made. |
| *Dict. An evil spirit or being. Devil is from the Greek diabolos literally meaning "slanderer". In Jewish and Christian faiths it is the personal supreme spirit of evil, the tempter of mankind.* | What am I afraid of? Do I feel like there are forces in my life beyond my control and understanding? Identify what these are. Dispel your fears of the unknown by bringing them into the light of your awareness. President Franklin Roosevelt said decades ago, "The only thing to fear is fear itself." Be willing to admit your intentions, changing those which are dishonorable and destructive to Self and others to those which are truthful and constructive to Self and others. |
| *Dict. A book containing the words of a language arranged in alphabetical order, with explanations or definitions of their meanings.* | Are you becoming well-versed in utilizing the Universal Language of Mind as presented in this Dreamer's Dictionary? Doing so will enhance your ability to communicate in more than one level of consciousness. This aids you develop a fuller use of your own mind and to communicate subconsciously through Universal Mind with other people. |

| Symbol | Meaning in Universal Language of Mind |
|--------|---------------------------------------|
| *Dining represents the mental action of receiving knowledge.* | Food in a dream represents knowledge. The action of eating indicates the reception of knowledge. Receiving knowledge occurs through the utilization of the five physical senses of the body. Vibratory impressions are received and transmitted to the brain for interpretation. Once interpreted, the impressions become part of the body of knowledge available for the thinker's use. |
| *Disease signifies unproductive attitudes held by the dreamer.* | Disease in the language of mind will represent mental and/ or emotional distress, discomfort, and distemper. The type of disease will give insight into the specific type of distress. For instance, a cold in a dream will indicate mental indecision. The area of the body where the disease is found will indicate how the unproductive thinking is impairing the natural function of the mind. For example, a brain tumor is relative to thoughts of feeling pressured or overwhelmed by information that has been received. (For more information of the relationship between attitudes and physical health see <u>Permanent Healing</u> by Dr. Daniel R. Condron.) |
| *Dishes are a receptacle for knowledge.* | Dishes in a dream indicate mental tools available for the thinker to use knowledge. An example of such a tool is concentration which enables the thinker to focus and direct his/her undivided attention upon a singular thought or object at hand. |
| *Divorce signifies breaking a commitment between your conscious mind and your subconscious mind.* | Marriage in the Universal Language of Mind indicates a commitment between the conscious mind and the subconscious mind for the fulfillment of desires. A divorce symbolizes a breaking of this commitment. The conscious and subconscious minds are autonomous in their duties and functions, yet they are allied in their relativity one to the other. Both minds must be utilized in order to produce any creative endeavor. |

| *Derivative Meaning* | *Thoughts to Consider* |
|---|---|
| *Dict. To eat a meal.* | What knowledge have I been adding to my Self recently? Examining the *dream-participants* and *dream-actions* will give further insight into the type and quality of knowledge relevant in the dream message. If everyone in your dream is eating but you, this will signify a need to integrate the knowledge into your awareness. The kinds of food being served and eaten will indicate the quality of the knowledge being received. Rich fare will signify highly valued knowledge; spoiled food would represent tainted knowledge that has outlived its usefulness or is no longer beneficial to the dreamer. |
| *Dict. Want or absence of ease; any morbid state of the body or any particular organ or part of the body; ailment, malady.* | Determine the nature of the disease appearing in your dream. Note who or what is diseased. Research its mental cause by using the book <u>Permanent Healing</u>. This will specifically tell you the nature of your unproductive attitude and will also give you suggestions for improvement. |
| *Dict. A broad open vessel made of various materials used for serving up meat and various kinds of food at the table.* | What knowledge have you recently gained? The condition of *dream-dishes* will give further insight: priceless china will indicate receptivity held in high esteem; dirty dishes will signify old, unwanted ideas that are interfering with your receptivity to new knowledge, broken dishes will represent aggressiveness where receptivity is needed. |
| *Dict. A legal dissolution of the bond of marriage.* | How have I deviated from previously created desires? How am I falling short of fulfilling obligations to my Self? Examine the aspects involved in the action of divorce in your dream. This will tell you which aspects are interfering with the creation and manifestation of your desires. |

| *Symbol* | *Meaning in Universal Language of Mind* |
|---|---|
| **Doctor** *symbolizes the superconscious mind.* | All people in dreams represent parts of Self. Doctors are a specific class of people distinguished by their extensive education and learning thus they signify the superconscious part of mind. The superconscious mind is the part of mind which holds the ideal and plan for becoming compatible to the Creator. |
| **Dog** *symbolizes a compulsive way of thinking. (see animals)* | Since dogs are domesticated animals, they usually represent familiar habits for which the dreamer holds attachment. |
| **Doll** *represents imagination.* | When a doll appears in a dream, it will indicate the use of imagination. If the doll belongs to a child in the dream, this will signify employing imagination in developing a relatively new idea. If the doll seems alive it can indicate pretense, which is imagination without will power. |
| **Door** *symbolizes access to places in mind.* | There are seven levels of consciousness comprising the whole mind of any individual. Within these levels are countless thoughts and attitudes, memories and creations. In the language of mind, doors symbolize a means to access any of these. |
| **Downhill** *indicates action taken following the accomplishment of a challenge or overcoming of an obstacle.* | In the language of mind hills or mountains represent challenges in life. Whether the thinker views a challenge as a question to be answered or an obstacle to be overcome will determine much of the significance and meaning of this symbol in a dream. |
| **Dragon** *symbolizes the conscious ego.* | Like a devil, the dragon is an imaginary creature, which by its universally accepted description, represents the ability to perceive the Self. In a dream it most often signifies the expression of the identity in the physical, known as the conscious ego. When the conscious ego is understood and |

| *Derivative Meaning* | *Thoughts to Consider* |
|---|---|
| *Dict. A learned man, a teacher; a person who has received the degree of this name from a university thus a doctor of divinity, laws, medicine, etc.; a person duly licensed to practice medicine.* | Observe the doctor's actions in the dream. They will tell you how you view your own superconscious mind. If the doctor is a healer it will signify recognition of wholeness that comes from realizing your purpose for existence and relationship with all of creation. If the doctor is a teacher it will indicate your learning about the superconscious mind. |
| *Dict. A well-known domesticated carnivorous quadruped, closely allied to the wolf and the fox, noted for its sagacity, acute senses and great attachment to man.* | Is the dog your pet? If so, look for a very familiar habit that gives you great joy or comfort. A strange dog that is attacking you will represent an unrecognized habit that is controlling your life. |
| *Dict. A puppet or small image in the human form for the amusement of children.* | Realize imagination is important in any creative endeavor, but it is only one of three ingredients required for creation. Direct your imaging skill on purpose and with purpose to ensure the manifestation of your desires. |
| *Dict. An opening or passage into a house by which persons enter.* | Why is the door prominent in your dream? Is this a door from one room to another, from the inside to the outside? Is it a door in a house or a building used for a purpose other than a home? Answering these questions will offer insight into how you are using your mind. |
| *Dict. A slope from a higher to a lower part; moving in descent.* | What have you recently accomplished and how are you responding to what has been acquired? If you are headed downhill in your dream, swerving out of control, you need to take stock of what has been gained and how you can use it to better your life. If you journey downhill is easy and pleasurable, you are relishing your accomplishment by taking time to assimilate the learning it afforded. |
| *Dict. A fabulous, imagined animal conceived as a sort of winged crocodile, with fiery eyes, crested head,* | How do I know myself? Do I define myself in physical terms only? Am I aware of what motivates my thoughts and actions? The actions of your *dream-dragon* will give you clues for using your conscious ego productively. If your dream |

| Symbol | Meaning in Universal Language of Mind |
|---|---|
| | used it will motivate the mind toward greater and greater awareness. When the thinker is unconscious of their own identity, the conscious mind is unaware of the source of motivation or the reason behind the actions. |
| *Dream* *signifies inner rapport and communication concerning the state of awareness.* | Dreaming that you are dreaming indicates an awareness of the inner Self. Dreams are messages from the inner subconscious mind to the outer conscious mind concerning the state of awareness of the dreamer. |
| *Dress* *signifies how the dreamer is expressing Self.* *(see clothes)* | |
| *Driving* *indicates control, use, and direction of the physical body.* | Small vehicles in a dream represent the physical body of the dreamer. The action of driving a vehicle indicates the control, use, and direction of the body. Through physical maturity, many bodily functions, such as walking, talking, eating, and elimination of waste, are learned and controlled by the conscious mind. There are other bodily functions, such as breathing and heartbeat, which most people do not learn to control thus leaving their function to the direction of the subconscious mind. Who is driving in the dream will offer insight into the meaning of the dream. |

| *Derivative Meaning* | *Thoughts to Consider* |
|---|---|
| *and enormous claws, spouting fire and often regarded as an embodiment of watchfulness. Dragon comes from the Greek* drakon *meaning "to see".* | dragon breathes fire it indicates your conscious ego motivating you toward expansion. If your *dream-dragon* is a friendly, cartoon figure, it represents your use of imagination in fashioning your identity. If the *dream-dragon* is slain, it will symbolize a change in your ego. |
| *Dict. The thought or series of thoughts of a person in sleep.* | How can I add to my awareness, building a rapport with my inner Self? Responding daily to the messages in your dreams is one way. Another is through daily meditation as a means of aligning the conscious and subconscious minds and attuning them to the superconscious mind. |
| *Dict. To impel or urge forward; to travel in an automobile.* | Note who is driving the car. If you are, then the dream indicates you are in control of your body. If a person of the opposite sex is driving this will signify a reliance upon the subconscious mind to control your body. If the person driving is determined, once interpreted, to represent the superconscious mind this will indicate a reliance upon the source of life force to control your body. |

| Symbol | Meaning in Universal Language of Mind |
|---|---|

*E*

*Eagles
represent
compulsive
thoughts in the
subconscious
mind.
(see birds)*

*Ears
symbolize
receiving
information
through listen-
ing.*

Ears are one of the five physical senses which specifically afford the conscious waking mind the power of distinguishing sounds. The sound waves received by the ears must be recognized by the attention in order for listening to occur. In a dream, ears will indicate the mind's ability for receiving vibration through the mental act of listening.

*Earth
represents
subconscious
mind substance.*

Earth in a dream represents the substance, known in Eastern philosophy as akasha, of the inner, subconscious mind. All physical matter is comprised of this metaphysical substance. All imaged desires are impressed in akasha for reproduction, just as a seed is placed in the earth for growth and maturity.

*Earthquake
indicates a lack
of control of
changes directly
related to how
subconscious
mind substance
is being used.*

Earthquakes result from the natural evolution of the earth. The inner exchange of gas and mineral causes a shifting of land mass. These in turn cause rifts in the outer surface of the planet. In dreams, earthquakes symbolize the alterations occurring within Self due to the exchange of energies acting upon the inner mind's substance. These alterations then produce effects in the outer, waking consciousness. Since most people have little awareness of the activity in the inner levels of mind, they only become aware of these transformations when the effects become physically known.

| *Derivative Meaning* | *Thoughts to Consider* |
| --- | --- |
| *Dict. The organ of hearing, which in man and higher animals is composed of a funnel for collecting the sound waves and directing them inward for reception by the auditory nerve.* | How attentive am I to listening? If the dream reports a disorder in the ears it will indicate a need to listen. The same would be true with misshapen or overly large or small ears. A lack of ears in a dream would indicate a refusal to listen. You will want to identify the aspect of Self failing to use this avenue of receiving for more complete understanding. |
| *Dict. The particles which compose the mass of the globe, particularly its surface.* | What is occurring with the earth in your dream will lend insight into how you are using the inner mind substance. If you are gardening, planting and weeding, this will symbolize the reproduction of desires and elimination of any counterproductive ideas. If earth is being moved in preparation for building a house, this will indicate the inner alterations occurring for the development of your mind. Mud in a dream will symbolize a confusing of inner level experiences and outer, waking experiences. |
| *Dict. A shaking, trembling, or concussion of the earth probably due to internal igneous forces.* | Are you acquainted with the parts of Self beyond the physical? If so, you will be more equipped to identify the meaning of your *dream-earthquake*. If not, begin study and practice that will aid you in expanding your consciousness with full awareness. Being attentive to your dreams will assist you. Meditation practices will aid. The more you are aware of the inner levels of consciousness, the intelligence, energy, and substance available to you, the more foresight you possess. |

| Symbol | Meaning in Universal Language of Mind |
|---|---|
| *Elevator signifies a means for movement between and to levels of consciousness.* | In the Universal Language of Mind, this mechanical device symbolizes willful attention. Attention is the only sense of the mind. Will is the faculty of mind by which we determine action and control the Self. When willful attention is directed to cause movement in mind, there is the ability to access different levels of consciousness. |
| *Examination signifies the mental action of discerning the truth.* | An examination in a dream symbolizes a time for reflection and evaluation. If the exam is a test it will indicate the dreamer's need to assess the truth of what has been gained. The subject of the test will give further insight into the theme for reflection. For example, a medical exam will indicate the need to identify attitudes producing wholeness or disease. |
| *Exercising indicates mental dexterity of attention.* | Exercising in a dream symbolizes the dreamer's command of willful attention. Just as physical exercise hones the muscles of the body, mental exercise hones the only muscle of the mind — will. |
| *Extrasensory Perception indicates the dreamer's use of intuition.* | Extrasensory perception is commonly used to describe the exceptional abilities beyond those tendered by physical senses. These are in the realm of telepathy or mind to mind communication, precognition, telekinesis, and so forth. All are abilities natural to the subconscious mind. When these abilities are prominent in a dream they will indicate the dreamer's use of intuition, the power of the subconscious mind. |
| *Eyes indicate receiving information through perception.* | Eyes are one of the five physical senses which specifically afford the conscious waking mind the power of delicate and accurate perception. The reflected light received by the eyes must be recognized by the attention in order for perception to occur. In a dream, eyes will indicate the mind's ability for receiving vibration through the mental act of perception. |

| *Derivative Meaning* | *Thoughts to Consider* |
|---|---|
| *Dict. A mechanical contrivance for raising passengers or goods from a lower place to a higher.* | Why is the elevator important in your dream? Is it filled with people or empty? Perhaps it is filled with something incongruous to physical reality, such as pigs or stacks of paper. By identifying the meaning of the other symbols appearing in your dream you will gain insight into your ability to use willful attention to access parts of your mind beyond the physical level. |
| *Dict. A careful search or inquiry, an attempt to ascertain facts.* | After interpreting the nature of your *dream-examination*, identify its relevance in your life. Consciously examine the quality of your thinking that is producing the circumstances and situations in your life, separating what is true from what is false. Then determine the action you will pursue based upon what you have gained from the identified endeavors. |
| *Dict. A putting into action the powers or faculties of (the eyes, the limbs, the mind); use; employment.* | How am I building my will? What thoughts and activities have I been pursuing that are increasing my will power? How you answer these questions will give you indications of which mental and physical activities are beneficial to pursue. |
| *Dict. The act or process of the mind which makes known an external object through the reception of impressions in such a way as to be more than what is usual and beyond what is expected.* | How have I experienced extrasensory perception recently? These types of dreams can assist you in becoming aware of your intuitive abilities that you might ordinarily ignore or take for granted. ESP in a dream will indicate a state of awareness receptive to and inclined toward spiritual development, many times indicating the dreamer's awareness of subconscious experience beyond that of dreams. |
| *Dict. The organ of vision in man and higher animals, consisting of a ball in an orbit forming an optical apparatus whereby external objects are received for sensible impressions.* | Are you looking but not seeing? If the dream reports a disorder in the eyes it will indicate a difficulty in clear, mental perception. Blindness in a dream will indicate a refusal to perceive and discern. You will want to identify the aspect of Self failing to use this avenue of receiving for more complete understanding. Remembering eyes in a dream due to size or color will often be a means for the subconscious mind to draw your conscious attention to acumen. |

| *Symbol* | *Meaning in Universal Language of Mind* |
|----------|------------------------------------------|

**F**

*Fabric*
*represents the*
*mental sub-*
*stance being*
*utilized in the*
*life.*

Usually appearing as material in a dream, fabric will signify the dreamer's manner of creating.   How the fabric is
used in the dream will indicate the nature of the creation.
For instance, if the dreamer is sewing fabric into an apparel, this will signify how the dreamer is creating his/her
outward expression. If the fabric is used to cover furniture
it will symbolize the way the dreamer utilizes mental abilities to create.

*Face*
*signifies the*
*dreamer's*
*identity.*

The face in a dream indicates how the dreamer sees him/
her Self. Distinctly different from clothing, the face is the
part of the body which reflects who the dreamer is. If the
features of the face are missing in a dream it will indicate
the dreamer's need to create an identity. If certain features
are outstanding, refer to the meaning in the Universal Language of Mind of those features in this dictionary.

*Factory*
*represents a*
*condition of*
*mind where*
*productivity*
*occurs.*

In the Universal Language of Mind a factory indicates a
specific state of mind held by the dreamer. It is characterized by its ability to cause something to be brought into
existence. The mind of the thinker is designed for creation
and re-creation; the conscious mind creates what is desired
in imaged form which the subconscious mind then recreates for manifestation in the physical life.

*Falling*
*symbolizes the*
*action of*
*returning to*
*awake con-*
*sciousness.*

In a dream, falling symbolizes the movement from the inner, higher levels of consciousness toward the outer, lower
level of consciousness — the physical.  There is an old
wives' tale which says if you dream you are falling and
you hit bottom you will die. This is not true. Falling symbolizes the mental action of returning to awake consciousness, therefore at the time the dreamer would "hit bottom"
he/she usually awakes and the dream images are no longer
present.

*Farm*
*indicates the use*
*of subconscious*
*existence to*
*produce what is*
*desired.*

In the physical, farming is the action of cultivating the earth
to produce potential food.  In the Universal Language of
Mind this indicates the mind's ability to use its substance
to produce experiences that will bear knowledge.  A farm
in a dream will indicate the dreamer's use of the inner subconscious mind for fulfilling desires.

| *Derivative Meaning* | *Thoughts to Consider* |
|---|---|
| *Dict. The structure of anything; the manner in which the parts are put together; often used as cloth manufacturer.* | Note how the fabric appears in your dream. This will give insight into what and how you are creating in your life. |
| *Dict. The front part of an animal's head, particularly the human head made up of the forehead, eyes, nose, mouth, cheeks, etc. Countenance, expression.* | Am I expressing my Self in the way I desire? Many people think one way and express another. This results in mental and emotional confusion. Endeavor to align your thoughts with your actions and words. Be the person you want to be. |
| *Dict. A building or collection of buildings appropriated to the manufacture of goods.* | How am I using my mental power to bring into being what I desire in life? Is my *dream-factory* running smoothly or does it have machinery breakdown? The action occurring in the factory will give guidance for causing what you desire to exist in your life. |
| *Dict. The act of sinking from a higher to a lower position; descending by the power of gravity.* | With knowledge and practice, you can learn how to move in and out of the inner levels of consciousness at will. Pursue studies that will aid you to develop this skill so you can access the considerable wisdom in the inner levels of your own consciousness. |
| *Dict. A farm is a tract of land cultivated by either the owner or a tenant and usually divided into fields.* | Note the activity of your *dream-farm*. Cultivating and planting will indicate an inner preparation for the fulfillment of your desires. Farm animals can indicate this preparation is, at least in part, a compulsive mental activity rather than one understood by you. However, if you are using the animals — milking a cow or driving horses — |

| Symbol | Meaning in Universal Language of Mind |
|--------|----------------------------------------|

**Fasting**
*is a ceasing of receiving new knowledge.*

Physically, fasting requires the body to draw upon reserves of potential energy already held or to draw directly upon cosmic energy. In the Universal Language of Mind, this action indicates drawing upon knowledge already possessed by the dreamer.

**Father**
*represents the superconscious mind.*

In the Universal Language of Mind, father represents the superconscious mind, the dreamer's inner authority and divinity. The purpose of the superconscious mind is to hold the seed idea for the thinker's maturity as a creator. The superconscious mind is the part of mind that is closest to the source, the Creator. Its duty is to supply the spark of life to the outer parts of mind, thus the origin of the word "father" meaning "to feed" becomes apparent.

**Fear**
*indicates what is unidentified and unknown to the dreamer.*

Although the common conception of fear is that of an emotion, this is incomplete. Fear is a refusal to identify cause, and this is its meaning in the language of mind. Since thought is cause, fear only arises when the thinker allows something to remain unknown. As this thought manifests through the mind, it eventually reaches the emotional level of consciousness. Here fear is registered by the outer, conscious mind as an emotion.

**Feet**
*represent spiritual foundation.*

In the language of mind, feet symbolize the dreamer's spiritual foundation. This foundation is the combination of the permanent understandings of creation previously gained and held in the soul plus the present conscious attitudes that foster and enrich spiritual progression. Feet in a dream will tend to indicate the dreamer's place of security.

**Female**
*an aspect of Self.*

In a dream, people of the same sex as the dreamer represent aspects of the conscious mind and people of the opposite sex represent subconscious aspects. If the dreamer is female, women will indicate conscious aspects of Self; if the dreamer is male, females will indicate subconscious aspects. If the *dream-female* is familiar to the dreamer, the aspect of Self can easily be identified by describing

| *Derivative Meaning* | *Thoughts to Consider* |
|---|---|
| | this will signify your direction of the driving forces operating in the inner levels of mind. |
| *Dict. Abstaining from food beyond the usual time; a withholding from the usual quantity of nourishment.* | What knowledge have I previously gained that can be useful to me now? Many people constantly seek new knowledge failing to assimilate what has already been received. Determine the nature of the knowledge you possess and put it to use in your life experiences. By using what you already have, you will prepare your mind to receive additional knowledge. |
| *Dict. He who begets a child; a male parent; The founder of a race, family, or line. Persian padar, Sanskrit pitri meaning father, from the root pa to feed.* | What is my relationship with my own superconscious mind? Am I aware of my own divinity, an inner sense of divinity, an inner urge toward spiritual progression? Your attitude toward and the activity of the father who appears in your dream will reveal the relationship with your own superconscious mind. |
| *Dict. A painful emotion excited by an expectation of evil or the apprehension of impending danger; holy awe and reverence for God and his laws.* | What am I afraid of? By identifying what stimulates the fear you will begin making what was previously unknown to you, known. If you are afraid of people in your dreams, you can easily identify your fear by interpreting the aspects of Self involved. This is also true for other dream participants and actions. With awareness, you can dispel any fear, freeing your Self to know the respect and awe of creation. |
| *Dict. The lower extremity of an animal's leg; the part of the leg which treads the earth in standing or walking.* | Am I investing my sense of security in spiritual matters or in things of the physical? The *dream-action* occurring will help you answer this question. If your *dream-feet* are huge it will indicate a need to give attention to your spiritual foundation. If your *dream-feet* are injured, you need to change errant thoughts concerning or impeding your spiritual foundation. |
| *Dict. Belonging to the sex which produces and bears young; feminine.* | First, determine the part of mind your *dream-female* represents. Second, identify the aspect of Self she symbolizes. Third, look to the activity in the dream to interpret what your inner Self is telling you about this aspect. If the female is unknown to you, remember your impression of her during the |

| Symbol | Meaning in Universal Language of Mind |
|--------|----------------------------------------|
| | the outstanding qualities of the person. If the *dream-female* is unfamiliar, it will signify an unknown aspect of the Self. |
| *Fence signifies a limitation in thinking.* | In the Universal Language of Mind, a fence symbolizes a limit in thinking. This can indicate a physical goal, an obstacle in the dreamer's life, or a barrier to what the dreamer desires. |
| *Field represents fertile mind substance.* | Earth in a dream represents the substance of the inner, subconscious mind. All imaged desires are impressed in this substance for reproduction, just as a seed is placed in the earth for growth and maturity. In the Universal Language of Mind, a field represents mind substance that is fertile, prepared and readied to receive imaged desires. |
| *Files indicate information stored in the brain that can be easily retrieved.* | In the language of mind files will indicate memory. If the files are lost, it will signify the dreamer's need to hone and develop memory recall. This is accomplished most easily by harnessing the mental attention. If the file is about a particular subject, refer to related entries in this dictionary for further understanding. |
| *Fingers symbolize purposeful use or action.* | Hands in the language of mind signify purpose. The fingers of the hands indicate purposeful use or action. Physically, the composition of the human hand, particularly the juxtaposition of the thumb and fingers, is one of the outstanding characteristics that elevates man above all other animals. This, combined with the ability to walk upright, gives the thinker the necessary physical vehicle, or body, for reasoning development. |
| *Fire represents expansion.* | In the Universal Language of Mind fire represents expansion; the ability to spread out becoming enlarged so as to embrace more. How fire appears in the dream will indicate where the expansion is occurring in the dreamer's thinking and life. |

| *Derivative Meaning* | *Thoughts to Consider* |
|---|---|
| | dream. This will assist you in identifying what part of you she is symbolizing. |
| *Dict. A wall, bank, railing, or paling forming a boundary to or enclosing some area; that which defends; the art of fencing.* | What function does the fence serve in your dream? This will give you clues for identifying what type of limit you are facing. If the *dream-fence* is keeping you in a restricted area in your dream, it is time to use your imagination to extend your thinking beyond what you have previously settled for or accepted. |
| *Dict. A field is a piece of land suitable for tillage or pasture; cleared or cultivated ground.* | Note the quality of your conscious thinking. Be attentive to the desires you are imaging, for this symbol indicates a readiness upon the part of the subconscious mind to fulfill those desires. |
| *Dict. A line or wire on which papers are strung that they may be conveniently found when wanted; a collection of papers arranged for ready reference.* | What does the *dream-action* say about my memory? Am I using it well and wisely or do I need to pay better attention to my experiences so they are easier to recall? By directing your mind toward what is occurring in the present, you will find your ability to remember at a later time is greatly improved. Keep ignoring the present, and you will continue to have a faulty memory. |
| *Dict. One of the five extreme members of the hand; any of them but the thumb. To have a finger in means to be concerned in; to have at one's finger ends means to be quite familiar with; to be able to make available readily.* | What purposeful actions am I making in my life? The answer to this question will reveal a significant part of your dream's message. Note why the fingers are a significant part of the dream action for more details. Keep in mind this symbol will indicate your intentions or motivations guiding your actions. Be willing to be open and honest with your Self concerning these and you will receive more benefit from the dream communication. |
| *Dict. The evolution of heat and light during combustion; fuel in combustion. Allied to the Sanskrit pu meaning "to* | Identify where the expansion is occurring. If your dream-house is on fire, this symbolizes an expansion of consciousness. In addition to interpreting what is on fire in your dream, note whether the fire is controlled or rampant, purifying or destructive. Who is involved with this fire in your dream? |

| Symbol | Meaning in Universal Language of Mind |
|--------|---------------------------------------|
| *Fish* *symbolize compulsive thinking, when used as potential food in a dream fish indicates knowledge of a spiritual nature.* | Animals in a dream symbolize habits. When the dream-action is fishing with the intention of procuring food, it will indicate seeking knowledge of a spiritual nature. |
| *Flood* *indicates a lack of control of conscious experiencing.* | In the Universal Language of Mind, a flood indicates that the dreamer is engrossed in physical life experiences. |
| *Floor* *signifies the separation of levels of consciousness in the mind.* | In the physical, a floor vertically separates stories and areas of activity in a building. In the Language of Mind, a floor will represent the separation of levels of consciousness. For example, the division between the conscious mind (first floor) and subconscious mind (second floor) of a house. |
| *Flowers* *are subconscious existence.* | Flowers spring from the earth. In the language of mind, earth is subconscious mind substance; flowers being a product of the earth represent subconscious existence. Subconscious existence includes the state of being within the dreamer's subconscious mind and it also indicates the condition of universal subconscious mind. |
| *Flying* *symbolizes the freedom to move in the inner levels of mind otherwise* | Flying in a dream here means the ability for flight, not flying with the means of a mechanical device such as an airplane. When you have the ability for flight in a dream it symbolizes mobility in the inner levels of consciousness. This is why people who remember flying in their dreams tend to realize the freedom associated with the experience. |

| *Derivative Meaning* | *Thoughts to Consider* |
|---|---|
| *purify"*. | This will tell you if your expansion is the result of forethought and premeditation or the result of reactions to what is occurring in your life. |
| *Dict. A vertebrate animal that lives in water, breathes by gills, and has cold blood, with limbs in the form of fins.* | Look to see how you are functioning from habit when you could be functioning from choice. Since this symbol is akin to spiritual knowledge, give special attention to your compulsive ways of thinking concerning spirituality. Give more thought to your spiritual nature and beliefs. Growing spiritually, rather than stagnating with old ideas that have become dogmas. |
| *Dict. A great flow of water; a body of water rising and overflowing the land.* | What are my thoughts about life? Do I believe the physical existence is all there is? Begin to become acquainted with your Self as a soul. This can be a first step to putting the physical, and all that it contains, in proper perspective. |
| *Dict. That part of a building or room on which we walk; a story in a building.* | Note the activity occurring in your dream that causes you to remember the floor. This will aid you to realize the importance of distinguishing the inner Self from the outer Self. For example, being able to separate your dream experiences from your waking experiences is necessary for Self control. |
| *Dict. The delicate and gaily-colored leaves or petals on a plant; a circle of leaves of some other color than green; blossoms: the organs of reproduction in a phenogamous plant.* | Why are flowers predominant in your dream? Are they growing in a garden or being offered to you by someone in the dream? How the flowers are used will indicate your awareness of your existence beyond the physical. This is why flowers are often seen as a token of love, respect, or gratitude in our physical lives. They symbolize an attitude of the giver beyond the physical gift itself. |
| *Dict. To move through air by the force of wind or other impulse; to rise in air as light substances.* | Are you scared by your *dream-flight* or relishing it, controlling the *dream-flight*? This will indicate how you are responding to the freedom you have in life. If flying dreams are common for you, begin to investigate astral projection or out-of-body experiences as a consciously induced en- |

| Symbol | Meaning in Universal Language of Mind |
|--------|----------------------------------------|
| *referred to as astral projection or out-of-body experiences.* | |
| *Food represents knowledge.* | Physically food nourishes the body. Mentally knowledge nourishes the mind, thus the old adage, "food for thought". In the Universal Language of Mind, food represents knowledge. |
| *Football symbolizes how the dreamer is using the life.* | Games in the Universal Language of Mind symbolize the manner in which the dreamer is approaching life. Football, a team sport, will indicate the dreamer's tendency to unite aspects of Self in a common endeavor where competition is a significant motive and mental dexterity is required. |
| *Foreign Country is an unfamiliar condition of mind.* | In the Universal Language of Mind, a foreign country will represent an unfamiliar or alien condition of mind. People of a foreign country will represent unfamiliar aspects of Self. |
| *Forest indicates subconscious existence.* | Similar to flowers in a dream, a forest will represent subconscious existence. Subconscious existence includes the state of being within the dreamer's subconscious mind; the recreative part of mind. Subconscious existence also indicates the condition of universal subconscious mind; the fact that all subconscious minds are connected. |
| *Freeze represents a static experience.* | In the language of mind freezing symbolizes a static existence. For example, frozen water will indicate unchanging life experiences; frozen food will signify knowledge that is retained for future use. |

| *Derivative Meaning* | *Thoughts to Consider* |
|---|---|
| | deavor. You don't have to wait until you are consciously asleep to experience the inner levels of consciousness! |
| *Dict. Whatever supplies nourishment to organic bodies; whatever feeds, sustains, or nourishes.* | Note what is happening with the food in your dream. Is it a huge banquet for you to choose from or is the food rancid? This will tell you how you perceive the knowledge available to you. If you are eating it will indicate receiving knowledge; if you aren't eating it will signify what is available to you that you are failing to utilize. |
| *Dict. A ball cased in leather, to be driven by the foot; a game played with a football by two parties of players.* | How am I approaching life? Is the competition friendly and beneficial or is it hostile and detrimental to my goals? Am I pleased with the way I approach life, does it accomplish what I desire? Or do I want to transform my ideals and motivations enabling me to approach life differently? |
| *Dict. Belonging or related to a nation other than that of one's birth or residence; alien or not belonging.* | What have you experienced lately that has challenged your sense of stability and security? Owing to the choices of others in your life, you may find a need to make new decisions about the direction of your life. By identifying the qualities you associate with the foreign country in your dream, you will be able to assess the frame of mind and become more aware of the dream's message. |
| *Dict. An extensive wood, or a large tract of land covered with trees.* | Am I aware of how my conscious thinking affects my inner Self? How are my conscious thoughts related to what I experience on deeper levels? Daily meditation will aid you to expand your conscious awareness beyond the confines of the physical level of consciousness. |
| *Dict. To be congealed by cold; to be changed from a liquid to a solid state by the abstraction of heat.* | Am I holding onto the past, wanting things to remain the same, unchanged? Do I confuse balance with stagnation? If you are trying to find equilibrium in your Self and your life by keeping things the same you are stagnating. Equilibrium occurs when you know what causes motion and use it every moment. |

| *Symbol* | *Meaning in Universal Language of Mind* |
|---|---|
| **Friends** *are familiar aspects of Self.* | People in dreams represent aspects of Self. Friends are aspects of Self well-known to you. |
| **Fruit** *represents knowledge.* | Fruit is a natural food. In the Universal Language of Mind fruit represents knowledge. |
| **Furniture** *symbolizes the means to implement the mind's desires.* | Drawing upon the origin of the word furniture gives deeper insight to its meaning in the language of mind. Furniture in a dream represents the means to implement the mind's desires; to perfect what is wanted, to complete what is started. Furniture can be symbolic of any number of mental actions required for creation, the foremost being memory, will, and imagination. |

## G

| | |
|---|---|
| **Galaxy** *signifies consciousness of Creator.* | With the advent of technology, images of the vast reaches of space and distant celestial orbs have been photographed. When this image appears in a dream, it will represent the consciousness associated with the creation of a Creator beyond the dreamer's present capabilities. |

| *Derivative Meaning* | *Thoughts to Consider* |
|---|---|
| *Dict. One who is attached to another by affection; one who has esteem and regard for another.* | Identify which aspects of Self your *dream-friends* represent. Whether desirable or not, realize you have a certain attachment to these aspects. Be willing to build upon the qualities that are productive and change those which are not. |
| *Dict. Whatever vegetable products the earth yields for the use of man and the lower animals; in a more limited sense, the reproductive product of a tree or other plant; especially the edible succulent products of certain plants.* | How is the fruit being used in your dream? Notice whether you are consuming the fruit or merely observing its presence. Eating a fruit indicates knowledge you have recently received. Sitting under a fruit tree would symbolize knowledge readily available to you. |
| *Dict. That with which anything is furnished; specifically, the seats, tables, utensils, etc. necessary or convenient for housekeeping; the necessary appendages in various employments or arts. Latin fornire, "to finish, perfect".* | Do I have what I require to fulfill my desires? Many people become dependent upon external means for having what they want in life. They rely upon others to fulfill their desires, or leave it to a higher power or fate. The furniture in your dream, its use and repair, will inform you of how you are employing your mental skills of creativity to fulfill your desires. |
| *Dict. The Milky Way, that long, white, luminous tract which is seen at night stretching across the heavens and which is formed by a multitude of stars so distant and blended as to be distinguishable only by powerful telescopes. Gr. galaxias: kyklos "circle" and gala "milk".* | What is occurring in my life that is beyond my understanding? This symbol will indicate an expansive awareness of creation yet a sense that what is occurring in the life is beyond your control. Begin honing and refining your ability to create so you can receive more of what is available in your experience. Use meditation as a means to establish a relationship with your Creator. |

| *Symbol* | *Meaning in Universal Language of Mind* |
|---|---|
| **Games** *represent the perspective of life held by the dreamer.* | Games in the Universal Language of Mind symbolize the manner in which the dreamer is approaching life. Individual games, such as solitaire, will indicate the dreamer's tendency for self-direction where excelling or enjoyment is a significant motive. Interactive games, such as chess, will indicate the dreamer's tendency toward challenge where competition is a significant motive. In either case, the dream will be highlighting the dreamer's mental dexterity. |
| **Garage** *represents a condition of the body; usually rest or healing.* | Small vehicles in a dream represent the dreamer's physical body. A garage, being physically a place for receiving or repairing motor vehicles, symbolizes the condition of rest or healing of the physical body. |
| **Garden** *represents subconscious existence.* | Gardens are the planned cultivation of substances that spring from the earth. In the language of mind, earth is subconscious mind substance; gardens being a product of the earth represent subconscious existence. Since physical gardens are the result of man's creativity, *dream-gardens* will indicate the imaged thoughts the dreamer is impressing in subconscious existence. |
| **Gas** *signifies energy.* | As you will note by the dictionary definition, man has created many uses for gas. In the Universal Language of Mind, gas represents energy. Energy is one of three principles of mind, and therefore is available to and throughout all of creation. Energy is necessary as a catalyst for change or motion. It can be physical as in the transformation of foodstuffs into energy for the human body or mental as in the transformation of information into energy for the mind's experience. Being able to determine energy in a dream is important because it gives an indication of the dreamer's willingness to put forth effort. |

| *Derivative Meaning* | *Thoughts to Consider* |
|---|---|
| *Dict. Sport of any kind; some contrivance or arrangement of sport, recreation, testing skill, and the like. O.G. gaman meaning "jest, sport".* | What is the dream telling me about my ability to respond to and direct my life? Am I Self motivated, continually striving to better my skill, or do I rely on competition, being better than someone else, for motivation? Cultivate the type of motivation you believe will aid you the most. Keep in mind this dream message is highlighting mental skills and dexterity that you can use in any life endeavor. |
| *Dict. A place for receiving and repairing motor vehicles.* | Am I giving sufficient attention to my body's physical needs? This dream will call your attention to the condition of your body advising you of your need for physical rest or recuperation. If your *dream-car* is in a garage for repairs, be aware that your body is experiencing healing and endeavor to cooperate with this. Positive and productive attitudes will foster healing, as well as physically healthy acts of proper nutrition, exercise, and relaxation. |
| *Dict. A piece of ground appropriated to the cultivation of plants, fruits, flowers, or vegetables.* | How aware am I of how my waking thoughts affect the inner me? Gardens in a dream will offer you insight for answering this question. For instance, a vegetable garden will indicate how your conscious desire for knowledge affects the mind substance in the inner levels of your consciousness. If the garden is flourishing, it will indicate your cooperation for manifesting your desire. If the garden is weed-infested, it will indicate your thoughts that are conflicting with and "choking" your desire. |
| *Dict. An elastic, airlike fluid; a substance such as air, the particles of which tend to fly apart from each other thus causing it to expand indefinitely. Coal gas used for heating, cooking; natural gas used as a fuel or illuminant; laughing gas used as an anesthetic.* | What is my dream saying about how I use energy? By interpreting the other symbols in your dream you will gain a clearly defined answer to this question. If the gas is being used for lighting, this will represent energy you are using toward greater awareness. If the gas is being used for cooking, it will signify the energy you are investing in gaining knowledge. |

| Symbol | Meaning in Universal Language of Mind |
|---|---|
| **Gas Station** *is a place to receive energy for the body.* | A gas station in a dream will represent an opportunity for replenishing the energy in the body. The *dream-action* will lend further insight; ie. filling a car with gasoline will indicate re-energizing the body, fixing a flat tire will indicate healing that is occurring in the body. |
| **Gems** *symbolize the value of subconscious existence.* | In the Universal Language of Mind, gems will indicate the value the dreamer places upon subconscious existence. The physical world is the external environment for the thinker. Within Self, are other dimensions of existence important to the well-being of the Self. The subconscious existence is a part of this internal environment. Gems in a dream indicate the dreamer's acknowledgement of the inner realms of Self. |
| **Geometry** *represents thought forms.* | When geometric figures appear in a dream they will indicate the form assumed by the thoughts of the dreamer. Each form will signify a specific quality of expression of thought. *(see circle, triangle, square)* |
| **Ghosts** *symbolize unidentified inner level bodies.* | In the Universal Language of Mind, ghosts symbolize the vehicles used for expression in the inner levels of consciousness. There are six inner levels of consciousness; the seventh being the physical. People are well-acquainted with the seventh level vehicle: the human body. Each inner level of consciousness also uses a vehicle for expression. When the thinker lacks knowledge of these inner level bodies they will appear as ghost-like forms in a dream. |
| **Gift** *indicates value.* | A received gift in a dream symbolizes value that is not a product of the dreamer's direct efforts; a given gift symbolizes value that is a result of the giver's effort. |

| *Derivative Meaning* | *Thoughts to Consider* |
|---|---|
| *Dict. A place where gasoline or oil are sold, chiefly for use in automobiles.* | Interpret the meaning of the *dream-action*. Energy is required to sustain bodily functions so your physical body is an efficient vehicle for your mind's experiences. Learn how to direct your mental and physical energy by practicing breathing exercises, tensing and relaxing groups of muscles, and learning to draw cosmic energy into the body. |
| *Dict. A precious stone of any kind, as the ruby, topaz, emerald, especially when cut or polished; a jewel.* | How do I know myself beyond the physical world? What credit am I giving to my inner Self as an intricate part of my happiness and well-being? Becoming aware of your existence beyond the physical is a predecessor to deeper states of Self awareness. Perhaps you are placing greater value upon your intuitiveness, for intuition is the power available in the subconscious existence. |
| *Dict. The science of magnitude; that branch of mathematics which treats of the properties and relations of magnitudes using lines, angles, surfaces and solids. Gr.* geometria: ge *meaning "the earth" and* metron *meaning "measure".* | What can I do to improve my ability to express my thoughts more clearly? Deeper thinking combined with a greater command of the meaning of words will assist you in defining and describing your ideas. The type of form appearing in your dream will give insight into the quality of thinking that you can use for more accurate Self expression. |
| *Dict. The soul or spiritual part of man; the visible spirit of a dead person. Greek* geist *meaning "a spirit".* | When ghosts appear in your dream, an appropriate response might be to become educated concerning out-of-body experiences and astral projection. By learning about the inner realms of consciousness, you will move closer to conscious knowledge of your whole Self. What was unknown and unidentified will become known and familiar. |
| *Dict. That which is given or bestowed; the act, right or power of giving. A natural quality or endowment regarded as conferred, faculty or talent.* | Note who is bestowing the gift as well as what the gift is. This will give you indications of the value you are receiving and what part of Self has earned it. Many times gifts in a dream will bring your attention to a quality or ability you possess but have been taking for granted, thus failing to use fully. By becoming aware of this attribute you can incorporate it into your conscious thinking. |

| Symbol | Meaning in Universal Language of Mind |
|--------|----------------------------------------|
| **Girl** *is an immature aspect of Self.* | As with all people in a dream, a girl will represent an aspect of Self, either conscious or subconscious depending upon the dreamer's physical sex. The youthfulness will indicate an underdevelopment or immaturity. If the girl is known by the dreamer, s/he can identify the outstanding quality the girl exhibits thus interpreting which aspect of Self is being addressed in the dream. If the girl is unknown, the dreamer can identify the aspect by remembering the girl's outstanding attribute during the dream |
| **Glasses** *symbolize a need to improve perception.* | Glasses alter the reception of light before it enters the eyes making adjustments that allow for perfect vision. Eyes in a dream symbolize perception. When an additional appliance is required for perfect vision this indicates the dreamer's need to enhance or improve perception. |
| **God** *signifies unknown creation.* | God is a concept of divine intelligence that transcends man's current capabilities for creation, therefore the idea of a Supreme Being who is the source of creation. In the Universal Language of Mind, God (or any of the other physical names describing this concept) represents unknown creation. Since God symbolizes a concept for man, rather than being a physically autonomous person or object, the dreamer who remembers God in a dream is drawing upon his own preconceived idea of what God is. For instance to one person God may be a giant, grandfatherly figure on a huge throne in the heavens; to another God may be the forces of nature; to another God may be blinding light that pervades all of creation. Because God is not a physical symbol like a person, vehicle, or building, in the language of mind it symbolizes unknown creation. |
| **Goddess** *signifies unknown creation. (See God)* | |

| *Derivative Meaning* | *Thoughts to Consider* |
|---|---|
| *Dict. A female child not arrived at puberty.* | Is this a part of Self I want to cultivate? If so, what can I do to foster its development and maturity? How can this part of me aid me to accomplish my aspirations in life? |
| *Dict. An optical instrument designed to enhance vision.* | Am I refusing to face facts, to see what is before me? Practice accurately receiving information from your environment, without prejudice or opinion. Once you have received what is available, then form your own ideas of your experience and fashion imaged ideals based on clear perception. Nearsightedness in a dream will indicate an ability to clearly see what is happening now but a lack of visionary thinking. Farsightedness will indicate an ability for clearly seeing the future but a lack of perception in the present. |
| *Dict. A being conceived of as possessing divine power and honored as the chief good; a deity; the Supreme Being; the Creator and the Sovereign of the universe.* | How does God appear in your dream? What made you determine that God appeared in your dream? Answering these questions will give you insight into how you understand creation. The dream message will be stimulating you to acknowledge your own concepts of the source of creation and what that source is capable of producing. |

| Symbol | Meaning in Universal Language of Mind |
|---|---|
| *Gold* *represents value in subconscious existence.* | Mined primarily in Southern Africa, gold has gained considerable world-wide respectability as a valued medium of exchange. Similar to gems, gold in the Universal Language of Mind indicates the value the dreamer places upon subconscious existence. *(see gems, jewelry, money)* |
| *Graduation* *indicates a point of achievement in learning, may indicate an understanding that has been reached through experience.* | Graduation in the Universal Language of Mind signifies an attainment reached through the dreamer's effort. Most graduations concern levels of schooling therefore indicating in a dream that a certain level of learning and mastery has been achieved. The area of the attainment can be discerned by the type of school, ie. musical conservatory will symbolize mastery in harmony; military academy will symbolize mastery in discipline. |
| *Grass* *is subconscious existence.* | In a dream, grass represents subconscious existence. Subconscious existence includes the state of being within the dreamer's subconscious mind; the recreative part of mind. Subconscious existence also indicates the dreamer's awareness of universal subconscious mind; the fact that all subconscious minds are connected. |
| *Greenhouse* *represents the caused and planned growth of intended desires.* | A greenhouse is the man-made cultivation of substances that spring from the earth. In the language of mind, it represents the process of visualization. Visualization begins with the formation of "seed" ideas in the conscious mind. These ideas are then "planted" in the receptive, subconscious mind substance where they grow and mature to fruition or manifestation in the physical life of their creator. A greenhouse represents this creative process available to every thinker. |
| *Grocery* *is the act of gaining or procuring knowledge.* | In the Universal Language of Mind food is knowledge. Physically, a grocery is a place to procure food, thus in a dream a grocery represents the act of gaining or procuring knowledge. |

| *Derivative Meaning* | *Thoughts to Consider* |
|---|---|
| *Dict. A heavy yellow metallic element, the most malleable and ductile of all metals; money, riches, wealth, a symbol of what is valuable or much prized.* | How is the gold used in your dream — as money or as a part of jewelry? The answer to this question will aid you to interpret the dream's meaning. Use this dictionary to decipher the elements of your dream. |
| *Dict. To mark relative position or standing by degrees, rank, or order. From grade, Latin gradus meaning "a step".* | What have I recently gained mastery in that I can now use to further my ideals and goals in life? Take stock of what you have gained in learning and understanding, for this is the foundation you will draw upon for every future endeavor. Mastery is often misappropriated to a single physical skill. This is a mistake in judgement. When mastery is achieved, mental capability and skill has been developed. With awareness of the power of thought, these skills can be used in any area, at any time by the one who has gained mastery. |
| *Dict. Herbage; the verduous covering of the soil.* | Am I aware of how my conscious thinking affects my inner Self? How are my conscious thoughts related to what I experience on deeper levels? Daily meditation will aid you to expand your conscious awareness beyond the confines of the physical level of consciousness. |
| *Dict. A building principally consisting of glazed frames or sashes for the purpose of cultivating plants which are too tender to endure the open air.* | Are you aware of the creativity you possess? Every imaged thought will seek to manifest itself in your life as a fulfillment of your desire. Realize the power you hold to create what you desire in your life and use that power wisely by creating images of the life you want. |
| *Dict. A merchant who deals in tea, sugar, spices, coffee, fruits; a retail purveyor of foodstuffs.* | Am I aware of the knowledge available to me? Am I actively seeking knowledge or passing it by? The activity in your dream will give you insight into the quantity and quality of knowledge currently available in your life and how you are using it. |

| Symbol | Meaning in Universal Language of Mind |
|--------|----------------------------------------|
| **Ground** *represents subconscious mind substance. (see earth)* | |
| **Group** *represents aspects of Self united for a common purpose; often signifying an attitude held by the dreamer.* | A group of people in a dream represent aspects of Self. The nature of the group, be it reporters, family members, athletes, sorority sisters, or a mob, will give insight into the united purpose of these aspects of the dreamer. This in turn will identify the attitude being addressed in the dream. |
| **Guns** *represent a means to cause change.* | In the Universal Language of Mind, guns are a means to cause change. |
| *H* | |
| **Hair** *symbolizes conscious thoughts.* | Hair in a dream represents the dreamer's conscious, waking thoughts. How hair appears in the dream will indicate the quality of the thoughts, thus giving the dreamer insight into the way s/he is thinking and what alterations can be made to enhance thinking. For instance, if hair is being cut this will symbolize the dreamer's current tendency to reorganize thoughts; baldness will indicate a need to exercise conscious thinking particularly relevant to the aspect of Self that appears in the dream. A hairy *dream-creature* will indicate an unknown part of Self consumed by conscious thoughts. |

| *Derivative Meaning* | *Thoughts to Consider* |
|---|---|
| *Dict. As assemblage, either persons or things; a number of individuals having some resemblance or common characteristic.* | Identify the nature of this group. This will tell you the purpose of these aspects of Self in your life. This element of your dream will indicate the intentions which promote the attitude being addressed in your dream. For instance, if the group is your family it will symbolize familiar aspects of all parts of Self that are wholistically relevant to the way you view and live your life. If the group is a mob of unknown people it will symbolize unknown aspects of Self that are promoting discord and conflict in your life. |
| *Dict. A name applied to every species of firearm for throwing projectiles by the explosion of gunpowder or other explosives.* | Do I want to change something about myself or my life? Determine what you want to change and initiate it by using reasoning. |
| *Dict. A small filament issuing from the skin of an animal.* | What thoughts populate my everyday thinking? Have I been changing my mind or altering my thoughts in some way recently? When hair is a significant dream symbol, the message is about how you construct your everyday thinking. Learning to still your conscious mind will aid you to separate who you are from the thoughts you create. |

| Symbol | Meaning in Universal Language of Mind |
|---|---|
| *Hallway* symbolizes access to parts of mind. | A house in a dream represents your mind. Buildings are ways of using your mind relative to the building's use in everyday life. Hallways will symbolize a means to access parts of mind, to use different mental activities. For instance a hallway leading to a kitchen would represent a way of accessing knowledge; a hallway to a bedroom will indicate a means for accessing assimilation of experiences. |
| *Hands* indicate purpose. | Purpose is the ability to conceive an intention for actions. Intention is important because it sets into motion karma, an indebtedness to Self for learning. When hands are outstanding in a dream it will usually indicate the dreamer's need to give attention to the intentions behind your actions. |
| *Harp* is means for harmony. (see musical instruments) | |
| *Hat* is a means of covering conscious thoughts. | Covering conscious thoughts can either be a way of protecting or hiding what the dreamer is thinking. The dreamer will need to determine if the *dream-hat* symbolizes defensiveness or secretiveness. |
| *Head* indicates the dreamer's ways of thinking. | Understanding, intellect, and will or resolution are indicated by this symbol. The capacities for mental acuity are important in this dream message. Identifying the meaning of the part of the head that is outstanding — eyes, hair, brain, and so forth — will give further insight into how the dreamer is utilizing thinking. |
| *Heal* shows a transformation from thinking which negatively affects Self to thinking which positively affects Self. | Healing is the ability to make whole. One of the creative powers man possesses, healing is usually left in the domain of the subconscious mind and Universal Law. Yet, by expanding conscious awareness, the thinker can learn to identify what causes wholeness and implement this awareness in the life. When healing appears in a dream it will signify the dreamer's interest in wholeness. |

| *Derivative Meaning* | *Thoughts to Consider* |
|---|---|
| *Dict. A corridor in a building.* | Note where the hallway leads for this will give you insight into your mind's activity. If the hallway is dark this will indicate a lack of awareness or familiarity with the parts of mind. |
| *Dict. The extremity of the arm, consisting of the palm and fingers; the power of performance; skill. O.E.* hent, *"to seize".* | Why me? Whose hands appear in your dream and how they are used will give you insight into the answer. Purpose combined with an ideal gives you motivation to achieve in life. Purpose is the ability to imagine how you will be enriched by accomplishing an ideal. Without purpose, your ideas will be empty goals and your life a series of crises. |
| *Dict. A covering for the head worn by men and women. From Icel.* hattr *meaning "to cover".* | Am I afraid of revealing my thoughts to others? Do I feel like I need to defend my ideas? Endeavor to be honest in expressing your thoughts. When your thoughts are well-developed, based on understanding and including purpose, you will no longer need to defend the truth you perceive. Likewise, you will be more willing to share the truth with others. |
| *Dict. The name generally applied to the anterior part or extremity of animals; the part which forms the seat of the brain and mental faculties.* | Am I using my full capabilities? This dream will indicate how you construct ways of thinking and many times highlight areas where further development can occur. If the head is overly large, you tend to embellish or exaggerate your thinking; if the head is absent, you need to think! |
| *Dict. To make sound or whole; to cure of a disease or wound and restore to soundness.* | What negativity am I releasing from my thinking and my life? How am I replacing unproductive and destructive thoughts with productive and creative ones? This dream will indicate a leaving behind of what retarded your well-being and growth, and the initiation into a more positive, wholistic experience of the essence and meaning of life. |

| Symbol | Meaning in Universal Language of Mind |
|---|---|
| *Heart*<br>*indicates the*<br>*dreamer's*<br>*awareness of*<br>*responsibility.* | The heart is the part of the body which sustains the movement of life force in the form of blood. The function and health of the heart is directly related to the thinker's awareness and understanding of responsibility. Responsibility is the thinker's ability to respond to his or her own desires. Gleaning understanding from each experience greatly enhances the ability to respond with awareness for it brings to the thinker wisdom concerning the nature of Self and the purpose for existence. |
| *Heaven*<br>*symbolizes the*<br>*superconscious*<br>*part of mind.* | Physically, heaven describes the vast reaches of the universe. Heaven has been used classically to denote the immensity of the universe, the abode of the Creator or Supreme being. In the Universal Language of Mind, heaven symbolizes the superconscious mind, the division of mind closest to the Source and where the divinity of man is housed. *(see authority figures)* |
| *Highway*<br>*represents the*<br>*path in life*<br>*chosen by the*<br>*dreamer to*<br>*accomplish his*<br>*goals.* | Physical life is the result of a series of choices made by each individual. Opportunities for Self betterment abound. A sequence of choices, based upon the initiation of and response to experience, creates an individual's path in life. A highway in the language of mind symbolizes this process. |
| *Home*<br>*indicates the*<br>*natural condi-*<br>*tion of mind.* | Although it seems foreign to many, the natural condition of the mind is stillness. This condition is alien to most because they attempt to think of two, three, or ten things at the same time thus scattering the attention producing restlessness. Stillness can be cultivated by focusing the mental attention upon one subject or object at a time. This skill produces calmness and opens the door to deeper states of consciousness. Home in the Universal Language of Mind indicates the familiar, inner frame of mind natural to the thinker characterized by peace. |

| Derivative Meaning | Thoughts to Consider |
|---|---|
| *Dict. A muscular organ which is the propelling agent of the blood in the animal body; the seat of the affections and passion. Sanskrit* hrid *from a root meaning "to leap".* | If the heart in your dream is sound and whole, it will draw to your attention your ability for understanding. Where understanding exists, there is the capacity to love. There is also the ability for excellence in any pursuit. A disorder in the *dream-heart* will indicate your tendency to become entrapped and overwhelmed by your experiences. Many times this will relate to a tendency to compete with others, rather than seeking your own personal best and the greater awareness it affords. |
| *Dict. The blue expanse which surrounds the earth, and in which the sun, moon, and stars seems to be set; the place where God manifests himself to the blessed.* | How do I understand my reason for existence? Do I believe the physical is all there is, or do I recognize unlimited power beyond what I presently possess? Dreaming of heaven indicates your need to know your Self beyond the limits of the finite world. Cultivate a deeper awareness of your spiritual nature by becoming familiar with the Universal Laws that govern creation and establishing a communion with the infinite through daily contemplation, prayer, and meditation. |
| *Dict. A public road; a way open to all travelers.* | Am I living the kind of life I want? What choices have I made that have led me to this point in my life? Knowing where you are going in life is largely dependent upon Self awareness, Self determination, and Self reliance. Think of your Self in these terms, imaging the type of person you want to become and choosing the avenues that will aid you in achieving your desire. |
| *Dict. One's own abode or dwelling. Latin* quies *meaning "quiet".* | What in your life brings you a sense of well-being, peace, and security? Realize these are the results of a focused and calm mind, and endeavor to strengthen your ability to cause this condition at will. You will find your ability to confidently respond to life's situations will increase. |

| Symbol | Meaning in Universal Language of Mind |
|--------|----------------------------------------|

*Horse represents compulsive thinking; when controlled by a person the horse will symbolize the dreamer's will.*

Animals, lacking sentience and conscious volition, function compulsively according to Universal Law. Therefore animals signify the dreamer's tendency to forfeit the opportunity for choice in favor of previously established habits in thinking. Because the horse has physically been used as a beast of burden by man, the horse in the language of mind will represent the dreamer's will. A white horse will indicate will power, the ability to make more productive choices than nonproductive; a black horse will indicate a lack of will power.

*Hotel symbolizes universal mind.*

Universal mind describes the interconnectedness of all minds experienced in the inner levels of consciousness. The subconscious, intuitive ability for telepathy is an example of this interconnectedness which transcends physical limitations of time and space. The power of influence has its origin in the ability to send and receive thoughts through the energy and substance of universal mind. This is one of the reasons why great thinkers can reach the same inventive discoveries seemingly simultaneously across the globe, or why someone can have knowledge of a distant loved one's thoughts or experiences.

*Hour is a means to identify and measure the dreamer's experiences and/ or understand- ings.*

Physical time is an invention of man to measure the passing of day through night and to expedite activities and communication. For the conscious, waking mind time is measured by experiences; the duration of an event. For the soul or subconscious mind of the thinker, time is measured by the gaining of understandings. Depending upon the aspects of Self involved in the *dream-action*, an hour will symbolize experiences and/or understandings.

*House represents the dreamer's mind.*

The mind is comprised of three major divisions: conscious, subconscious, and superconscious. Within these divisions are a total of seven levels of consciousness. A house in a dream will symbolize the dreamer's mind. The floors of the house will represent different parts of the mind *(see attic, basement, etc.)* and the activity in the house will signify how the dreamer is using this structure for thinking.

| *Derivative Meaning* | *Thoughts to Consider* |
|---|---|
| *Dict. A well-known quadruped, The most important to man of all animals that are used as beasts of burden and of draft.* Latin curro *meaning "to run".* | How do I understand will power? Many people confuse will power with "won't" power. They believe will power is denying something, like refusing to eat certain foods or perform certain activities. This is not will power. Will power is the ability to engage the will toward an imaged desire. It is a positive action of the mind that promotes growth and always leads to the fulfillment of a desire. |
| *Dict. A house for entertaining strangers or travelers.* | Become more aware of your intuitive ability for thought projection and reception by developing your concentrative and visualizing skill. By knowing your own thoughts, you will be more equipped to distinguish your thoughts from those of others. You will also be able to distinguish when you are sending thoughts you have visualized and when you are receiving impressions from someone else. Command of your own mind brings awareness of the wisdom available to you in universal mind. |
| *Dict. The twenty-fourth part of a day; sixty minutes; a fixed or appointed time.* Greek hora *meaning "a season, an hour".* | Am I gaining everything possible from my everyday experiences? Do I wait for experiences to come to me or do I initiate experiences purposefully? The best use of life occurs when you use your mind's capabilities to image the fulfillment of your desires. This means drawing upon the experiences you have understood to create new experiences that will add to your permanent learning. |
| *Dict. A building serving or intended to serve as an abode; a building for the habitation of man or for his use or accommodation.* | Note the ownership, kind, repair, and any other details about the house which are outstanding to you. These will give you indications of how you can more fully use your mind to create your desires and for soul progression. If you own the house, the dream action will revolve around the way you use the structure of your mind. If the house is unfamiliar, the dream is advising you to become aware of abilities or skills of mind currently unrecognized. A beautiful mansion symbolizes the value you place upon your mind and its capabilities. An abandoned shack indicates a lack of care and respect for your mind. |

| Symbol | Meaning in Universal Language of Mind |
|--------|----------------------------------------|
| *Husband is an aspect committed to wholeness. (see spouse)* | |

*II*

| | |
|--------|----------------------------------------|
| *Ice signifies unchanging life experiences.* | Many people try to keep the same situations and circumstances in their lives. They want their job to continue, their spouse to be the person they married, the children to remain the same age, and so forth. This type of thinking restricts the thinker for it works against the universal principle of motion. In the Universal Language of Mind water symbolizes life experiences. When its state is altered it ceases to flow naturally, thus ice in a dream represents unchanging life experiences. |
| *Illness symbolizes unproductive attitudes held by the dreamer. (see disease)* | Thought is cause. When the individual directs the mind toward productive, loving thoughts and spiritual growth and maturity there is wholeness in mind and body. When the mind is in disarray, filled with the negativity that stems from misunderstanding, there is dis-ease in the mind and body. In a dream illness will reveal dis-eased attitudes held by the dreamer. Specific illnesses will indicate specific attitudes that need to be changed for wholeness and health. For more insight into dis-eases and their mental causes use the book <u>Permanent Healing</u> by Dr. Daniel R. Condron. It is an excellent reference book based on decades of research conducted by the author and faculty of the School of Metaphysics. |
| *Insurance indicates an expectation of loss.* | Insurance is a relatively new business based upon principles of gambling. The client purchases insurance with the hope of never having to use it or as a protection against financial ruin. Meant to give peace of mind to its owner, insurance acts on the fears of the purchaser; a fear of dying, a fear of being sick, a fear of having an automobile accident. |

| *Derivative Meaning* | *Thoughts to Consider* |
|---|---|
| *Dict. Water or fluid congealed or in a solid state as result of abstraction of heat necessary to preserve its fluidity.* | What am I resisting in my life?  In what ways am I attached to things being the same rather than moving forward?  Realize the nature of the physical is change.  Cease trying to keep the conditions and circumstances in your life the same.  Increase your adaptability by initiating changes you want to occur. |
| *Dict. The state or condition of producing evil or misfortune; sick or indisposed. Not proper, rude or unpolished.* | Note who is ill in the dream and the type of disease they are experiencing.  Interpret which aspect of Self is involved in the detrimental thinking.  Using <u>Permanent Healing</u> you can identify the nature of the unproductive thought.  When these factors are determined, you can respond by initiating a change for the better by using the suggestions Dr. Daniel Condron gives in his book. |
| *Dict. A contract by which a person or company, in consideration of a sum of money, becomes bound to indemnify the insured or his representatives against loss by certain risks.* | What am I afraid of losing?  How am I gambling that there would be recompense should my fears manifest?  Cease allowing fear to control your life by directing your own mind toward productivity, success, and fulfillment.  Come to terms with your fears of the unknown or unexpected by expanding your awareness of the purpose of physical life and your purpose for existing. |

| Symbol | Meaning in Universal Language of Mind |
|--------|----------------------------------------|

*Invent is discovery made by the employing of full reasoning capability.*

Every invention is the result of creative genius. Each individual has the capacity for outstanding visionary thinking. When a man discovers a truth that has universal application, when he has the courage to communicate his ideas to the world, he becomes outstanding because humanity progresses as a result of his desire and willingness to create a better world. Reasoning is the power in the conscious mind which fosters inventiveness through the full use of memory, attention, and imagination.

*Invitation represents a stimulus for action.*

An invitation is a request for action upon the part of the receiver. In a dream, it indicates a stimulus which will set visualization into motion. Visualization is a skill employing the conscious and subconscious minds which enables the individual to conceive a desired image and experience its manifestation. Shaping Your Life by Laurel Fuller Clark is an excellent book on the power of creative imagery.

*Island represents the removal of attention from the physical.*

The only time most people remove their attention from the physical is when they go to sleep. Even then the process is automatic and not understood. The attention can also be forced to move away from the physical through anesthetics, mind-altering drugs, or hypnosis. These methods also lend little, if any, understanding to the nature of attention and its destination when not engrossed in physical matter. However, an individual can learn to consciously, with purpose and on purpose, remove the attention from the outer environment and physical body and place the attention within the mind. This process is known as astral projection. One way to understand this process and develop this skill is through daily practice of meditation.

*J*

*Jail signifies limitations arising from errors in thought and action.*

Manmade laws are an attempt to align with the Universal Laws that govern creation. Jails are places for those who will not abide by the laws of society. They exist for the protection of those who are willing to obey those laws and cooperate with others. In a dream, a jail will represent the limitations experienced by the dreamer arising from his failure to productively use the laws of creation. When an individual refuses to create what will satisfy his inner urge toward growth, s/he is severely limited.

| *Derivative Meaning* | *Thoughts to Consider* |
|---|---|
| *Dict.* To contrive or produce; make or construct as the originator of something that did not before exist. | What new discoveries am I making about my Self and life? What experiences have fostered these discoveries and how can I use them to promote greater understanding? Look for ways you can aid others with your newfound knowledge or insight. Become familiar with your potential for creative genius. For research, read <u>Kundalini Rising</u> by Dr. Barbara Condron. |
| *Dict.* A solicitation, asking, requesting, or calling upon its receiver to do something. | What arrests my interest? Am I aware of the ideas, people, or places currently in my life that are stimulating me into action? Knowing what stimulates you and why it grabs your attention, will increase your ability to control your own destiny. Without this awareness you are a victim of circumstance, reacting to your environment. |
| *Dict.* A tract of land surrounded by water whether of a sea, a river, or a lake. | Is my drawing away from physical experience an automatic, defensive reaction or a premeditated, intentional response? If it is the former, realize your escape is a temporary remedy for what you find unpleasant. No matter what your form of escape, you will return to what you are trying to avoid. Stop scattering your thoughts with pretense and daydreams and begin harnessing the creative power of your mind. If you are intentionally removing your attention from the physical for the purpose of greater awareness, this dream will be significant feedback to your efforts. |
| *Dict.* A prison; a building or place for confinement of persons arrested for a crime. | Am I feeling trapped by my past? Have choices I previously made in life resulted in confinement and restriction? What have I learned from these experiences and how can I use my creative ability to imagine a different life for my Self? |

| Symbol | Meaning in Universal Language of Mind |
|---|---|
| *Jewelry* *represents value expressed in the outer presentation.* | Jewelry is used to adorn the outer appearance; for beautification or as a reflection of wealth and position. When it appears in a dream it will indicate the value the dreamer holds in the way s/he expresses Self to others. The assessment of value will be indicated by the genuineness of the metals or stones. |
| *Judge* *represents the superconscious mind.* | Judges are authorities and administrators of justice. In the Universal Language of Mind, a judge symbolizes the power of the superconscious mind to determine what is just and right. The superconscious mind holds the ideal for the spiritual maturation of thinker. This ideal is in alignment with the Universal Laws that govern creation. What serves to promote the fulfillment of this ideal is what is "right". This is well described in Buddhist's teachings as the Eightfold Path: *right* beliefs, *right* intentions, *right* speech, *right* actions, *right* means of livelihood, *right* endeavoring, *right* mindfulness, and *right* meditation. |
| *Jungle* *is subconscious existence.* | Jungles, or in today's vernacular "rain forests", are specific areas of land near the equator of the earth; the tropics. Unless the dreamer lives in this area, it is foreign to him. Therefore when a jungle appears in a dream it conveys the alien mystery of the dreamer's subconscious existence. Most people are only familiar with the physical self, having little awareness of the inner realms of existence. Earth is subconscious mind substance; jungles being a product of the earth represent subconscious existence. |
| *Jury* *symbolizes aspects of Self.* | All people in dreams represent aspects of Self. A jury is a collection of people united for a common purpose: to determine truth based upon facts. In a dream, a jury will symbolize a united effort to use experiences to discern Universal Truth. Universal Truths describe Universal Laws, for instance "as you sow, so shall you reap" is a Universal Truth describing the Universal Law of Cause and Effect. Universal Truths apply to anyone, anytime, any where in our universe. |

| *Derivative Meaning* | *Thoughts to Consider* |
|---|---|
| *Dict. A personal ornament in which precious stones form a principal part. Anything of exceeding value or excellence.* | Note who is wearing the jewelry and why it is outstanding in your dream. This will give you insight into the quality of outer expression that you value. If the jewelry includes fake jewels, you need to evaluate the worthiness of how you are expressing your Self outwardly to others. Stolen jewelry indicates a lack of awareness of your own influence. Admit how you think and express to others makes a difference in your life and in theirs. |
| *Dict. A civil officer invested with the power to hear and determine causes, civil or criminal, and to administer justice between parties in courts held for the purpose.* | How do I consciously understand righteousness and justice. Do these concepts pervade my thinking or are they foreign to me? Expand your awareness of what is right according to the Universal Laws that govern creation by contemplating and acting upon the Eight-fold Path concepts noted. |
| *Dict. Land covered with forest trees, thick, unimpenetrable brushwood, or any coarse, rank vegetation.* | Am I acquainted with my existence beyond the physical body and environment? Do the inner parts of me remain unknown to me, vast and mysterious? If this is true, then you are equally unaware of how the conscious thoughts you create affect your inner mind. Begin developing Self awareness through a daily practice of concentration. Honing your ability to focus your mind will serve as the foundation for using your conscious mind more fully and exploring the inner levels of your consciousness. |
| *Dict. A certain number of people selected according to law and sworn to inquire into or to determine facts, and to declare the truth according to the evidence legally adduced. Latin* jurare, *"to sear"; same origin as* Jus *meaning "right, law".* | Am I seeking to understand Truth that is universal or am I only concerned with the truth as I see it? Learning how to determine the difference can be an appropriate response to this element of your dream message. Realize Universal Truth shows no favoritism. These concepts reflect the universal cause for an effect produced. The world's Holy Scriptures are filled with truths that are universal; read them! |

| Symbol | Meaning in Universal Language of Mind |
|--------|----------------------------------------|

# K

**Key**
*symbolizes
access to
solutions.*

In the language of mind a key is a means whereby any mystery is disclosed or anything difficult is explained. When a key appears in a dream it will indicate a solution or a guide which affords the dreamer greater understanding or control. How the key is used will indicate the specific understanding gained.

**Killing**
*indicates
changes
occurring within
the dreamer.*

Death in a dream represents change. The aware thinker recognizes physical life as temporary existence for the soul; one of many brief sojourns offering opportunity to further progression. When killing is part of the *dream-action*, it will indicate a change occurring in the dreamer and his/her life. The dreamer is performing the action symbolizes a premeditated, intentional change. The type of change will be signified by who or what is killed in the dream. For instance, if the dreamer is killing a tiger this will represent a change in a habit.

**King**
*is the
superconscious
mind of the
dreamer.*

Kings rule by divine authority established by bloodline. In the language of mind, a king will represent the superconscious mind of the thinker. The superconscious mind is the part of mind closest to the point of origin, the Source, or Creator. It is the divinity in man; the inner authority in individual consciousness.

**Kiss**
*represents loving
acknowledgement
of a part of Self.*

A kiss is a sign of affection, and as such in the Universal Language of Mind it represents a loving acknowledgement of a part of Self.

**Kitchen**
*is a condition of
mind where
knowledge is
available.*

A kitchen is a specific room of a house used for the storage, preparation, and often consuming of food. Food in the Universal Language of Mind is knowledge. A kitchen represents the frame of mind that is conducive to giving and receiving, preserving and serving knowledge.

| *Derivative Meaning* | *Thoughts to Consider* |
|---|---|
| *Dict. A key is an instrument used for shutting or opening a lock.* | What understanding have I recently gained that has added to my sense of Self control? A key will draw your attention to an understanding gained that might otherwise be overlooked. If you've lost your keys in a dream it will indicate your need to answer a question or solve a problem in your life. |
| *Dict. To deprive of life, animal or vegetable, in any manner or by any means; to render inanimate.* | Note who is killing what in your dream. If someone you recognize is killing an unknown person in the dream, you can identify the change being experienced by 1] interpreting the familiar aspect, 2] realizing this aspect is causing greater awareness of another part of your Self that you were previously unaware of. Although these types of dreams can be shocking to your conscious mind, remember in the language of mind killing and death indicates change and change is the nature of the physical existence. |
| *Dict. The sovereign of a nation; a man invested with supreme authority over a nation, tribe, or country.* | What is your attitude toward the king in the dream? Are you honorably respectful or defiantly rebellious? This will give you insight into your own conscious attitudes toward your own superconscious mind, your inner authority. |
| *Dict. To touch with the lips in salutation or as a mark of affection. Love and respect.* | Note the aspects of Self symbolized in this dream activity. These are aspects which are rooted in love and harmony. Draw upon them for they will assist you in fulfilling your desires. |
| *Dict. The room of a house appropriated to cookery.* | Be attentive to the recent condition of your mind for it is one you will want to continue. A mind that is open to learning is a curious mind invested in discovery. |

| *Symbol* | *Meaning in Universal Language of Mind* |
|----------|------------------------------------------|
| *Kite* *represents a thought form.* | A kite is a recreational device which provides entertainment. Its operator's enjoyment is derived from causing the kite to become airborn so it can become suspended in air by wind currents. In the language of mind, a kite represents a thought form in the deepest level of the subconscious mind. |

*L*

| *Labor (pregnancy)* *symbolizes the physical manifestation of a new idea.* | Labor describes the final preparation and stages of giving birth. In the language of mind this symbolizes the interaction between the emotional level of consciousness and the physical level of consciousness. Every imaged thought is recreated in the inner levels of the subconscious mind. The final subconscious level before physical manifestation is the emotional level. Here the thought undergoes its final development and, once complete, the thought is emoted or pushed from the inner levels to the outer physical level. Labor in a dream indicates an impending manifestation of an idea. |
| *Labor (work)* *symbolizes a vehicle for the dreamer's learning and growth.* | The thinker's work or career is his/her chosen path in life. Ideally, the work is a vehicle during the adult years for learning and growth and this is its meaning in a dream. When the workplace appears in a dream it will give the dreamer insight into his/her attitudes toward productive learning. |
| *Ladder* *is a means to gain access to levels of consciousness.* | There are seven levels of consciousness available to man. Each level is distinguished by specific qualities of energy which promote the development and maturation of imaged thought. The physical level of consciousness, that of the waking consciousness, is the level farthest from the Source and point of origin of individual consciousness. The six inner levels of consciousness are higher or deeper levels that can be accessed through conscious development; al- |

| *Derivative Meaning* | *Thoughts to Consider* |
|---|---|
| *Dict. A light frame of wood and paper constructed for flying in the air for amusement.* | What desire have you recently imaged? This symbol in your dream will indicate that thought is now being recreated in the inner levels of your subconscious mind and is on its way to becoming a manifested physical reality in your life. |
| *Dict. The pangs and efforts of childbirth.* | What have you been anticipating in your life? What desires have you been seeking to fulfill? Be attentive in your life for physical manifestations of what you have wanted for this dream indicates imminent fulfillment. |
| *Dict. Exertion, physical or mental or both, undergone in the performance of some task or work; particularly the exertion of the body in occupations by which subsistence is obtained.* | What is my dream imparting about my attitudes towards learning? Am I being productive, thus continuing to foster growth and Self improvement? Or am I stagnant, seeing my life as a series of obstacles to overcome, a chain of activities that must be endured? Enhance your productivity by setting your mind into action by creating an ideal of what you desire to accomplish. Add purpose to your ideal by envisioning how the pursuit of this ideal will add to your whole Self. Let these guide your mental and physical actions for productivity in your life. |
| *Dict. An article of wood, metal or rope consisting of two long side pieces and connected by crosspieces at suitable distances forming steps by which a person may ascend.* | What steps are you taking to expand your consciousness beyond the physical, waking level? If these are unconscious, endeavor to take control of your experiences by learning how to develop your conscious will for access to the inner levels. Practices in concentration and meditation will serve as cornerstones for inner level access, opening new worlds of awareness to you. |

| Symbol | Meaning in Universal Language of Mind |
|--------|----------------------------------------|

though most people access these levels in an unconscious fashion through sleep, hypnosis, or mind-altering drugs. A ladder in a dream will indicate a way to access these inner levels.

*Lake*
*represents*
*conscious life*
*experiences.*

Lakes are water surrounded by land mass. Water in a dream symbolizes conscious life experiences. A lake will represent the nature of the dreamer's attitude in everyday experiences. If the lake waters are calm and clear this will signify a relaxed and enlightened attitude. If the lake waters are turbulent and potentially dangerous it will indicate a restless and fearful attitude about life.

*Lamp*
*is a tool for*
*awareness.*

A lamp is a vessel for creating light, thus in a dream it symbolizes the ability to create awareness. Awareness results from employing the mind's innate capacities for reasoning and intuition for new realizations. For instance, a *dream-lamp* that does not perform its function, giving light, will indicate the dreamer is remaining in ignorance. Turning on a light in a dream will signify a new awareness.

*Land*
*indicates*
*subconscious*
*mind substance.*
*(see earth)*

Man's experience of his native planet is divided into land or bodies of water. The land is comprised of earth. Earth in a dream represents the substance of the inner, subconscious mind. This is the finer substance which precedes what we know as physical matter. Every imaged thought undergoes a re-creative process whereby the idea draws substance from the inner levels of subconscious mind for manifestation of the thought. Land in a dream indicates this subconscious mind substance.

*Laundry*
*indicates the*
*need to review*
*and organize.*

Laundry in a dream indicates the dreamer's need to bring order into how he expresses Self. The articles being laundered will lend further insight into the areas requiring the dreamer's attention. For instance, clothes will indicate how the dreamer is presenting Self to others; linen will signify the dreamer's ability for dexterity and purity in thought.

| *Derivative Meaning* | *Thoughts to Consider* |
|---|---|
| *Dict. A body of water wholly surrounded by land and having no direct communication with the sea or having so only by means of rivers.* | Note the condition of the lake for it will indicate your general attitude toward life. Life is more readily embraced by those who possess a calm mind and relaxed body. Make time daily to still your mind endeavoring to reach deeper and deeper states of mental and physical relaxation. Then image the quality and kind of life you desire to live. Using your will, direct your creative energies, both mental and physical, toward the fulfillment of this image. |
| *Dict. A vessel for containing oil or other liquid inflammable substance to be burned by means of a wick; any contrivance adapted to contain artificial light. Something metaphorically communicating light.* | Note how your recent thinking and activities have affected your awareness. Embrace new ways of thinking for the insights they afford. Extend your Self to new people and situations, thus giving your Self the opportunity for further growth in Self awareness. |
| *Dict. The solid or fixed part of the surface of the globe, in distinction from the sea or other waters.* | The appearance of land in your dream will inform you of how you are using your inner mind's substance for the recreation of your desires. To fully use your mind's potential employ visualization for it is your ability to image thought that will call upon the inner resources available to you and mold mind substance for the fulfillment of your desires. |
| *Dict. The place or room where clothes are washed.* | Is your mind clear and focused or cluttered and scattered? By determining what you desire and using your will to accomplish that image, your mind becomes focused. Eliminating extraneous, unrelated thoughts clears the mind to discern truth. When you find your mind wandering, becoming distracted away from your desire, use your will to redirect your attention toward your desire. |

| Symbol | Meaning in Universal Language of Mind |
|---|---|
| *Law* symbolizes universal principles governing creation. | The function of law at anytime, in any society, is to establish order and provide for the rights of its citizens. Beyond physical, manmade laws, exist the Universal Laws that govern creation. These laws apply to anyone, anywhere, at anytime in our universe. They are the principles which guide the evolutionary and involutionary development of humanity. When symbols relative to law appear in a dream they will indicate these universal principles. |
| *Lawn* represents receptive and readied subconscious mind substance. | Lawns are planned and cultivated areas of ground usually surrounding manmade buildings or houses. Thus in the Universal Language of Mind they indicate receptive and readied subconscious mind substance. |
| *Left* indicates the past. | Drawing upon the meaning of the word origin as "worthless, weak or infirm", left in the Universal Language of Mind represents what has already transpired and is active only as a product of the function of memory. "Left" is worth less because memory alone is insufficient for reasoning. |
| *Letter* signifies a communication from one aspect of Self to another. | A letter is a means of communication. When it appears in a dream, note the contents of the message and who it is from and to. These will give the dreamer specific insight into the way s/he communicates. |
| *Library* represents wealth of information available. | A library is an extensive collection of recorded thoughts penned by writers around the world and from different time periods. A library in the Universal Language of Mind symbolizes the limitless information available to the dreamer. |

| *Derivative Meaning* | *Thoughts to Consider* |
|---|---|
| *Dict. A rule of action or conduct laid down or prescribed by authority; the whole body of rules regulating and controlling the individuals of a state or community. Rights established by law; justice; one of the principles by which any matter or proceeding is regulated.* | Become acquainted with the workings of Universal Law in your life. Universal Laws are described in all the Holy Scriptures of the world. For instance the Universal Law of Relativity is described in the Bible by "do unto others as you would have them do unto you", in the Koran by "no one of you is a believer until he desires for his brother that which he desires for himself", in Buddhist teachings as "hurt not others in ways that you yourself would find hurtful." When law appears as part of your dream it will be indicating one or more of these principles which govern creation. |
| *Dict. A glade in a forest; a space of ground covered with grass.* | What ideas am I cultivating? The thoughts you create consciously are re-created in the substance of your subconscious mind. Give attention and care to the quality of your thoughts. Make them ideas that you will embrace and will joyfully look forward to living. |
| *Dict. Denoting the part opposed to the right of the body. A. Sax. left meaning "worthless"; O. Sax. lef meaning "weak" or "infirm".* | Am I drawing upon past experiences as a springboard for imaging a new, more productive future? Or are you enslaved by past memories, repeating the same old patterns of thought and action? Only you can determine how you are using the past. Respect memory for what it is, an integral element of the power in your conscious mind for reasoning. |
| *Dict. A written or printed message.* | How aware am I of inner communication? Do I value Self awareness as much as I value awareness of my external relations with others? Self awareness is strengthened by acknowledging the many parts of Self and establishing firm lines of communication. This can be heightened by realizing the many conscious roles you use and the many understandings available for you to draw upon in your everyday life. |
| *Dict. A collection of books belonging to a private person or to a public institution.* | Realize the wealth of information available to you by learning to organize your thoughts about your experiences. Put the information to use, incorporating it into your life. Move beyond intellectual pursuits into the realm of applied knowledge that will change your life and influence the lives of others. |

| Symbol | Meaning in Universal Language of Mind |
|---|---|
| *License signifies the acknowledgement of proficiency and ability.* | In the language of mind, a license symbolizes an authoritative acknowledgement. It will indicate the dreamer's proficiency and ability in a particular area of endeavor. For instance a marriage license will signify the dreamer's skill in commitment to Self; a driver's license will signify the dreamer's skill in operating the physical body. |
| *Light symbolizes awareness.* | Light is the means by which we can see and therefore identify the physical world. In the Universal Language of Mind light symbolizes awareness which is the means by which we can perceive and therefore identify the inner worlds and creation. Awareness is the beginning of all creation. |
| *Liquor indicates a potential loss of will power.* | Liquor is a chemical, like any other drug, which alters the balance of natural substances required for efficient functioning of the body. These chemicals enter the body and affect all systems including the brain. For man to utilize his full capacity the physical body must be whole and healthy. When the natural balances are artificially disrupted by foreign chemicals they interfere with the electrochemical impulses which stimulate brain activity thus impairing the mind's capacity for reasoning. The effects of liquor are apparent in diminished will power which is why the imbiber will think, act and react in ways that are foreign to him in a sober state. When liquor appears in a dream it will symbolize the dreamer's potential loss of will power. |
| *Lock represents a means for security.* | A lock joins or restrains providing security. When a lock appears in a dream it indicates a means for inner security. When mental abilities are united the individual is free from apprehension. For instance when memory, will, and imagination are joined the past, present, and probable future are known. Where there is knowing there is no fear; there is security. |

| *Derivative Meaning* | *Thoughts to Consider* |
|---|---|
| *Dict. Authority given to act in a particular way; power conferred upon a person by proper authority, to do particular acts, practice in professions, conduct certain trades. Latin* licet *meaning "it is permitted".* | After interpreting the particular meaning of your *dream-license*, realize this symbol is informing you of skills you possess. Endeavor to build upon this skill, drawing upon your proficiency for increased autonomy and Self control. |
| *Dict. That agent or force by the action of which upon the organs of sight objects from which it proceeds are rendered visible. Mental or spiritual illumination.* | What new awarenesses have you experienced recently? How have these awarenesses changed the way you see your Self and others? Many times awareness will appear in the form of a new idea which prompts fresh perspectives. Sometimes they are the result of unexpected experiences or new people entering your life. Be attentive to what promotes new awarenesses in your Self and pursue them intentionally thus adding to your awareness daily. |
| *Dict. An intoxicating liquid beverage.* | How am I demonstrating a lack of will power? Am I being indecisive, allowing situations and conditions to determine the course of my life? Do I make judgments based upon what I don't want instead of what I do desire? Build your will power by listing each morning ten desires to accomplish during that day. Use this list to guide your thoughts and actions throughout your day. Rest only when you have fulfilled your desires. |
| *Dict. An appliance used for fastening doors, chests, drawers, etc. its main feature being a bolt moved with a key.* | What is the source of my security? Is it in external factors: friends, money, possessions, positions? Or do I derive security from inner confidence to create the life I desire? When the source of security comes from within, you are free from fear and your ability to respond to life is greatly enhanced. |

| Symbol | Meaning in Universal Language of Mind |
|--------|----------------------------------------|
| *Love Making symbolizes harmony between the inner and outer Self.* | Love making is a loving and progressive interaction between a male and female. In the language of mind love making symbolizes the cooperative effort between the inner and outer Self for creation. |

# M

| | |
|--------|----------------------------------------|
| *Machine represents the mechanics or sequence of events in the action of thinking.* | Machines are evidence of man's ability to be a creator. Designed to ease the amount of physical effort in accomplishing a feat, they expedite work and often offer uniformity in creation. In the Universal Language of Mind, machines represent a sequence of mental actions commonly referred to as thinking. For instance, reasoning is a type of thinking employed by the conscious mind. Reasoning is a result of a sequence of mental actions. First, the thinker accesses his present experience by receiving information through the senses and the brain. Second, the thinker identifies the nature and quality of the experience by using will to draw upon information previously stored in the brain as memory. Third, the thinker judges his present experience based upon his immediate response and memory of how he has responded before. Fourth, the thinker determines if and how this response is aligned with his ideals or desires. Fifth, the thinker employs imagination to mentally alter his future response thus setting into motion his creative faculties. This is the sequence of events in the action of reasoning. |
| *Magazines represent a body of information.* | Magazines are a means for disseminating timely information of interest to a particular type of person. News magazines attempt to inform a broad audience of readers of immediate world developments while "women's" or "men's" magazine cater to the difference in the sexes. In a dream magazines will symbolize a particular body of information immediately pertinent to specific aspects of Self. For instance a bride's magazine will signify information the dreamer is receiving concerning commitment to Self; an automobile magazine will signify information the dreamer is receiving concerning the physical body. |

| Derivative Meaning | Thoughts to Consider |
|---|---|
| *Dict. Courtship; to woo; expression of strong feeling of affection and devoted attachment especially to a person of the opposite sex.* | Identify and interpret the meaning of the people engaged in love making in your dream. This will give you indications of the parts of Self that are actively invested in the fulfillment of your desires. |
| *Dict. Any appliance which serves to increase or regulate the effect of a given force or to produce motion. From Greek* mecho *meaning "expedient".* | How much do you know about the nature of thinking? Begin investigating what is known about the mind and its relationship to the body and brain. Seek information and research that is rooted in experience rather than conjecture only. Look for suggestions that will aid you in exercising the power of your mind and strengthen your command of your abilities. |
| *Dict. A receptacle in which anything is stored; a publication issued in a series of numbers or parts containing papers of an instructive or entertaining character.* | What type of information have you recently gained in your life? Realize acquiring this information is the result of your own desires and efforts and is relative to your life right now. By interpreting your dream you now have insight into the greater purpose this information can serve. |

| Symbol | Meaning in Universal Language of Mind |
|--------|----------------------------------------|
| **Magic** *indicates the dreamer is unaware of cause.* | Whatever man does not understand he calls magic. Whether it is the illusion of making something disappear or the reason two people fall in love, magic is man's temporary answer to an experience that tests the boundaries of what is accepted and commonly known. To the uneducated, anything can seem magical from playing a piano to false teeth, from life in the universe to the nature of dreams. When the dreamer deems something in his dream as magical this will indicate his lack of awareness of cause. |
| **Maid** *is an aspect of Self.* | In the Universal Language of Mind a maid will represent an aspect of Self; a conscious aspect for a female dreamer, a subconscious aspect for a male dreamer. Service is assistance or kindness rendered to another reflecting attitudes of giving. *(See people)* |
| **Mail** *signifies a communication from one aspect of Self to another. (see letter)* | |
| **Main Floor** *represents the conscious part of the mind. (see house, building, floor)* | The dwelling place for the thinker is the mind. The mind is comprised of three major divisions: conscious, subconscious, and superconscious. A building in a dream symbolizes the dreamer's mind. The floors of the house denote these divisions, the main floor indicating the conscious mind. |
| **Males** *are aspects of Self.* | Throughout physical evolution the principles of aggressiveness and receptivity manifest through the male expression and the female expression, respectively. When these two principles are active creation can occur. The male signifies aggressive action. For a male dreamer, a male will represent a conscious aspect of Self; for a female dreamer, a male will represent a subconscious aspect of Self. This is owing to the manifestation of these principles in the conscious and subconscious mind of any individual which enables the thinker to create with thought. |

| *Derivative Meaning* | *Thoughts to Consider* |
|---|---|
| *Dict. The art of producing effect by superhuman means, as by spiritual beings or the occult powers of nature.* | Do you think some events occur in your life without or beyond your control? Do you believe in fate or do you think there are some things that are not meant to be understood? This dream is stimulating your conscious mind toward greater understanding of cause and effect in your life. Nothing ever happens by chance. Thought is cause and the physical is its manifest likeness. The other symbols in your dream will give you insight into what you are capable of understanding from the point of cause. |
| *Dict. A young unmarried woman; a virgin; a female servant.* | After identifying this aspect of Self, note its activity in the dream. This will give you insight into your attitudes toward service. Is your dream conveying a joyous attitude of giving or a reluctant attitude of being burdened? |
| *Dict. Main meaning principal, chief, or most important; floor meaning that part of a building or room on which we walk.* | When dream activity occurs in the main floor of a building the message will revolve around how you are using your conscious, waking mind. Be attentive to the people and their activities, interpreting the meaning. This will give you valuable information for more fully using your conscious mind in everyday experiences. |
| *Dict. Pertaining to the sex that begets young; masculine.* | Is the male someone you know or a stranger? If it is a known aspect, determine if it is productive by interpreting the meaning of his actions in the dream. If it is an unknown aspect, begin to identify this unfamiliar part of Self by noting your assessment of him in the dream. For instance, was the male polished and beneficent or surly and dictatorial? |

| Symbol | Meaning in Universal Language of Mind |
|--------|----------------------------------------|
| **Man** *represents all aspects of Self.* | From the Sanskrit, man refers to the thinker therefore representing all of humankind. In the Universal Language of Mind man will indicate all aspects of Self, for these aspects are the expression of the dreamer's capacity for thought. |
| **Manager** *represents superconscious mind.* | A manager is a person with authority. People of authority appearing in a dream represent the superconscious mind of the dreamer. This part of Self, symbolized by those who hold authority in the dreamer's waking life, demonstrates the power and right to command that is reflective of the dreamer's superconscious mind. |
| **Mansion** *represents the mind. (see house)* | A house in a dream symbolizes the dreamer's mind. A mansion, by virtue of its richness, will further indicate the value and respect the dreamer holds for his mind. |
| **Manual** *signifies purposeful use of structure for learning.* | Manuals are intended to offer step-by-step instructions for a particular accomplishment and to make that work easily understandable. In the Universal Language of Mind a manual will represent the dreamer's use of structure for his/her learning. For instance, if the *dream-manual* gives instruction in operating a computer program it will signify the dreamer's use of the brain (structure) for learning. If the dream-manual tells how to better manage people it will signify the dreamer's use of the mind (structure) toward leadership. |
| **Map** *indicates the identification of opportunities available.* | A map is a representation, a picture, of what exists. It can be a representation of a city, a solar system, or even a building. Whatever the map represents, it will offer a means for easy identification and access to what exists. In the language of mind, a map symbolizes the identification of opportunities available to the dreamer. |

| *Derivative Meaning* | *Thoughts to Consider* |
|---|---|
| *Dict. A human being; a person; mankind. Sanskrit* man *meaning "to think"; manas, meaning "mind".* | Note the activity in this dream for it will offer insight into your whole Self. Most dreams involve several aspects of the dreamer. This dream speaks to you as a whole Self and will offer significant guidance for expanding your consciousness and realizing your purpose for existence. |
| *Dict. One who has the guidance or direction of anything.* | What is my attitude in the dream toward this authority figure? Am I respectful and cooperative or disparaging and rebellious? The former will indicate a seeking for divine inner guidance that can be cultivated by daily meditation upon your Creator. The latter will indicate a rejection of inner authority characterized by attachment to the finite, physical world. |
| *Dict. A dwelling or residence, especially one of considerable size and pretension.* | A beautiful mansion symbolizes the value you place upon your mind and its capabilities. An abandoned shack indicates a lack of care and respect for your mind. |
| *Dict. Performed or done by the hand; a small book of instructions or orders. From Latin* manualis *meaning "pertaining to the hand".* | Determine the function and meaning of the type of manual that appears in your dream. This will reveal the type of learning that is important to you at this time in your life. Because the word manual stems from the Latin meaning pertaining to the hand, and is commonly used as a handbook, this symbol will be highlighting your purpose in learning. Reach beyond knowing why you are pursuing your chosen activities and identify how the pursuit will expand your consciousness. This will serve as an impetus toward the realization of higher purposes and ultimately knowledge of your reason for existence. |
| *Dict. A representation of the surface of the earth or of any part of it usually on paper.* | Am I aware of the opportunities open to me? How readily do I recognize them and respond? Once opportunities are acknowledged there must be a response to them for growth and learning to occur. You can have many job offers or marriage proposals but until you accept one, the opportunities will continue to pass you by. Learn how to evaluate opportunities and readily respond to them for your soul progression. |

| Symbol | Meaning in Universal Language of Mind |
|--------|----------------------------------------|
| **Mare** *represents compulsive thinking; when controlled by a person the horse will symbolize the dreamer's will.* *(see horse)* | |
| **Market** *represents the giving and receiving of what is assessed as having value.* | A market is a public place where goods and services are bought and sold. In the Universal Language of Mind a market symbolizes the giving and receiving of what is valuable. |
| **Marriage** *symbolizes a commitment between the conscious mind and the subconscious mind for the fulfillment of desires.* | Marriage is the union of a male and female. In the Universal Language of Mind, marriage symbolizes the commitment between the conscious and subconscious minds. In order for this commitment to occur there must be a conscious willingness for cooperation with the inner Self. This type of dream indicates the initiation of a new awareness for the dreamer. |
| **Mask** *indicates the dreamer is assuming an identity.* | Masks are used to cover the face thus obscuring the identity. In dreams the face represents the dreamer's identity or the person the dreamer sees Self as being. When the face is disguised this indicates an alteration of that identity. For instance the mask of another person symbolizes the dreamer assuming the identity of that aspect of Self; a mask of an animal will indicate a habitual identity. |
| **Massacre** *symbolizes change without reason.* | Killing in a dream signifies change. A massacre is indiscriminate killing symbolizing a lack of purpose for the change. It also indicates a failure to employ reasoning to create the change. Change for the sake of change is a poor replacement for intentional change initiated with foresight. |

| *Derivative Meaning* | *Thoughts to Consider* |
|---|---|
| *Dict. A public place in a city or town where goods are exposed for purchase or sale.* | Are you giving (selling) or receiving (buying)? Note your attitude toward your dream action for it will give you clues for which action is appropriate in your waking life. |
| *Dict. The legal union of a man and woman for life; the ceremony by which they are so united; a wedding.* | What kinds of thoughts have populated your thinking recently? These thoughts and subsequent actions are causing a unification of your inner and outer Self. Strengthen this new commitment by dedicating your thoughts and actions to learning and growth. |
| *Dict. A cover for the face, often intended to conceal identity; a disguise, pretense, or subterfuge.* | Stop the pretense and start being who you are. Instead of trying to be something you aren't, bring out the Real You. Be forthright and honest with your Self and others. Give your Self and others an opportunity to know who you are. |
| *Dict. The indiscriminate killing of human beings, especially without authority or necessity.* | Purposeless change arises from reactions to the choice of others. You get mad at your boss and declare "I quit" without any idea of what your next job will be. You discover your spouse is having an affair so you have an affair. This type of change is purposeless, promotes undesired problems in your life, and destoys opportunities. Before initiating a change THINK! What will this cause in my life? Is this the kind of change I want to live? |

| Symbol | Meaning in Universal Language of Mind |
|---|---|
| **Mathematics** *is the understanding of identity and relativity.* | Mathematics is the science of numbers. Numbers were invented to represent form. Forms represent universal principles. In dreams mathematics symbolize the understanding of identity and relativity, two of the universal principles of creation. |
| **Meditation** *symbolizes communion with the Creator.* | The common usage of meditation is contemplation. Beyond focusing the mind on any object is the ability to direct the mind toward knowing the Source of creation — the Creator. Meditation is specialized concentration devoted to knowing and communing with your Creator. This is what meditation represents in the Universal Language of Mind. |
| **Melody** *represents harmonious vibratory pattern.* | Beyond your favorite song that conjures memories, melodies are pleasing vibratory patterns. In a dream, melodies represent harmonious patterns of vibration that arise from the dreamer's attitudes. For instance melodies can indicate attitudes of joy, cooperation, love, and peace. |
| **Menu** *indicates the knowledge available.* | Food in a dream is knowledge. A menu is a listing of foods available to the diner. In the Universal Language of Mind a menu will symbolize knowledge available to the dreamer. If the menu is blank it will symbolize a lack of knowledge in the dreamer's life. If the menu repeats the same entry it will indicate the need to assimilate a particular idea presently available to the dreamer. |
| **Microscope** *represents a means to reveal what was previously not perceived.* | A microscope makes it possible to see what is invisible to the human eye without aid. It magnifies what is viewed. In the language of mind a microscope symbolizes a means to reveal what was previously not perceived. |
| **Midget** *signifies the dreamer is misusing the will.* | When the thyroid gland is underdeveloped or functioning at a diminished capacity it will affect the development of the physical body producing limited physical growth. For the thinker, limited mental growth arises from a weakened will. A midget in a dream will symbolize the dreamer's |

| *Derivative Meaning* | *Thoughts to Consider* |
|---|---|
| *Dict. The science that treats of the properties and relations of quantities. From Greek* mathesomai *meaning "to learn".* | Are you adding in your dream or subtracting? How is math used in your dream — to calculate the number of people as in a census or to calculate monetary change due from a purchase? How math is used will reveal how you understand what something is and how it relates to other parts of Self, hence your life. |
| *Dict. To dwell on anything in thought; to turn or revolve any subject in the mind.* | Relish your growing awareness of your true nature as spirit. Reach to understand the cause of creation by filling your mind with Truth that is universal. Seek this Truth at all times and all else will be opened to you. Continue to strengthen your relationship with your Maker through daily prayer and meditation. |
| *Dict. An agreeable succession of sounds; sound highly pleasing to the ear. From Greek* melodia *meaning "a tune, a choral ode".* | Examine your thinking patterns. Note those attitudes which serve as a magnet for goodwill and productivity. Strengthen these attitudes to raise your vibratory pattern attracting the people, places, and things that will assist you in fulfilling your desires. It requires less energy to think positively and with love than thinking negatively and with hate. |
| *Dict. A list of dishes to be served at dinner or supper.* | Use the knowledge available to you. Cease taking this knowledge for granted, acting as though it will always be there, and begin to choose knowledge that will enhance your learning and growth. Assimilate the knowledge you have to gain understanding and ultimately wisdom. |
| *Dict. An optical instrument consisting of a lens or combination of lenses for rendering minute objects distinctly visible.* | What have you recently become aware of that has existed all along but you just didn't see? Develop your perception by being willing to use your mental perception as well as your physical sight. Things are not always as they appear, so be willing to delve more deeply, study at length and in detail. |
| *Dict. A small creature; a dwarfed body produced by malfunction of the thyroid gland.* | Am I procrastinating or avoiding making decisions in my life? Use your will productively by visualizing what you desire so your will has a positive image to act upon. Decisions can only be made toward a positive image. Choosing whether or |

| Symbol | Meaning in Universal Language of Mind |
|--------|---------------------------------------|

misuse of the will.

*Military symbolizes discipline.*

There are ideals worth fighting for in life. Anything worth accomplishing requires discipline to overcome inertia and the discord of laziness. Until the thinker establishes Self discipline he/she will experience inner conflict arising from fear and doubt. This is the inner war waged until the thinker takes command of all aspects of Self, directing Self toward a singular ideal and purpose of Enlightenment.

*Mine represents the activity of thought occurring in the subconscious mind.*

Earth is subconscious existence. The action of mining represents the activity occurring in subconscious mind which re-produces the desires of the dreamer. Every imaged thought created in the conscious mind is re-produced and developed in the inner workings of the subconscious mind until the thought is matured enough for manifestation.

*Minister represents the superconscious mind.*

A minister or clergyman of any religious faith is viewed as a spiritual parent and as such will represent the superconscious mind of the dreamer. In the Universal Language of Mind, father represents this innermost part of mind, the dreamer's inner authority and divinity. The purpose of the superconscious mind is to hold the seed idea for the thinker's maturity as a creator. The superconscious mind is the part of mind that is closest to the source, the Creator. Its duty is to supply the spark of life to the outer parts of mind, thus a minister is one who serves on behalf of the Creator's authority.

*Mirror represents a means for objective viewing.*

Mirrors reflect what exists. In the language of mind a mirror will represent a means to view something objective. If the dreamer is looking at the Self in a mirror it will signify the dreamer's willingness to see the Self objectively, free from prejudice.

| *Derivative Meaning* | *Thoughts to Consider* |
|---|---|
| | not to take an action is not a decision. Choosing which action to make is a decision and employs the will productively. |
| *Dict. Pertaining to soldiers or the profession of a soldier; pertaining to a war. From Latin* milito *meaning "to fight".* | Do I lead a disciplined life? How do I understand discipline — is it something I am forced to do to get what I want or is it a refined ability to create what I desire? Discipline is the acquired awareness and personal implementation of the Laws of creation. |
| *Dict. A pit or excavation in the earth from which coal, metallic substances, or other mineral substances are taken by digging.* | What desires have I been actively pursuing that I have begun to recognize as manifesting in my life? Cooperate with the inner workings of your subconscious mind by continuing to direct your conscious thinking toward your desires, never deviating from your ideal. Be steadfast in your belief that you will have what you desire. This will lead to the knowing you crave when you receive the manifest likeness of your image. |
| *Dict. One who acts under the authority of another; a servant; one authorized to conduct Christian worship.* | What is my relationship with my own superconscious mind? Am I aware of my own divinity, an inner sense of divinity, an inner urge toward spiritual progression? Your attitude toward and the activity of the minister who appears in your dream will reveal the relationship with your own superconscious mind. |
| *Dict. A looking glass; any polished substance that forms images by the reflection of rays of light. Latin* miror *"to admire", French* miroir *"to look at".* | What new awarenesses about your Self have come to light recently? Build upon these by strengthening your ability to be objective about your Self. Be willing to admit what is productive, beautiful, attractive about your Self so you can add to these qualities. Be willing to admit what is destructive, ugly, repulsive so you can transform these limiting ideas of Self. |

| Symbol | Meaning in Universal Language of Mind |
|---|---|
| *Miscarriage indicates the abandonment of a manifesting desire.* | A miscarriage is usually the result of an imperfect seed whether the expelling of an imperfect fetus from the womb or the abandonment of an ideal such as a miscarriage of justice. In the Universal Language of Mind it will symbolize the abandonment of a manifesting desire. *(see pregnancy)* |
| *Mistake signifies a misconception or erroneous judgment.* | A mistake in the language of mind symbolizes a misconception or erroneous judgment. Mistakes become less frequent as the thinker utilizes the power in his conscious mind: reasoning. By drawing upon the memory of what was productive in the past, activating the imagination to create greater productivity, and employing the will to set the mind into action, the thinker will be certain of his conceptions and his judgment will be sound. |
| *Money represents exchange of value.* | Money in a dream symbolizes the value assessed by the dreamer. How the money is being used in the dream will indicate what is being valued. For instance, if money is being used to buy a house this will symbolize the value the dreamer places upon his own mind; if it is being invested for future use it will indicate the wealth derived from experiences which is permanent understanding. |
| *Monster symbolizes an unknown aspect of Self.* | Monsters are unfamiliar life forms, usually a grotesque and frightening animal-type creature that does not physically exist. In a dream these unidentified aspects of Self will appear in a form unfamiliar to the conscious mind and be described by the conscious, waking mind as a monster *(see God, devil)*. If animal-like, a monster signifies a compulsive aspect of Self foreign to the image of Self held by the dreamer but a product of the dreamer's imagined fears. |
| *Moon symbolizes awareness in the subconscious* | The earth's moon orbits the planet, reflecting the light from the sun. By itself it is not luminous and there is significant evidence to support the theory that the moon's origin is the earth itself. In the language of mind the moon rep- |

| *Derivative Meaning* | *Thoughts to Consider* |
|---|---|
| *Dict. Unfortunate issue or result of an undertaking; failure; abortion.* | Have I recently given up something I wanted? Sacrificing leads to resentment in life, for the desire remains unfulfilled. Giving up is not compromise or cooperation. Compromise is the result of weighing your desires with another's and determining how both can be fulfilled. Always pursue what is most important to you. Complete what you begin, being willing to grow in wisdom through the actions that lead to accomplishment. |
| *Dict. To take in error; to select wrongly.* | Am I repeating the same situation over and over again? Am I experiencing similar unwanted circumstances in my life, thus feeling like a victim? Break the pattern of self-imposed limitation by calling upon your reasoning power. You need never be a slave to your past. Reach for the freedom that is rightfully yours by responding to life with intelligence and vision. |
| *Dict. Coin, gold, silver or other metal stamped by public authority and used as the medium of exchange; in a wider sense any equivalent for commodities and for which individuals readily exchange their goods and services.* | Value in a dream can relate to your own sense of Self worth or to the worth you are willing to give and receive. The action in your dream will indicate which is appropriate. |
| *Dict. A plant or animal of abnormal structure or greatly different from the usual type; a person looked upon with horror on account of extraordinary crimes, deformity, or power to do harm. Latin monstrum meaning "a marvel".* | Have I been allowing fears to rule my thinking? Fear arises when the imagination is allowed to scatter due to an undisciplined will. Although you may attach specific people and situations to your fear, the only fear that ever exists is fear of the unknown. As President Franklin D. Roosevelt said the only fear we ever have is fear, itself. Conquer your fear by admitting what you do not know. This will free you to learn, and where there is learning there is the potential for knowing. Where knowing resides, fear cannot live. |
| *Dict. The heavenly orb which revolves round the earth. Sanskrit mas from root ma "to* | What talents do you possess that no one taught you this lifetime? These talents are one indication of the past understood experiences housed in your soul or subconscious mind. Look for these |

| Symbol | Meaning in Universal Language of Mind |
|---|---|
| *mind.* | resents the awareness in the subconscious mind. The subconscious mind reflects the inner light of the superconscious mind, and it is made of mind substance. Awareness in the subconscious mind is the result of understood experiences whether in the present lifetime or in past lifetimes. |
| *Mortuary symbolizes an attitude of holding onto what is past or has been changed.* | Death in dream symbolizes change. To dream of mortuaries or dead bodies indicates the dreamer's attachment to what is past, what has been changed. |
| *Mother is the superconscious mind.* | A mother is a female who has given birth to offspring. In the Universal Language of Mind, mother represents the superconscious mind, the dreamer's inner authority and divinity. The purpose of the superconscious mind is to hold the seed idea for the thinker's maturity as a creator. The superconscious mind is the part of mind that is closest to the source, the Creator. Its duty is to supply the spark of life to the outer parts of mind, thus a mother "brings forth". |
| *Mountain represents a challenge or obstacle in the dreamer's life.* | Mountains in the Universal Language of Mind represent challenges or obstacles. Which one will depend upon the dreamer's own attitude. If the dreamer is using his/her mind and abilities to move forward in life the mountain will signify a challenge to be met and understood. If the dreamer is unaware and unenlightened concerning his own thinking capacities the mountain will indicate an obstacle to overcome. |
| *Movie or Motion Picture symbolizes imagination.* | In the Universal Language of Mind movies represent the dreamer's imagination. The capacity for imaging is unique to mankind. This conscious faculty separates him from all other life forms. Imagination is the power of creating with thought. |

| *Derivative Meaning* | *Thoughts to Consider* |
|---|---|
| *measure"*. | abilities and cultivate conscious use of them. They will enhance your ability to draw upon the awareness in your subconscious mind. |
| *Dict. A place for the temporary reception of the dead. Latin* mortuus *meaning "dead".* | What change has recently occurred in your life that you wish had not transpired? Realize the nature of the physical is change. Everyone and everything is in constant motion. Endeavor to look forward rather than holding onto a past which no longer exists. By envisioning a future you find desirable you will more easily relinquish your attachment to what was comfortable and familiar in the past. Learn to love free of attachment by expanding your circle of loved ones. |
| *Dict. A female parent, especially of the human race; that which has produced anything; source of anything. Sanskrit* mata *Persian* mader *"to bring forth, the term".* | What is my relationship with my own superconscious mind? Am I aware of my own divinity, an inner sense of divinity, an inner urge toward spiritual progression? Your attitude toward and the activity of the mother who appears in your dream will reveal the relationship with your own superconscious mind. |
| *Dict. A huge mass of earth and rock rising above the common level of the earth or adjacent land; something very large or great.* | Which kind of mountain are you facing? Turn any mountain into a molehill by drawing upon your reasoning skills. Remember when the mountain wouldn't come to Mohammed, Mohammed went to the mountain. Be willing to meet the challenges in your life with courage, dignity, and confidence. |
| *Dict. A form of drama produced by means of a series of photographs projected upon a screen to give an illusion of continuous, lifelike motion.* | Am I using my imagination to create what I desire in life? Develop your imaging capacity by assessing the facts in your life and asking your Self "what if...". This is an excellent way to strengthen imagination. Read descriptive classical literature, imaging the characters and scenes. Train your Self to think in pictures rather than in words. |

| Symbol | Meaning in Universal Language of Mind |
|--------|----------------------------------------|
| **Mud**<br>*signifies the merging of conscious life experiences and subconscious life experiences.* | Mud is the result of water mixing with earth. In a dream water signifies conscious life experiences and earth represents subconscious mind substance. Mud in a dream symbolizes the blending of these two and often indicates the dreamer's failure to separate the two existences. When the thinker fails to acknowledge the integrity of these two divisions of mind s/he will experience disorientation and confusion. An example of this is no longer being able to distinguish what has actually occurred in the physical life from what has occurred in a subconscious dream state. |
| **Murder**<br>*is change with disregard to effects of intention.* | Death in a dream represents change. The aware thinker recognizes physical life as temporary existence for the soul; one of many brief sojourns offering opportunity to further progression. When killing is part of the *dream-action*, it will indicate a change occurring in the dreamer and his/her life. When the dreamer is performing the *dream-killing* this symbolizes a premeditated, intentional change. The type of change will be signified by who or what is killed in the dream. For instance, if the dreamer is killing a tiger this will represent a change in a habit. |
| **Museum**<br>*is a condition of mind where valued and longstanding ideas are held.* | Museums in a dream represent a longstanding frame of mind valued by the dreamer. The type of museum will indicate the particular ideas that contribute to the dreamer's mental affluence. For instance an art museum will indicate creativity used by the dreamer over a long period of time; a historical museum will signify the value derived from lifetimes of experience. |
| **Music**<br>*represents harmony.* | Music in a dream indicates harmony, the ability to connect and combine for accord and peace. Dreams where music is a significant part of the action will indicate the dreamer's |

| *Derivative Meaning* | *Thoughts to Consider* |
|---|---|
| *Dict. Wet and soft earth or earthy matter as in a puddle; mire. Icelandic* mod *meaning "dust".* | Look for ways to maintain awareness of the separation of conscious experiences and subconscious experiences. Attention will be your key. By fully directing your attention in the present moment you will find it easier to gain the most from your experiences. Realize there are no short-cuts to Self awareness. Mind altering drugs, hypnosis, or sleep may throw your consciousness into the inner levels of mind but you will lack the control of your experiences there. By creating specific constructs, such as concentration practices, you will refine your mind's powers — with purpose and on purpose. |
| *Dict. The act of unlawfully killing a human being with premeditated malice. Sanskrit* mri *meaning "to die".* | Note who is killing what in your dream. If someone you recognize is killing an unknown person in the dream, you can identify the change being experienced by 1] interpreting the familiar aspect, 2] realizing this aspect is causing greater awareness of another part of your Self that you were previously unaware of. Although these types of dreams can be shocking to your conscious mind, remember in the Language of Mind killing and death indicates change and change is the nature of the physical existence. |
| *Dict. A building or apartment appropriated as a repository of interesting objects connected with literature, art, or science. Greek* mouseion, *originally a temple of the Muses. The Muse was one of the daughters of Zeus and Mnemosyne, who presided over the different kinds of poetry, and the sciences and arts, nine in number.* | After interpreting this symbol in context of your dream, realize it is very easy for you at this time to assess your worth. Consciously review the ideas addressed in your dream, evaluating your progress over time and seeing how these ideas have matured and now affect your consciousness. |
| *Dict. A succession of sounds so modulated as to please the ear; melody* | What connections are you making in your thinking? How are you combining different elements of your Self or your life into a workable and uni- |

| Symbol | Meaning in Universal Language of Mind |
|---|---|

ability to adapt individual parts to each other thereby creating agreement.

*Musical Instruments are the means by which harmony is produced within Self.*

As music in a dream is harmony, instruments are the means by which this harmony is produced. One example of such an instrument is imagination. Imagination enables the thinker to combine different and separate ideas or objects into a new and unified creation. Imagination is what stimulates the artist to mix pigments creating a new hue or the inventor to combine material, wood, and steel to form an umbrella.

*Mute symbolizes a barrier in the expression of thoughts.*

When one is mute he lacks the power of speech. In the language of mind this indicates an inability to express the thoughts accurately and fluently. Most communication difficulties arise from careless words spoken habitually and carrying little if any meaning. The mastery of communication requires precision in thought and description. The ability to think deeply and completely, then convey those thoughts through the use of language and action is a skill that can be developed. It is also the mastery of Truth.

# N

*Naked symbolizes openness and honesty.*

Being naked in a dream symbolizes an attitude of openness and honesty. Honesty is the result of the alignment of the thinker's thoughts and words or actions. When someone appears nude in a dream this will represent an aspect of Self that is being expressed openly; the ideas manifest in their true form without alteration or limitation.

*Name is identification.*

In the Universal Language of Mind a name signifies the sameness of a person, place or thing giving the thinker a means to establish the identity. For instance, personal identity, symbolized by the individual's name, denotes the same

| *Derivative Meaning* | *Thoughts to Consider* |
|---|---|
| or harmony. *Greek* mousike *meaning "music, art, culture". Muse.* | fied whole? Realize this kind of mental accord is a cornerstone for the peace of mind you desire. |
| *Dict. That by which a work is performed or anything is effected; a tool, utensil, implement for producing melody.* | Note the quality of your recent thinking. Has it been imaginative, directed, intuitive, reminiscent, visionary? Whatever the quality, this will be the means by which you have caused cooperation and unity in Self. By acknowledging the quality you know how to ensure your continued peace of mind. If your *dream-instrument* is broken you need to add this productive quality to your thinking. |
| *Dict. Silent; incapable of utterance, not having the power of speech. Latin* mutus *meaning "silent" or "dumb".* | Practice meaning what you say and saying what you mean. Stop tailoring your words to suit your audience. Think before you speak or act. Let intelligence guide your tongue rather than habit. |
| *Dict. Bare; not having clothes on.* | After determining the aspect of Self that is being open and honest, note your reaction to the *dream-nakedness.* Many people are embarrassed by nakedness in a dream because this is how they would react if the nudity occurred in their everyday waking life. Remember the people and events in your dream are symbolically revealing your state of consciousness. Although relevant to your waking consciousness, they are distinctly separate from the people and events in your everyday life. |
| *Dict. That by which a person or thing is called or designated, in distinction from other* | Note why a name is outstanding in your dream. Combine the symbolism of the *dream-factors* involved in the name to understand what you are currently learning to identify in your Self. When |

| Symbol | Meaning in Universal Language of Mind |
|--------|----------------------------------------|
| | person from birth to death while the body, disposition, habits, thoughts are continually changing. |

| | |
|--------|----------------------------------------|
| *Narrow symbolizes limits.* | When narrowness is highlighted in the dream it will indicate the limits existing for the dreamer relevant to the symbolic meaning of what is narrow. For instance, a narrow road will represent the limits existing in the dreamer's path or direction in life. Limits can be real or imagined. The goals a thinker creates are limits, so are prejudices formed from reactions to previous experiences. |
| *Nation represents all aspects of Self.* | A nation is a means of uniting, by physical birth, a wide variety of people for a common ideal that enables them to live together productively and in harmony. In the Universal Language of Mind, nation represents all aspects of Self that have developed from a common spiritual origin, that have a common ideal of spiritual maturity, and that have a common language — the Universal Language of Mind. In a dream a nation will be indicative of the dreamer's awareness of this inner unity and the inner urge for spiritual progression. |
| *Nature signifies creation.* | Nature is the creation, especially that part of it by which man is more immediately surrounded. In current society, most people live in artificial, manmade environments. This can promote appreciation for man's creative ability while simultaneously separating him from manifestations of creation from the Creative Source. Nature in the language of mind symbolizes creation from the Creative Source and is reflective of the inner realms of man's existence. |
| *Neat indicates order and brevity.* | Neatness in a dream indicates order, as in a neat or tidy room, and brevity, as in neat diction. It is worthy of noting that the origin of the word *neat* comes from the Latin *nitidus* meaning "shining" and this is the meaning of neatness in the language of mind: that which is radiant and full of awareness. |

| *Derivative Meaning* | *Thoughts to Consider* |
|---|---|
| *persons or things; reputation; character, renown.* Sanskrit naman *meaning "name" from same root as* know. | a name is predominant it will indicate a way you are moving beyond believing to knowing and in this way utilizing one of the Universal Laws of creation. |
| *Dict. Of little breadth; having little distance from side to side; of little extent.* | Do the limits you accept in your life serve a valuable purpose? Realize all limits are self-imposed. If the limits are restrictive, holding you back from being the best you can be, free your Self by imaging more than you have before. Use goals to stretch beyond previously accepted limitations, continually expanding your awareness, your circle of associates, your endeavors and accomplishments. |
| *Dict. A people inhabiting a certain extent of territory, and united by common political institutions; an aggregation of persons speaking the same or a cognate language.* Latin natio *from* natus *meaning "born".* | To build upon the information in this dream, continue to study, learn, and apply the Universal Language of Mind for it is a cornerstone for your spiritual progress enabling you to unite with full awareness the varied aspects of Self. Strengthen your awareness of your spiritual origin through daily communion with your Creator through prayer and meditation. Live the highest ideals you are capable of conceiving. |
| *Dict. The universe; the system of things of which ourselves are a part; the world of matter or of matter and mind. From* Sanskrit jan *meaning "to produce".* | Become sensitive to the workings of creation as it manifests in the air you breathe, the plants you eat, the animals you care for, the people in your life. Realize the cause for what exists within and around you is thought, therefore think positively and with love. Give at least as much attention to the cause of life as you do to the effects. Expand your awareness of the Creative Source through daily communion with your Maker. |
| *Dict. Having everything in perfect order; tidy; expressed in few and well-chosen words. From Latin* nitidus *meaning "shining".* | Whatever is neat in your dream indicates a point of awareness in your consciousness. Here is potential for understanding and soul progression. Build upon this awareness by imaging ways to turn awareness into understanding. For instance, you may be aware of your ability to influence others through the power of speech. By using this ability and honing it into a skill that will aid others to abundance, you will understand how to use it wisely. You will also know how to teach it to oth- |

| *Symbol* | *Meaning in Universal Language of Mind* |
|---|---|

*Neglect
signifies
inattention.*

When neglect appears in a dream it will signify the dreamer's inattentiveness thereby highlighting an aspect, an attitude, or an area of thought and endeavor that requires investigation. Attention is the only sense of the mind. The body has five senses — seeing, hearing, tasting, smelling, and touching. These are utilized by the mind to gather experience. The attention of the mind must be directed in order to fully receive sensory impressions. Neglect symbolizes a breakdown in this process.

*Negotiate
represents inner
cooperation
assessing value.*

In everyday life, negotiation is a means to reach mutual accord. In the language of mind, negotiation signifies inner cooperation between aspects of Self that brings new insight into the value or worth of the Self. When the *dream-negotiation* is transpiring between members of the opposite sex it will indicate cooperation between the conscious and subconscious minds. As mentioned before, these two parts of mind have an interdependent relationship based on the fulfillment of compatible needs that enables the thinker to create and manifest desires.

*News
symbolizes
timely and
readily available
information.*

News in a dream will symbolize information that is fresh and timely to the dreamer. It will reflect the dreamer's capacity to add new awarenesses by responding to what was previously not available to him.

*Night
indicates a lack
of awareness.*

In the Universal Language of Mind, night will represent a lack of awareness. This lack of awareness is characterized by obscurity, ignorance, or intellectual and spiritual darkness. Throughout all Holy Scriptures of the world, which are written in the language of mind, night will represent a lack of awareness.

*Nightmares
are repeated
messages from*

A nightmare will elicit an emotional reaction in the conscious mind causing you to retain the message or dream. Nightmares are repeated messages from the subconscious

| *Derivative Meaning* | *Thoughts to Consider* |
|---|---|
| | ers. A mark of understanding is the ability to teach another what has been made known. |
| *Dict. To treat with no regard or with too little; to slight; to leave undone. Latin* negligo *meaning "not to pick up".* | What am I ignoring in my life? Most often people ignore what they do not understand because it is unpleasant. Resolve to live your life by higher standards, embracing all of life for the opportunities for growth it affords. Move beyond your attachment to pleasure and pain by establishing ideals based upon the progression of your soul rather than temporal pleasures of the flesh. |
| *Dict. To treat with another respecting purchase and sale; to hold intercourse in bargaining or trade. Latin* negotior *from* negotium *meaning "want of leisure, business".* | How have I recently experienced a sense of inner accord? Note the specific aspects involved in your *dream-negotiation*, interpreting their meaning to you. Increase your sense of Self worth by consciously responding to this dream. Draw upon these aspects of your Self, purposefully integrating them into your everyday thinking. |
| *Dict. Recent intelligence regarding an event; fresh information of something that has lately taken place, or something before unknown.* | Review the recent events in your life to identify what is new to you. When noted, analyze how you became aware of this new information — your frame of mind, the circumstances that brought about the new awareness. Then determine how you can utilize this new information to improve the quality of your life now. |
| *Dict. That part of the natural day when the sun is beneath the horizon, or the time from sunset to sunrise. Sanskrit* nakti *meaning "night" from root* nak *meaning "to vanish or perish".* | This dream will highlight the area of your consciousness which is deficient in awareness; an area where you are limited and bound by effects. Interpret the other symbols in your dream to assist you in defining this area. Purposely pursue awareness in this area by making choices that will bring information and knowledge of the cause for your experiences. To accelerate this, learn how to control your thoughts beginning with concentration practices. |
| *Dict. A state of oppression or feeling of suffocation felt during* | The best way to stop nightmares is to recall, record, interpret, and respond to the message. When you have accomplished these four steps you |

| *Symbol* | *Meaning in Universal Language of Mind* |
|---|---|

*the subconscious mind that have gone unheeded.*

mind that have gone unheeded. The specific people and action of the dream will be interpreted according to each symbol's meaning. Once the message is received and understood, the nightmares cease because there is no longer a need for subsequent messages to relay the old message.

*Nuclear War is an unknown fear of change.*

Nuclear war has yet to occur in mankind's experience. Therefore whatever can occur in nuclear war is unknown, a product of the imagination only. It is known that nuclear energy utilized in warfare will cause destruction or death. Death in a dream is change. Therefore in the language of mind nuclear war indicates an unknown fear of change; widespread change affecting all aspects of Self.

*Nudity indicates honesty and openness. (see naked)*

*Numbers represent the universal structure of developing thought.*

Numbers most often appear in dreams as a means of highlighting the import of certain thoughts or ways of thinking. For instance, noting Interstate 10 in a dream will bring the dreamer's attention to the highway in the dream, stressing its importance in the message. In the Universal Language of Mind, numbers do signify the universal structure of developing thought. Each thought created in the conscious mind undergoes a development process dictated by Universal Principles and Laws. This process is the thought as it experiences a series of structural principles represented by specific forms that have been identified mathematically as geometric forms. These forms are arithmetically described as numbers. The following is a list of the first thirteen numbers and a single word description of the quality of the form that number describes: *1* individuality, *2* duality, *3* creation, *4* stability, *5* reasoning, *6* intuition, *7* creative imagery, *8* value, *9* manifestation, *10* power of unity, *11* power of opposites, *12* power of generation, *13* power of realization. For more information on the meaning of numbers refer to The Universal Language of Mind: The Book of Matthew by Dr. Daniel R. Condron.

| *Derivative Meaning* | *Thoughts to Consider* |
|---|---|
| *sleep, and accompanied by a feeling of intense anxiety, fear, or horror.* | need have no fear of a repeat of the nightmare. People who regularly remember their dreams rarely experience nightmares because they value this internal communication and strive to understand the meaning of the dream messages. |
| *Dict. A state of violent opposition or conquest pertaining to or having the character of a nucleus.* | Am I passively waiting for life to happen to me? Do I fear disaster, believing that something terrible is bound to happen to me or those I love? Take control of your Self! Harness your power for belief by imagining what you do want to happen in your life. Use this known, desired image to guide your will, thinking and acting in ways that will produce what you want in life. |
| *Dict. That which may be counted; an aggregate of units or a single unit considered as part of a series. From Greek* nemo *meaning "to distribute".* | Realize when you remember numbers in a dream the import is found in what the number describes. Further insight can be gained by utilizing the descriptive qualities of the form the number represents, but this will be secondary in importance. For numbers larger than thirteen, digit the number down to its lowest single denomination. For instance 34 will be 3 + 4 which is the number 7. |

| Symbol | Meaning in Universal Language of Mind |
|---|---|

*Ⓞ*

*Object*
*signifies what*
*captures the*
*attention of the*
*dreamer.*

An object in a dream will signify what is presently capturing the attention of the dreamer. By identifying what the object is — a ball, a hat, a book — the dreamer can further interpret the meaning of the object in the dream. If the object is unidentified it will indicate that the dreamer has no awareness of what is attracting and holding his attention.

*Observe*
*indicates*
*objective*
*perception.*

Being an observer in a dream indicates the dreamer's ability for objective perception. When the dreamer is not a part of the dream action s/he is watching the interaction, therefore removed from it. Positively this indicates the dreamer's capability to objectively view the aspects, attitudes, choices, and direction of the Self. Negatively this indicates the dreamer's self-imposed exile from who s/he is. The dreamer must determine which is true at the time the dream occurs.

*Occasion*
*represents an*
*opportunity.*

In the Universal Language of Mind an occasion represents an opportunity. Opportunities are available anywhere, at anytime, when the thinker is alert to their presence. Ultimately physical life is the opportunity for soul progression under the Law of Karma, sometimes called the law of opportunity. When an occasion is highlighted in a dream it often signifies a karmic opportunity presently available to the dreamer.

*Ocean*
*symbolizes*
*conscious life*
*experiences.*

Water in a dream symbolizes conscious life experiences. An ocean will represent the nature of the dreamer's attitude in everyday experiences. If the ocean waters are calm and clear this will signify a relaxed and enlightened attitude. If the ocean waters are turbulent and potentially dangerous it will indicate a restless and fearful attitude about life.

| *Derivative Meaning* | *Thoughts to Consider* |
|---|---|
| *Dict. That toward which the mind is directed in any of its states or activities; what is thought about, believed or seen. Latin* objectum *meaning "something thrown before" or "against".* | What has occupied my thoughts recently? Am I giving my attention with full awareness of what I am thinking and doing or am I unconscious of where my attention is, seemingly obsessed? Your attention is like an object. It can be moved by your will at any time and directed toward whatever you choose. Begin to use your attention in this manner and experience the benefits of the control it brings. |
| *Dict. To look on with attention; to regard attentively, to watch. Latin* observe *meaning "before, to keep or hold".* | If your dream observation is positively employed develop this into a skill of Self evaluation for the purpose of growthful change. If your dream observation is negatively employed drop the aloof pretense and begin to experience life more fully by investing your Self in activities that will bring fulfillment to your life. |
| *Dict. Time of an occurrence, incident, or event; favorable time, season, or circumstances. A cause acting on the will; a motive or reason.* | Recognize the meaning of experiences beyond what is physically obvious. There is always a point of cause for what is experienced in the physical and that point is thought. Examine the thoughts you hold — are they productive, loving, eager, progressive, prosperous? Learn to look for the treasure of understanding inherent in your experiences, whether pleasant or unpleasant. |
| *Dict: The vast body of water which covers more than three-fifths of the surface of the globe. Greek* okeanos, *"the ocean, the deity of the ocean".* | Note the condition of the ocean for it will indicate your general attitude toward life. Life is more readily embraced by those who possess a calm mind and relaxed body. Make time daily to still your mind endeavoring to reach deeper and deeper states of mental and physical relaxation. Then image the quality and kind of life you desire to live. Using your will, direct your creative energies, both mental and physical, toward the fulfillment of this image. |

| *Symbol* | *Meaning in Universal Language of Mind* |
|---|---|
| *Office*<br>*indicates a*<br>*place in mind*<br>*where learning*<br>*and growth can*<br>*occur.* | An office is a place of employment or business. During the early years of physical life, the soul's learning manifests through educational avenues. As an adult, learning manifests through a career or chosen occupation which comprises the primary activity of life experiences. Therefore in the language of mind an office will indicate a place where learning and growth can occur. |
| *Oil*<br>*represents*<br>*energy.* | In the Universal Language of Mind, oil symbolizes energy. Energy is the manifestation of one of the three principles of mind known in Eastern philosophies as prana. Prana is the omnipresent power that vitalizes all of creation giving motion and vigor to all life forms. In a dream, oil will symbolize this energizing power. For instance, oil used for a car represents energy that is useful to the body; oil used in a lamp symbolizes energy used for awareness. |
| *Ointment*<br>*represents*<br>*potential*<br>*healing.* | Ointments are used to sooth diseased body parts and promote restoration. In the language of mind, an ointment symbolizes potential healing. Healing is the ability to create and sustain wholeness. The only limits man experiences in his ability to heal are those he is willing to accept. The mind working in conjunction with Universal Law has no limits in fulfilling the inner urge toward wholeness and completeness. When thoughts are productive for Self and others, healing can take place. |
| *Old*<br>*signifies*<br>*duration, a*<br>*long-standing*<br>*condition.* | There are four stages of man: infancy, adolescence, adulthood, and old age or wisdom. When someone in the dream is considered old, this will symbolize the dreamer's wisdom. Wisdom is gained through the application of understandings of creation. Characteristic of old age or wisdom is the ability and urge to impart to others what has been gained; to teach. In a dream, when an object is deemed old, such as an old building or old song, interpret the object's meaning in the language of mind to gain insight into the dream's message. |
| *Open*<br>*indicates free*<br>*accessibility.* | Open implies freedom without limitation or restriction. In the language of mind, open indicates free accessibility such as an open door symbolizing free accessibility to places in mind, or an open market symbolizing free accessibility in |

| Derivative Meaning | Thoughts to Consider |
|---|---|
| *Dict. Employment or business; duty or duties falling on or entrusted to a person. From Latin* officium *meaning "duty".* | Do I view life for the learning it brings or as a series of burdensome crises to be solved? Once interpreted, the dream action occurring in the office will reveal much about your attitude concerning life. Endeavor to embrace life from the soul's perspective becoming open to the opportunities for learning and progression. Set ideals for your Self, giving your Self something to anticipate with joy. |
| *Dict. A substance of animal and vegetable origin, liquid at ordinary temperatures, insoluble in water, and burning with a more or less luminous flame.* | Become more sensitive to the energy expended in thought and action. Every exertion of mental will requires energy just as physical exertion does. It requires less energy to think positively, directing the mind toward something that is desirable, than to think negatively, trying to avoid or escape something feared or unwanted. To utilize energy efficiently, use your creative mind to guide your thoughts and actions toward the fulfillment of your desires. |
| *Dict. Any soft unctuous substance used for smearing, particularly the body or a diseased part. From French* oindre *meaning "to anoint".* | How the ointment is used in your dream will indicate the area where healing needs to occur in your life. Become open to the power of faith as a stimulant toward healing. When the cause for dis-ease is understood, wholeness and health are experienced. Keep in mind the cause exists in the thoughts you create and maintain, therefore endeavor to make your thoughts those which will lead to an enhanced understanding of Self and life. |
| *Dict. Advanced far in years or life; long made or produced. Latin* alo *meaning "to nourish".* | Your wisdom is your gift to the world. Be willing to share it with others without hesitation, condition, or apology. All great thinkers throughout history have been remembered for their contributions to humanity. They employed their wisdom toward the benefit of all mankind. Strive to be like them. |
| *Dict. Not shut; unsealed; free to be used or enjoyed; not restricted.* | Being open enables you to embrace new people and situations in your life. It enables you to be open-minded thus increasing your capacity to learn rapidly. Most importantly, your ability for |

| Symbol | Meaning in Universal Language of Mind |
|--------|----------------------------------------|
| | giving and receiving what is valuable. What is open in the dream tells the dreamer where he is experiencing freedom in his/her life. |
| *Operate* *indicates cause that produces an effect.* | Operate is a verb describing an action that will produce a specific result, such as operating machinery or operating on the physical body. In the Universal Language of Mind operating symbolizes causing something to occur with the intention of producing an effect. In a dream, if the body is being operated on symbolically this indicates removing specific thoughts of dis-ease; operating a piece of machinery such as a computer indicates controlling the functions of the brain. |
| *Opponent* *symbolizes inner conflict and discord.* | An opponent is an adversary. In a dream, an opponent will be an aspect of Self that is working against the ideas, goals, and actions of the dreamer. The result is inner conflict, arguing with the Self. By identifying the aspect in the dream that is viewed as an opponent, the dreamer can understand the source of his inner turmoil and change it. |
| *Orchestra* *represents cooperation of many aspects.* | An orchestra is a combination of instruments played by many individuals and under the direction of a conductor who unifies their efforts. In the language of mind this symbolizes the harmonious cooperation of many aspects of Self. |
| *Orphan* *symbolizes an immature aspect of Self.* | An orphan is a child without his natal parents. In the language of mind this represents an immature aspect of Self, one that is new and undeveloped. It is significant that the orphan does not have a relationship with his natal parents indicating the aspect is unaware of its origin. A lack of confidence arising from an undetermined origin or a tendency toward willfulness to recognizing cause, could be an example of the meaning of an orphan in a dream. |

| *Derivative Meaning* | *Thoughts to Consider* |
|---|---|
| | openness initiates the working of Universal Law in your life. An open mind is a learning mind. |
| *Dict. To exert power or strength, physical or mechanical; to work, to have agency.* | This dream indicates where you are exhibiting control and direction in your life. The interpretation of the dream action will usually reveal what is being controlled, how it is being directed, and the aspects of Self being used for the control. Self control is a prerequisite to not only living a full and fruitful life but more importantly to gaining Self awareness and access to the inner levels of consciousness. |
| *Dict. Opposing; antagonistic; an adversary; one that supports the opposite side in controversy, disputation, or argument. Latin* opponens *meaning "to place against".* | Arguing with your Self produces stagnation in life. If allowed to continue, the stagnation will lead to dis-ease mentally, emotionally, and physically. If you are fighting your Self internally, you will fight the world around you. Do not wait for something outside your Self to cause accord. Assert your desires for happiness by recognizing and employing all aspects of Self toward a common goal of your choosing. |
| *Dict. The part of a theater appropriated to the musicians. Greek* orchestra *meaning "to dance".* | This dream indicates the fulfillment of your desire for harmony and cooperation. Note your recent thoughts and actions for they are the keys that have produced this state of mind. What connections are you making in your thinking? How are you combining different elements of your Self or your life into a workable and unified whole? Realize this kind of mental accord is a cornerstone for the peace of mind you desire. |
| *Dict. A child bereft of both parents.* | What aspect of Self is this dream addressing? You will find this is an aspect that is relatively new in your manner of expression and more importantly one that you do not remember initiating. Identifying this aspect will be a step toward remembering the reason you created this part of your Self. By recalling the origin of this aspect you can more fully direct its development and maturity as a valuable part of Self. |

| Symbol | Meaning in Universal Language of Mind |
|---|---|
| **Outdoors** *signifies the external environment.* | What is apart from the dreamer is symbolized in a dream by the outdoors. Owing to the workings of the Universal Law of Duality, the thinker experiences both internal and external environments. A dream outdoors will indicate the external environment. What occurs in the outdoors will reveal the dreamer's attitudes towards that outer environment. |
| **Outer Space** *represents the inner levels of consciousness.* | Limitlessness is characteristic of outer space and is symbolic of the inner worlds of Self found in the inner levels of consciousness. Including the physical level, there are seven levels of existence where the consciousness of the thinker resides. In the language of mind, outer space symbolizes these inner levels of consciousness. |
| **Owe** *indicates responsibility to give.* | To owe means an individual is indebted. In an expanded realm, each individual is indebted to his soul for existence and maturity as a creator. In the language of mind, owing symbolizes the responsibility to give. Consciously, each thinker is responsible for gaining experiences so understanding can be produced through the power of reasoning. These understood experiences are then given to the subconscious mind to become part of the permanent memory thus advancing soul progression. |
| **P** | |
| **Paint** *indicates the attitude used in imaging.* | As a verb, paint describes creative action. In the Universal Language of Mind, this indicates an attitude used in imaging. All thinkers can learn the sequence of events that causes thought to manifest, yet it is the individual's unique understandings comprising his/her attitude that will determine what, when, and where imagery is used. |
| **Paralyzed** *indicates passivity in thinking.* | Physically, paralysis is the inability to cause the body to move. In the language of mind paralysis signifies a lack of will characterized by passivity in thinking. Being paralyzed in a dream symbolizes the need to give attention to the desires of the inner Self and cause movement through creative thinking. |

| *Derivative Meaning* | *Thoughts to Consider* |
|---|---|
| *Dict. That which is toward the outside; abroad.* | Your attitude toward the people, places, and things in your life will determine your happiness, health, prosperity, and success in life. Don't try to fight the world. Rather appreciate the world for the wealth of opportunity it provides you. |
| *Dict. Degree of extension in all directions; any portion of extension; quantity of time.* | When this type of dream occurs it is time for you to investigate wholistic education for the mind. Acquaint your Self with meditation practices, astral projection, intuitive skills, mystical experience. Do more than read, seek a teacher wise in these areas who has attained a degree of mastery greater than your own. Learn from that teacher, and apply what you learn in your life. |
| *Dict. To possess or own; to be indebted in; to be bound to pay.* | Have I recently responded to opportunities in my life by giving or am I waiting for a chance to take what I want? The most reliable way to ensure the attainment of your desires is to give. Refine your ability to give by initiating the action of giving at least five times each day. Give freely, without placing any condition on the receiver. |
| *Dict. To lay color or colors on with a brush or otherwise; to color; to form a likeness or representation of in colors.* | Do I look forward to each day with hope and excitement? When you think positively and with love your attitude toward your Self, others, and experiences is transformed. You have the power to create the quality of your life through the choices you make. Ensure that your choices will bring to you what you desire, not what you fear. |
| *Dict. A diminution of the power of motion in some part of the body or a loss of sensation in any part. Greek* paralyo *meaning "to loosen".* | What is immobilizing you? Fear and doubt are the most common inhibitors of will. There are three kinds of people: those who make things happen, those who watch what happens, and those who wonder what happened. To overcome inertia, be the kind of person who makes things happen. |

| *Symbol* | *Meaning in Universal Language of Mind* |
|---|---|
| *Park* <br> *symbolizes* <br> *subconscious* <br> *existence.* | Similar to a forest in a dream, a park represents subconscious existence. Because parks are manmade spaces, in the language of mind they represent the recreative, subconscious part of mind. The subconscious mind will re-create only what the conscious mind has first created through imaged thought. |
| *Path* <br> *represents the* <br> *direction the* <br> *dreamer is* <br> *taking to* <br> *achieve a goal.* | In the Universal Language of Mind, a path represents the goals the dreamer has set and his progress toward their attainment. The kind of path will further signify the ease or difficulty the dreamer encounters in accomplishing his goals. For instance a steep path filled with debris will indicate obstacles in achieving goals; a clear path surrounded by nature's beauty will signify enjoyment and ease in attaining goals. |
| *People* <br> *represent* <br> *aspects of Self.* | People in dreams represent the many aspects of Self. An aspect is a particular way of thinking and expressing. An easy way to recognize aspects of Self is to acknowledge the roles the thinker plays in life — the devoted spouse, loving parents, reliable employee, the good friend. Shakespeare said, "All the world's a stage, and we are merely players." What becomes most important in interpreting the aspects of Self in a dream is noting the qualities the dreamer attributes to them. Aspects reflect characteristics of the dreamer — the comic, the shy one, the ambitious one, the generous one. Whatever quality the dreamer attaches to that person is the quality of Self being addressed in the dream message. |
| *Pets* <br> *symbolize* <br> *compulsive* <br> *ways of* <br> *thinking.* | Pets are animals cared for by people. As with all animals, in a dream they represent habits or compulsive ways of thinking, and in the case of pets they will indicate habits the dreamer is attached to. Habit is a mental construction of thinking which has been repeated over and over therefore easily accessed through memory. Since the pattern has imbedded itself in nerve pathways in the brain, habit can be drawn upon immediately without creative thought. The dreamer must determine if the habit is beneficial to his growth or a retardant to it. |

| *Derivative Meaning* | *Thoughts to Consider* |
|---|---|
| *Dict. A large piece of ground enclosed and set apart for beasts of chase; a piece of public ground in or near a large town, laid out and kept for the sole purpose of pleasure and recreation.* | How do I understand the relationship between my outer, conscious mind and my inner, subconscious mind? Do I realize and accept my own power of creative thought? One of the great joys in life is realizing your subconscious mind's readiness to assist you in the fulfillment of your desires. Cultivate an appreciation of the constant helper who resides within you. |
| *Dict. A way beaten or trodden by the feet of man or beast, or made hard by wheels; a narrow road. Greek patos meaning "a trodden way".* | What kind of path are you following? Goals are necessary in life as a way to use the physical for learning and as a stimulus for reasoning power. A goal can be a response to something previously accomplished, such as deciding to pursue a higher degree of education than you currently hold or deciding to start a family following a marriage. Goals are most effective when they add to the experience and understanding of the Self rather than merely repeating what has already been accomplished. |
| *Dict. The body of persons who compose a community, race, or nation; a community.* | To interpret the aspects in a dream, describe the outstanding qualities you see in the person. Describe their characteristics as if you were telling a stranger about them. This will be the quality of Self being addressed in your dream. Also remember, people of the same sex will be aspects of your conscious mind, people of the opposite sex will be aspects of your subconscious mind, and people in positions of authority will symbolize your conscious awareness of your superconscious mind. |
| *Dict. A fondling; an animal fondled and indulged. (see animals)* | Is this habit one I want to keep or change? Being Self aware means having full recognition of what and how you think. Therefore, the degree of compulsive thinking you allow will determine the degree of lack of awareness you are willing to abide. Keep in mind the spirit's urge toward constant, omniscient, and omnipresent awareness. |

| Symbol | Meaning in Universal Language of Mind |
|--------|----------------------------------------|
| **Phone** *is a means for communication. (see telephone)* | The telephone is the lazy man's telepathy for it enables communication to occur between two parties separated by physical distance. In the language of mind, a phone represents mind to mind communication. Mind to mind communication often occurs between a parent and child, between spouses, or between best friends. The same mental actions which produce telepathy in these instances can be identified, practiced, and honed into an intuitive skill that can be used at anytime with anyone. |
| **Photograph** *represents the manifestation of an imaged desire.* | A photograph is a physical reproduction of a likeness. The thinker has the power to image in his likeness through visualization. In the language of mind a photograph symbolizes the manifestation of imaged desires. When a photo appears in a dream it indicates the manifestation of the dreamer's desire. How the photos are used in the dream and what appears in the photo give more specific details aiding the dreamer to identify what the desire is that has recently manifested. |
| **Physician** *represents superconscious mind.* | In the Universal Language of Mind a physician represents the superconscious mind. The superconscious mind is the part of Self that holds the complete plan for spiritual development and maturity. It is the part of Self that knows the destiny of Self as a spiritual being, an offspring of the Creator. |
| **Piano** *is a means for producing harmony.* | As with all musical instruments, a piano in a dream represents a means for producing harmony. Becoming Self aware of positive traits frees thinker to utilize more of mind's potential. For instance, when an athlete recognizes his power of concentration is the basis for physical success in a sport endeavor, the mental skill of concentration can be transferred to relationships with others or another professional endeavor. |
| **Pictures** *are manifested thought forms.* | Similar to photographs, pictures in a dream symbolize what the dreamer's thoughts have created in his life. |

| *Derivative Meaning* | *Thoughts to Consider* |
|---|---|
| | Am I effectively communicating my ideas to others? Do my words accurately convey my thoughts so I can employ mental, intuitive communication as well as physical, conscious communication? Be aware that your thoughts affect those around you. Others may not be able to identify specifically what you are thinking, but most can vaguely sense the vibration you emanate as a "feeling" of love or the "smell" of greed or the "noise" of confusion. |
| *Dict. To produce a likeness or representation of by means of the action of light on substances treated with certain chemicals. Greek* photos *meaning "light" and* grapho *meaning "to describe".* | What have you recently acquired in your life that you fervently desired? This dream will give insight into a manifested desire, how it is presently affecting you and how you can now respond more fully to your own creative power. Use this manifestation as a springboard for bigger and better situations in your life. |
| *Dict. A person skilled in the art of healing; one whose profession is to describe remedies for diseases. Greek* physikos *meaning "pertaining to nature, natural". Sanskrit* bhu *meaning "to be".* | Since the activity of a physician is to diagnose the state of health, a physician in your dream will reflect your attitudes toward the wholeness present in your superconscious mind. Strive toward the highest ideals you can consciously imagine, without hesitation or restriction. Align your waking thoughts with superconscious awareness. |
| *Dict. A musical metal-stringed instrument with a keyboard, by means of which the metal strings are struck by hammers; soft.* | Which thoughts do I hold that bring a sense of contentment and peace? Identify these so you can build upon them. By learning the quality of thinking that produces harmony in your life you will be free to draw upon these thoughts during times of stress or conflict. |
| *Dict. A painting, drawing, or engraving exhibiting the resemblance of anything; a likeness. Latin* pictura *meaning "to paint".* | What is my opinion of the pictures in the dream? Do they arrest my attention because of their beauty and artistry or are they scenes which repel me? Are they pictures I have created or are they alien? Answering these questions will lend insight into how much control of your life you believe you possess. |

| Symbol | Meaning in Universal Language of Mind |
|---|---|
| *Pills represent dependency in the mental attitude.* | Pills are chemicals intended to interrupt, replace, or recognize, the chemical balance existing in the body. Prescribed medicine is usually meant to artificially provide the body with substances it is not for some reason producing on its own. All drugs affect the body as a whole, not just the area immediately needing relief, and these are called "side effects". In the language of mind, pills represent dependency upon someone or something outside of Self for a sense of well-being. |
| *Planes (small) signify the physical body. (see airplane)* | |
| *Planes (large) indicate an organization of people.* | Large vehicles are a means of conveyance for a group of people. In a dream, large airplanes will indicate an organization comprised of many people in the dreamer's life such as a company, a church, or a club. Such organizations afford many people to strive toward and reach a common destination. |
| *Planets indicate the mode or activity that can be used to bring about learning for soul progression.* | Space is the largest factor in our universe whether in the microcosm or macrocosm. Outer space is occupied by planets that emit a vibratory influence just as people, places, and things immediately surrounding the thinker do. Planetary influences are manifestations of the macrocosm, affecting humanity as a whole. In a dream, planets symbolize the mode or activity that can be used to bring about learning for soul progression. |
| *Plants (factories) symbolize a place for learning.* | Any place of productivity symbolizes a field of activity where potential learning can take place. In the early years of life educational systems symbolize this process. As an adult the place of employment symbolizes the activity where skills and talents can be used for personal enrichment and benefit of others. The entire lifetime is a series of opportunities for learning that will support soul progression. |

| *Derivative Meaning* | *Thoughts to Consider* |
|---|---|
| *Dict. A little ball or small round mass of medicinal substance to be swallowed whole.* | What am I dependent upon for a sense of security? This may be a person, such as a friend or spouse, a place, such as your hometown, or a thing, such as car or job or the clothes you wear. How the drugs are used in the dream will give indications of where your dependency lies. Strive to become Self reliant. This will enable you to give and receive in life rather than drain others by only taking from them. Independence is a sign of maturity. It frees you to cooperate with others. |
| *Dict. abbreviated form of airplane meaning any one of different kinds of flying machines.* | Determine which organization is being highlighted in your dream. The action of the plane in your dream will tell you how this organization is aiding or impairing the achievement of your goals in life. The people on the plane will give you insight into the aspects of Self invested in the accomplishment of these goals. |
| *Dict. A celestial body which revolves about the sun or other center, whence it receives light. (see astrology)* | Your soul's progression is dependent upon your conscious ability to gain understandings from the experiences at hand. As understandings are gained and used in your waking life they become a part of permanent memory. Permanent memory is easily recognized in the demonstration of what is considered a talent or ability that you exhibit which has not been learned in your present lifetime experience. Planets in a dream will indicate the understandings that are or can become a part of your permanent memory thus adding to your soul |
| *Dict. A collective term for the fixtures, machinery, tools, apparatus, etc. necessary to carry on any trade or mechanical business.* | What have I been learning in my life? This could be a physical skill such as using machinery or running a marathon, or it can indicate a mental skill such as communicating or parenting. Give more attention to that learning, extending its benefits into all areas of your life. |

| Symbol | Meaning in Universal Language of Mind |
|---|---|
| *Plants (vegetation)* represent subconscious knowledge. | Most plants are edible, providing a source of energy and sustenance to other life forms including man. In the language of mind, plants symbolize the knowledge available in the subconscious mind of the dreamer. The subconscious mind stores all past understood experiences therefore holds a wealth of knowledge for the comparatively novice conscious mind. |
| *Play* signifies the use of imagination. | The symbology of play is dependent upon the activity in the dream. A stage play signifies the dreamer's use of imagination, the ability to perceive what exists and mentally alter it based upon desire. If the *dream-play* describes recreation, it is indicative of daydreaming, a purposeless and frivolous use of imagination. If someone in the dream is playing an instrument this signifies actions producing harmony in the dreamer's life. |
| *Poison* symbolizes destructive mental attitudes. | In the language of mind, poison symbolizes that which destroys health — spiritually or physically. The quality of the thinker's thoughts will promote wholistic health, growth and productivity or will erode them through destructive negativity. That which is poison to the dreamer is that which undermines his reason to exist and works against Universal Law. |
| *Police* represent discipline. | In the language of mind, police represent aspects of the dreamer that are disciplined. Discipline is the command of thought and will that enables the thinker to prepare the Self to use Universal Laws wisely. |

| *Derivative Meaning* | *Thoughts to Consider* |
|---|---|
| *Dict. One of the organisms which form the vegetable kingdom; an organized living body deriving its sustenance from the organic world; generally adhering to another body and drawing from it some of its nourishment.* | How intuitive am I? Do I give credence to flashes of brilliance or unexpected insights I experience? Realize these abilities are a natural part of your inner, subconscious mind. Use your dream messages to establish a rapport with your subconscious mind and give you a means to draw upon its extensive knowledge. |
| *Dict. To act a part on the stage; to do something not as a task or for profit but for amusement. To act wantonly or thoughtlessly; to move irregularly; to dally or trifle. To perform on an instrument of music.* | Sharpen your imaginative skills. Every invention is the result of directed imagination. Every ideal you set is the result of directed imagination. To control your destiny, to live life completely, to become the person you desire to be, appreciate your imaginative ability and hone it into a skill. |
| *Dict. Any agent capable of producing a morbid, noxious, dangerous or deadly effect upon the animal economy, when introduced either by cutaneous absorption, respiration, or the digestive canal. That which taints or destroys moral purity or health.* | Note what is poisonous in your dream. For instance poisoned food will indicate knowledge that is destructive to you. A poisonous snake will indicate your aversion to using your own wisdom. Seek to direct your thoughts toward positive action to create the life you desire. |
| *Dict. The means instituted by a government or community to maintain public order, liberty, property, and individual security; the body of men by whom the municipal laws and regulations are enforced and public order maintained.* | Release any misunderstandings of discipline being hard, boring, or a means of punishment. Discipline is none of these. Discipline is the intelligent use of your freedom to think thereby producing greater enlightenment of your purpose for existing. A disciplined mind is a mind free to experience the innate, unlimited potential of the whole Self. |

| Symbol | Meaning in Universal Language of Mind |
|--------|----------------------------------------|
| *Pool represents conscious life experiences.* | Water in a dream symbolizes conscious life experiences therefore a pool of water will represent particular life experiences. The dream action will give more information about the experiences being addressed in the dream. For instance, note who or what is around or in the pool and what action is occurring interpreting those symbols for the dream's message. |
| *Post Office symbolizes what facilitates communication.* | In the Universal Language of Mind a post office signifies what facilitates communication. Since the post office operates under the auspices of the government, the "what" would indicate Universal Laws. Communication occurs as a result of individual efforts to fully utilize the mind's capabilities in cooperation with the laws of creation. Communication is possible because of the structure of creation and the structure of the mind. |
| *Pots & Pans are tools for preparing knowledge.* | Food in a dream represents knowledge. Pots and pans are utensils used to prepare food therefore in the language of mind they represent tools available to the dreamer for preparing knowledge. Examples of the mental tools the dream may indicate can include attentiveness, receptivity, recall, will, imagination. |
| *Poverty indicates the dreamer's attention dwells upon what is lacking.* | In the language of mind, poverty indicates lack or want. When poverty appears in a dream, it symbolizes the dreamer's attention dwells upon what is lacking. Low esteem, jealousy, worthlessness, greed, avarice are all examples of the frame of mind such a dreamer is experiencing. |
| *Praying indicates the aggressive communication toward unknown creation.* | Praying is an aggressive act whereby the suppliant makes his or her desires known to a Supreme Being. Prayer is a means of communication with a power greater than Self. In the language of mind prayer symbolizes the aggressive communication toward unknown creation — the desire to know more, to grow in wisdom. |

| *Derivative Meaning* | *Thoughts to Consider* |
|---|---|
| *Dict. A small collection of water or other liquid in a hollow place.* | By determining the elements of the dream you can more readily identify which experiences are being highlighted in this dream message. For instance, if someone is drowning in the pool it will indicate an aspect of self that is overwhelmed by the experiences in the life. If the pool is crystal clear and inviting it will indicate your positive attitude about life experiences. |
| *Dict. An office or house where letters or parcels are received for transmission to various parts and from which letters are delivered that have been received from places at home and abroad.* | Are you easily understood by others? Do your words convey your thoughts clearly and precisely or do you often speak without thinking? Make it your practice to think before speaking or acting. Know your own thoughts and intentions. This will aid you in communicating with others. When receiving communication from others, still your mind so you can receive their thoughts as well as their words. This will facilitate your communication. |
| *Dict. A hollow vessel more deep than broad, used for various domestic and other purposes.* | Note how you are preparing your Self to receive knowledge. One of the most important prerequisites to receiving knowledge is a desire to learn. Stimulate your own sense of curiosity. Become inquisitive about your Self, others, and life. Actively seek to learn thereby increasing the knowledge available for your use in everyday life. |
| *Dict. The state of being poor or indigent; a deficiency of necessary or desirable elements. Barrenness. Latin* paupertas *meaning "poor".* | Have you been pessimistic, perhaps thinking you are not as good as others or that you are unappreciated? Rise above these wasteful attitudes by admitting your own abundance. Situations in life are neutral, neither good or bad. You can think positively and with love, so endeavor to control your own mind by dwelling upon the beauty in life. Make a list of what you have to be thankful for. |
| *Dict. The act of asking for a favor with earnestness; to make petition to the Supreme Being.* | Endeavor to identify your own desires. Make them known in your conscious, waking mind. Strengthen your relationship with your God, whatever you conceive it to be, through daily meditation. |

| Symbol | Meaning in Universal Language of Mind |
|---|---|
| *Precognitive Dreams signify the subconscious mind's ability to perceive probable future events and occurrences.* | Physical experience is measured by the rising and setting of the sun. Subconscious experience does not have these linear limitations and is measured by understanding. The subconscious mind is free to perceive the past, present, and probable future at will. Precognitive dreams are conscious remembrances of subconscious perceptions of probable future events. It is important to note that these are only probabilities based upon current choices; should any of those choices change the outcome will be altered also. |
| *Pregnancy symbolizes the recreation of an imaged idea transpiring in the inner levels of the subconscious mind.* | Pregnancy is the result of a female egg and a male sperm uniting to reproduce the species. In the language of mind, it symbolizes the recreative ability of the conscious and subconscious minds to reproduce imaged thoughts. Pregnancy in a dream symbolizes the incubation period of an imaged idea that is developing in the inner levels of the subconscious mind. When the *dream-baby* is born the idea it represented during the *dream-pregnancy* will be a manifested reality in the dreamer's life. This is why it is possible for a male to be pregnant in a dream. |
| *Premarital Sex indicates creation for its own sake without benefit of a commitment between the conscious and subconscious minds. (See marriage, sex)* | Sexual intercourse between members of the opposite sex provides the potential for creation. In the language of mind the dreamer will signify the conscious mind and the person of the opposite sex will signify the subconscious mind. Sexual activity outside of marriage symbolizes potential creation without benefit of commitment between the conscious and subconscious minds. An example of this is expecting the subconscious mind to fulfill conscious desires with no conscious intention of gaining understanding from the manifested experiences. |
| *Price indicates worth or the value assessed.* | When price is significant in a dream it will indicate the value of that specific symbol to the dreamer. For example noting the price of a car in a dream represents the value of the physical body as a vehicle for experiences; the price of a college education signifies the value of higher learning to the dreamer. *Dream-prices* will highlight worth. |

| *Derivative Meaning* | *Thoughts to Consider* |
|---|---|
| *Dict. To foretell; to possess knowledge prior to the occurrence. Latin* prae *meaning "before" and* cognitio *meaning "knowledge".* | In time as you record and actively work with your dreams, you will find some dreams actually occur in the physical. Some will involve you directly, others will involve others. Seek to develop your use of this subconscious ability apart from the dream state. You can learn how to access the inner levels of subconsciousness with conscious awareness and control. You do not have to put the conscious mind aside in sleep for precognition to occur. Investigate study programs that teach the development of your whole Self. |
| *Dict. Being with young.* | What idea have you created that has yet to manifest in your life? This will be the idea symbolized in your dream by pregnancy. Nurture this idea, cooperating with its growth in the inner subconscious levels of mind, and preparing to receive it as the manifestation of a greatly wanted desire. |
| *Dict. Physical sexual contact between the sexes occurring before a legal or religious union for life has been tendered.* | How do you view commitment in your life? Are you dependable, reliable, loyal, true? Explore and develop these qualities in your Self, then extend your awareness beyond the physical. There is much more to you than the physical body and brain. You have existed before this lifetime and you will exist after this lifetime. Endeavor to know your Self beyond the physical so what you desire and create in your life can reflect a commitment between your conscious, waking Self and your subconscious, inner Self. |
| *Dict. The sum of money or the value which a seller sets on his goods in market. Latin* pretium *meaning "a price"; same words as* praise *and* prize *meaning "to value".* | Examine what has recently occurred in your life. Did these events make you feel worthy and valuable or worth-less. Realize you determine your sense of worth; the situations in your life are merely a stimulus for you to evaluate your Self. Valuable people undertake valuable activities. They are worthy of trust, loyalty, love, kindness, appreciation. Be such a person and fill your life with worthwhile activities that aid others. |

| Symbol | Meaning in Universal Language of Mind |
|---|---|
| **Priest** *represents the dreamer's awareness of superconscious mind.* | A priest or clergyman of any religious faith is viewed as a spiritual parent and as such represents the superconscious mind of the dreamer. In the Universal Language of Mind, father represents this innermost part of mind, the dreamer's inner authority and divinity. The purpose of the superconscious mind is to hold the seed idea for the thinker's maturity as a creator. The superconscious mind is the part of mind that is closest to the source, the Creator. Its duty is to supply the spark of life to the outer parts of mind, thus a priest is one who serves on behalf of the Creator's authority. |
| **Prince** *represents the superconscious mind.* | A prince is the male offspring of royalty or the sovereign of a nation. In the language of mind, a prince represents the superconscious mind of the thinker. The superconscious mind is the part of mind closest to the spiritual origin of Self. |
| **Princess** *represents the superconscious mind.* | A princess is the female offspring of royalty or the sovereign of a nation. In the language of mind, a princess represents the superconscious mind of the thinker. |
| **Principal** *represents the dreamer's awareness of superconscious mind.* | A principal oversees the education of a child, performing in the parent's stead. In a dream a principal represents the superconscious mind of the dreamer. The superconscious mind is the innermost part of mind, the dreamer's inner authority. The superconscious mind holds the seed idea for the thinker's maturity as a creator. |
| **Prize** *indicates acquiring of value.* | A prize in a dream indicates the manifestation of value to the dreamer as the result of his/her efforts. |
| **Pupil** *is an aspect of Self.* *(see student)* | |

| *Derivative Meaning* | *Thoughts to Consider* |
|---|---|
| *Dict. A clergyman of the Roman Catholic, Greek Catholic, Orthodox or Episcopalian church; a person consecrated to the ministry of the gospel.* | What is my relationship with my own superconscious mind? Am I aware of my own divinity, an inner sense of divinity, an inner urge toward spiritual progression? Your attitude toward and the activity of the minister who appears in your dream will reveal the relationship with your own superconscious mind. |
| *Dict. A male holding the first or highest rank; a sovereign who has the government of a particular territory, but owes certain services to a superior.* | What is your attitude toward the king in the dream? Are you honorably respectful or defiantly rebellious? This will give you insight into your own conscious attitudes toward your own superconscious mind, your inner authority. |
| *Dict. A female of the same rank as a prince; female sovereign.* | What is your attitude toward the princess in the dream? Are you honorably respectful or defiantly rebellious? This will give you insight into your own conscious attitudes toward your own superconscious mind, your inner authority. |
| *Dict. Chief; highest in rank, character, authority, or importance; first. One who takes a leading part; the chief executive of an educational institution.* | What is my relationship with my own superconscious mind? Am I aware of my spiritual purpose for existence? Am I pursuing the manifestation of that purpose in my life? Your attitude toward and the activity of the principal who appears in your dream will reveal the relationship you presently have with your own superconscious mind. |
| *Dict. That which is deemed a valuable acquisition; any gain or advantage; that which is obtained or offered as the reward of exertion or contest.* | Examine the recent events in your life. How have they aided you to realize a deeper sense of worth? How have they enriched your life? By identifying your experience completely, you can readily re-create similar experiences in the future. |

| Symbol | Meaning in Universal Language of Mind |
|--------|----------------------------------------|
| *Puppet* *represents a use of imagination.* | In the language of mind a puppet represents a use of the imagination. The imagination is employed by the will to bring about what is desired. When the will is missing, pretense is the result. |
| *Purse* *symbolizes the storage of value.* | A purse in a dream symbolizes the retaining of value or what is highly prized by the dreamer. A stolen purse signifies a loss of value, buying a new purse indicates reassessing value. |
| *Puzzle* *indicates need to identify cause.* | A puzzle promotes thinking, answering questions. Whether a jigsaw or crossword, puzzles challenge the solver to think. In the language of mind, a puzzle indicates the dreamer's need to identify cause. Cause will always be found in thought. The physical life and experiences are the effect. |
| *Pyramid* *represents the full use of the mind's energy.* | The pyramid as a structure has fascinated mankind for millennia. Significant research concerning the way the pyramid form traps and focuses energy has been conducted throughout the world. A two dimensional form depicting the structure of mind is a triangle. A three dimensional form depicting the structure of the mind is an equilateral pyramid. In the language of mind the pyramid represents the full use of the mind's energy because of how the energy is utilized in the space of the pyramid structure. |

| *Derivative Meaning* | *Thoughts to Consider* |
|---|---|
| *Dict. A small figure in the human form, moved by cords or wires, in a mock drama; one actuated by the will of another.* | Are you becoming what you desire or are you pretending that you are something you are not? Pretense is a form of lying, and you will eventually be caught in your own lie. Be honest with your Self and others. When you desire to become something, use imagination and will to bring it about, then there is no place for fear to take root. |
| *Dict. A small bag or case in which money is contained or carried in the pocket.* | Examine what has recently occurred in your life. Did these events make you feel worthy or worthless? Realize you determine your sense of Self worth; the situations in your life are merely a stimulus for you to evaluate your Self. Valuable people undertake valuable activities. Fill your life with worthwhile activities that aid others. |
| *Dict. To perplex; to discover or resolve by long cogitation. From pose to perplex with a question.* | Begin by asking your Self "why?" Most people wait until something goes wrong, a crisis arises, to ask "why?" Learn to ask why when things are going well in your life. As you answer your "why" delve deeper and deeper into your own thinking. Do not settle for external answers such as "because he said so" or "because that's the way she is". This will keep you from identifying cause in your thinking. Look for answers that are Self revelatory: "because I expect that kind of response" or "because I wanted/was afraid this would happen". These answers you can do something productive with. |
| *Dict. A solid structure whose base is a rectilinear figure and whose sides are triangular and meet at a point.* | What has recently occurred in your life that brought you a profound sense of joy, peace, power, or well-being? Examine this peak experience. You need not passively wait for such an exhilarating experience to happen again. You can actively pursue the thrill of using more of your mind, more of your potential, by continuing to interpret and respond to your dreams, by meditating daily, by honing mental skills such as memory recall and concentration. Each of these align the inner levels of consciousness thus enabling you to draw upon more of your mind's power. |

| Symbol | Meaning in Universal Language of Mind |
|--------|----------------------------------------|

## Q

**Queen**
*represents the*
*superconscious*
*mind.*

Queens rule by divine authority established by bloodline or through marriage. In the language of mind, a queen will represent the superconscious mind of the thinker. The superconscious mind is the part of mind closest to the point of origin, the Source, or Creator. It is the divinity in man; the inner authority in individual consciousness.

**Quicksand**
*symbolizes a*
*loss of control*
*in the use of*
*subconscious*
*mind substance.*

In the language of mind, quicksand symbolizes the lack of control using subconscious mind substance. This could be brought on by overindulgence in alcohol or drugs, excessive sleep, coma, or any lack of conscious will. When quicksand appears in a dream, the dreamer needs to exercise conscious will by making definitive decisions toward action. This will restore control of thoughts and therefore how the substance of mind is being used.

## R

**Rabbi**
*is the*
*superconscious*
*mind. (see*
*minister, priest)*

**Race  (contest)**
*indicates a need*
*for conscious*
*stimulation.*

In the language of mind a race symbolizes a drive for expeditious accomplishment indicating a need for conscious stimulation.

| *Derivative Meaning* | *Thoughts to Consider* |
|---|---|
| *Dict. The consort of a king; a woman who is the sovereign of a kingdom.* | What is your attitude toward the queen in the dream? Are you honorably respectful or defiantly rebellious? This will give you insight into your own conscious attitudes toward your own superconscious mind, your inner authority. |
| *Dict. A movable sandbank in the sea, a lake, or river, dangerous to vessels or to persons who trust themselves to it.* | Eliminate "will busters" from your life. If you want to regain control of your inner faculties, do not relinquish your conscious will, rather strengthen it through daily concentration exercises. An exercise to perform for ten minutes each day is to direct your gaze and all of your mental attention upon the tip of your finger. Think only of the tip of your finger. When your mind wanders to something else bring your thoughts back to the tip of your finger. Practice this faithfully each day for ten minutes. As with physical exercise you will in time begin to see results in your ability to control your attention. |
| *Dict. A title of respect given to Jewish doctors or expounders of the law. Hebrew rabi meaning "my master".* | |
| *Dict. A rapid course; a contest of speed. A strong or rapid current of water.* | Do you know what stimulates you to action? Is it desire or fear? Are you Self-motivated or other-motivated? Relax. Explore stimulation beyond your five physical senses. Seek stimulation in your dreams or in the meaning of fine poetry or in a breath-taking sunset. |

| Symbol | Meaning in Universal Language of Mind |
|---|---|
| **Race (body structure)** *symbolizes a collection of thoughts comprising an attitude foreign to the dreamer.* | Race is determined by body structure not skin color as is often mistakenly believed. The structure of the human body is basically the same. Slight variations in genetic codes constitute variations of the structure which can be noted in what is described as race, similar to the variations which produce either a male or female body structure. In the language of mind, people of a different race will signify a collection of thoughts comprising an attitude foreign to the dreamer. |
| **Radio** *symbolizes a means for receiving mind to mind communication.* | In the language of mind, a radio signifies the ability to receive thoughts. Telepathy is the sending and receiving of thoughts from one person to another. The radio symbolizes the means to receive thoughts from another whereas a broadcasting station symbolizes the means to project or send thoughts. A radio announcer will indicate an aspect of Self involved in sending thoughts. |
| **Railroad** *represents a predetermined direction of an organization.* | A railroad is the track used by a train. Similar to a road which enables easy movement from one place to another, the railroad symbolizes a direction or goal. In this case, it is a goal for an organization symbolized in the language of mind by the train. |
| **Rain** *represents conscious life experiences. (see water)* | |
| **Rainbow** *signifies identification of levels of awareness in conscious experiences.* | The interaction of water and light which produces a rainbow symbolizes the relationship of awareness to conscious life experiences. The prismatic display of the light signifies the dreamer's level of awareness. For instance, a thinker can be heavily engrossed in the physical senses and life, rarely thinking of anything beyond sensual gratification. A thinker can be aware of the cause of creation and attuned to the universe. These illustrate distinct differences in perceptions of reality which are examples of levels of awareness in conscious experience. |

| Derivative Meaning | Thoughts to Consider |
|---|---|
| *Dict. A class of individual sprung from a common stock; a perpetuated variety of animals or plants.* | What is perplexing you? Rather than prejudging it, explore it. Find out more about this foreign attitude. Become informed and educated. You may discover something new about your Self or something that you did not previously know that can help you attain your desires. |
| *Dict. The transmission or reception of electromagnetic waves without conducting wires intervening between transmitter and receiver.* | Mind to mind communication or telepathy is a daily occurrence. Most people are unaware of the sending and receiving of thoughts, yet they will insist, without discernable cause, that certain people make them feel great and certain places make them uncomfortable. Become aware of the thoughts you project, your aura or influence, and likewise be attentive to that of others. It will expand your sense of well-being. |
| *Dict. A permanent roadway consisting of one or more pairs of rails laid parallel to each other and several feet apart, making a track over which locomotives, freight or passenger cars may run.* | Which organization is your dream referring to — your job, a club, a religious group, or perhaps a political affiliation. Do your goals align with those of that organization? If so, seek further involvement or leadership in the group as a field of greater learning and contribution. If not, find a group of people who do share your ideals. |
| *Dict. A bow or arc of a circle, consisting of all the prismatic colors, formed by the refraction and reflection of rays of light from drops of rain, appearing in the part of the heavens opposite to the sun.* | Be willing to admit where you are in learning. The mind of a college graduate is filled with a wider range of information and experience than the mind of a kindergartener. This does not make one better than the other. Identify whether you are a novice, an apprentice, an adept, a master, or a teacher. This will aid you to identify your level of awareness and reach for your next step in your personal evolution. |

| Symbol | Meaning in Universal Language of Mind |
|--------|----------------------------------------|
| *Rape symbolizes fighting creation.* | Rape in a dream symbolizes forced creation. If the dreamer is female and dreams a male is raping her, it signifies a conscious refusal to receive what the subconscious mind is offering. The dreamer is fighting the manifestation of her own desires. If the dreamer is male and dreams he is raping a female it signifies the conscious mind trying to force the subconscious mind to fulfill desires. He is fighting the natural creative process within Self rather than co-operating. Rape in a dream will show how and why the dreamer is failing to achieve what s/he desires. |
| *Refrigerator is a means for preserving knowledge.* | In its common usage, a refrigerator is an artificially cooled container for storing and extending the life of food. Food in a dream represents knowledge. For knowledge to be sustained over a period of time it must be put to use. Therefore, the means for preserving knowledge is memory, plus action. |
| *Rehearsal symbolizes preparation toward an imagined goal.* | In a dream, rehearsing indicates the dreamer's willingness to work toward the manifestation of what s/he desires. In the language of mind, rehearsal symbolizes the preparation toward an imagined goal. For man to create with thought, he must be willing to keep his mind and body moving in the direction he has imaged. |
| *Repair indicates the need to repeat successes.* | Repair in a dream symbolizes the individual dreamer's need to repeat previous successes. What was at one time valuable and useful is no longer of benefit until there is a restoration, a re-creation. Once the thinker's desires manifest, they begin to deteriorate — the car depreciates and rusts, the delicious food is either used by the body or eliminated as waste. For man to learn how to become a mental creator, he must learn to use creation fully. The means to do so is to create and re-create again and again. |
| *Restaurant is a place in mind to receive knowledge.* | Again, we have a dream symbol connected with food. Food in the language of mind is knowledge. A restaurant is a place in mind where knowledge can be received. Places in mind signify specific internal, mental conditions. For instance, when the mind is still and focused a place of calmness is created conducive to receiving new input. |

| *Derivative Meaning* | *Thoughts to Consider* |
|---|---|
| *Dict. The act of snatching by force; the carnal knowledge of a woman forcibly and against her will.* | Cease fighting against your Self. Take full responsibility for what you have imaged, and prepare to receive the manifestation of your desires. Your subconscious mind does not have the capacity to force something on you of its own volition. It can only recreate what you have consciously imaged. If your desires have changed, determine how you will respond to the manifestation of desires already set into motion. Cooperate! |
| *Dict. A box or room in which materials, usually foods, are kept cool.* | To insure knowledge gained is accessible to you at a future time, repeatedly draw upon that knowledge, applying it to your life. This strengthens memory and also aids you to build understandings so the fruit of the knowledge will remain with you as permanent memory. |
| *Dict. To repeat what has already been said or written; a trial performance made before exhibiting to the public.* | Preparation aids in causing the inner and outer minds to work harmoniously. It assures the cooperation of the conscious mind with what has already been set into motion and is manifesting through the subconscious mind. Anyone desiring excellence will work toward what they desire. |
| *Dict. To execute restoration or renovation on; to restore to a sound or good state after decay, injury, dilapidation, or partial destruction. Latin reparo meaning "again to get" or "make ready".* | How can your life be changed for the better? Maybe your dream is encouraging you to change jobs or friends. Perhaps your inner Self is offering guidance on how to adjust your attitudes to receive more from what already exists in your life. Note what is being repaired and by whom in your dream to help answer these questions. |
| *Dict. A commercial establishment for the sale of refreshments.* | What kind of knowledge are you gaining in your life? Every person has every possible opportunity for a positive and productive existence when they choose to respond to it. You choose the people you associate with, the books you read, the work you do, the place you live, the very fabric of your existence. Make sure it meets your standards. |

| Symbol | Meaning in Universal Language of Mind |
|---|---|
| **Right** *indicates what is in alignment with Universal Law, therefore productive.* | The origin of the word "right" comes from Latin words meaning to rule. The universe is ruled by Universal Laws and Principles which establish order otherwise we would experience chaos. References to right in a dream occur when the thinker is cooperating with the natural function of Law. This kind of thinking is productive toward growth, realization, and liberation of the Self as a Creator thus unfolding the destiny of the individual. For this reason "right" can also symbolize the future in a dream. |
| **Ring** *symbolizes commitment.* | The circular structure of a ring symbolizes unity and completeness. Worn as an apparel on the hand, a ring symbolizes a purposeful commitment. The use of the ring in the dream will reveal the nature of the commitment. For instance if used in a wedding ceremony, it will symbolize the commitment between the conscious and subconscious minds; a graduation ring will symbolize learning accomplished through commitment. |
| **River** *indicates the movement and direction of the dreamer's conscious life experiences.* | Another dream symbol connected with water, a river symbolizes a direction the dreamer's experiences are taking. A clear, peaceful river will indicate ease and enjoyment in life experiences; a polluted, turbulent river signifies a life filled with waste and turmoil. |
| **Roads** *symbolize the dreamer's direction in life.* | In the Universal Language of Mind, a road represents the direction of the dreamer's life. The direction in life is determined by the goals and ideals the thinker makes his own. These can be imaged, created from the thinker's desire for a better life, or remembered, an imitation of what the thinker has seen others accomplish. The dream activity will reveal the nature of the dreamer's goals. |

| *Derivative Meaning* | *Thoughts to Consider* |
|---|---|
| *Dict. In conformity with the rules which ought to regulate human action; in accordance with duty, truth, and justice, or the will of God. Latin* rectus *meaning "straight"; rectum meaning "to rule or direct". To restore to the natural or proper order.* | Universal Laws guide creation in our universe. They function whether you know about them or not. Learning about these Laws increases your understanding of nature, your Self, others, and creation. Living in harmony with the Laws brings fulfillment, peace, security, and enlightenment. Be willing to become more educated about the universe; it will aid you in being a more productive part of it. |
| *Dict. Anything in the form of a circular line or hoop; a circle of gold or other material worn on the fingers.* | Commitment means to give over in trust. Your physical existence is entrusted to your conscious waking mind. How well you know your Self physically, emotionally, mentally, and spiritually determines the degree of responsibility you can demonstrate. Responsibility is your ability to respond, and this requires Self trust and awareness of your purpose for existence. |
| *Dict. A large stream of water flowing through a certain portion of the earth's surface and discharging itself into the sea, a lake, a marsh, or into another such stream.* | How are you responding to life — with full awareness of what you are creating or unconsciously, reacting to situations in your life. The *dream-action* will give you insight to answer this question as well as suggestions in symbolic form of what you can do to improve the quality of your experiences. |
| *Dict. An open way or public passage; a piece of ground appropriated for travel, forming a line of communication between one city or place and another for foot passengers or vehicles. A.Sax.* rad *meaning "a riding; a journey on horseback".* | Do you know where the road is leading? If the *dream-road* is a dead end, it's time to set new goals for your Self. If it leads to an unfamiliar town, it is time to redefine your goals. If it takes you where you want to go, the dream is supporting your efforts and progress in achievement. |

| *Symbol* | *Meaning in Universal Language of Mind* |
|---|---|
| **Rock** *represents the will in subconscious mind.* | In the Universal Language of Mind, matter or earth represents subconscious mind. Rock indicates how the will is operating in subconscious mind. Will is the mental muscle that enables movement to occur in the outer and inner levels of consciousness. |
| **Roof** *symbolizes the separation between the superconscious mind and the Creator.* | A house symbolizes the dreamer's mind, with the floors or levels indicating different parts and functions of the mind. The roof separates the house from the uppermost environment — the sky. Thus in a dream the roof represents the separation between the superconscious mind and the Creator. |
| **Room** *indicates a particular part or activity of mind.* | In the Universal Language of Mind, rooms indicate particular places in mind. In a dream look for the activities performed in the room as an indication of the symbology. For instance: an *Attic* will represent the superconscious mind, a *Basement* - unconscious awareness, a *Bathroom* - place for purifying/cleansing, a *Boardroom* - place for determining goals, a *Classroom* - place for learning, a *Dining room* - place for assimilating knowledge, a *Family room* - place for rejuvenation, a *Library* - place for receiving information, a *Nursery* - place for new ideas, an *Office* - place for learning/growth, a *Storage room* - place for memories, a Secret *room* - place of obscurity, a *Waiting room* - place for expectant nonaction. |
| **Rose** *signifies subconscious thought form.* | Flowers spring from the earth. In the language of mind, earth is subconscious mind substance; flowers such as a rose are a product of the earth and represent subconscious existence. Subconscious existence includes the state of being within the dreamer's subconscious mind and it also indicates the condition of universal subconscious mind. |
| **Run** *indicates rapid mental motion.* | Running indicates rapid motion. In a dream running toward something indicates quick action toward a goal. Running from signifies energy expended to escape or avoid an aspect or part of the Self. Running in slow motion indicates that the dream action has moved from one subconscious level to a more outward level where the vibration is |

| *Derivative Meaning* | *Thoughts to Consider* |
|---|---|
| *Dict. A large mass of stony matter; the matter constituting the earth's crust, as distinguished from soil, mud, sand, gravel, clay, peat.* | To strengthen your will, make positive choices and follow through with action. Deciding not to do something keeps you and conditions the same, thus the will has nothing to empower. When the conscious mind creates desired images, the subconscious mind has something positive to reproduce. Thus strengthening your conscious will also strengthens your subconscious will. |
| *Dict. The cover of any house or building irrespective of the materials of which it is composed.* | What is you concept of deity? How do you understand your Maker? How do you commune with your transcendent spiritual parent? Dreams featuring prominent roofs or activity involving a roof highlight these types of thoughts. |
| *Dict. Space; any division separated from the rest by a partition.* | The rooms in a dream will offer you insight into where your attention is focused during your waking state. No matter where your physical body is, you, the thinker, can be anywhere through the power of thought. When this ability is not understood and therefore not directed with intelligence it is called daydreaming. When it is harnessed with wisdom it becomes visualization. |
| *Dict. A well-known and universally cultivated plant and flower of many species and varieties, found in almost every country of the northern hemisphere.* | Why are flowers predominant in your dream? Are they growing in a garden or being offered to you by someone in the dream? How the flowers are used will indicate your awareness of your existence beyond the physical. This is why flowers are often seen as a token of love, respect, or gratitude in our physical lives. They symbolize an attitude of the giver beyond the physical gift itself. |
| *Dict. To pass over the ground by using the legs more quickly than in walking; to retreat hurriedly.* | Take inventory of your ideals and goals. Face your desires, making them worthy of your intelligence and effort. Procrastinating or ignoring only prolongs the situations you are attempting to avoid. Such attitudes require more energy than honest Self-revelatory action. Make sure you are expend- |

| Symbol | Meaning in Universal Language of Mind |
|--------|----------------------------------------|
| | slower. The dream action appears in slow motion because the consciousness has yet to adjust to the change in the rate of vibration. When the adjustment occurs, the dream action will appear at "normal" speed. |

## S

| Symbol | Meaning in Universal Language of Mind |
|--------|----------------------------------------|
| **Saddle** *represents a tool for using the will.* | A saddle provides a rider with stability. Beasts of burden, work animals, or horses represent the dreamer's will. The will can be described as the muscle of the mind. It is the power that gives mental mobility. A saddle in a dream will indicate the dreamer's ability to control the will. |
| **Sailing** *signifies observing life experiences.* | In the Universal Language of Mind, water signifies conscious life experiences. When there is sailing in a dream it will indicate the dreamer's movement through life without participating in life. Thus sailing signifies observing life experiences. |
| **Salary** *symbolizes value assessed on learning.* | In the Universal Language of Mind money symbolizes value and work symbolizes productive learning. A salary is the money received for work performed. Thus in the language of mind a salary symbolizes the value assessed on learning. |
| **Salt** *indicates the use of knowledge over a prolonged period of time.* | Although many think of salt as a flavor enhancer, it is more widely used throughout the world as a food preservative. Food in a dream symbolizes knowledge. The addition of salt to food, in the language of mind, indicates the use of knowledge over an extended period of time. |

| *Derivative Meaning* | *Thoughts to Consider* |
|---|---|
| | ing energy toward what you desire in life. |
| *Dict. A seat to be placed on an animal's back for the rider to sit on.* | Be sure to direct your will with intelligence. When this is present, the power of the conscious mind — reasoning — can be used. Without intelligence, willfulness becomes stubbornness. |
| *Dict. To begin a voyage across water.* | Are you observing life in order to learn or is observing a means of avoiding life experiences? Be honest in your assessment for the full meaning of the dream to be clear to you. Much can be gained by observing others, their successes and failures, but it is only useful to the observer when the knowledge acquired is put to use in his or her own life to produce understandings. |
| *Dict. The recompense or consideration stipulated to be paid to a person periodically for services.* | Do you see your life's work as contributing something to others or society? Is it worthwhile, providing a needed service? This type of attitude will aid you to see the value of your activity and will promote your own learning and sense of productivity in life. |
| *Dict. A well-known substance in common use for seasoning and preserving food.* | Be attentive to the knowledge you draw upon repeatedly in your everyday life. How does this knowledge enrich your life? Does it add to your enjoyment? Become determined to use your knowledge to gain understandings that will become a part of your soul. When the physical body dies all knowledge acquired and added to the brain's memory will also pass away. Only that which fosters compatibility to your Creator will become a part of permanent memory and remain with you forever. |

| Symbol | Meaning in Universal Language of Mind |
|---|---|
| **Scales** *indicates a means for measuring and differentiating substance.* | In the Universal Language of Mind, scales will represent the dreamer's use of discrimination. Scales, rulers, compasses, and any other tool used to measure something signify a means to identify substance. How the scales are being used in your dream will give further insight into what you are attempting to identify. For instance, a balancing scale like the one the lady of justice holds in her right hand will indicate the dreamer's desire to balance two elements of the life. |
| **Scar** *signifies attachment to past misunderstanding.* | A scar is the result of an incomplete healing of a wound. It is incomplete because the wounded tissue has not returned to its original, healthy state, rather a mark remains as a result of the damage. Not all wounds result in a scar. In the language of mind, wounds are the result of destructive thinking or misunderstandings that require change and learning in order to produce wholeness. When the thinker attempts to move forward yet remains attached to the misunderstanding which caused pain complete healing will not take place, thus a "scar" remains. |
| **School** *symbolizes a place for learning.* | In a dream, a school will indicate the dreamer's thoughts are centered on his or her learning. Mankind exists in the physical level of consciousness for the purpose of learning and growing in understanding that will feed the soul. In the language of mind, a school signifies the dreamer's awareness of this purpose. |
| **Science** *symbolizes a pursuit of truth to perceive with certainty.* | Science is the yearning to understand physical cause and to use what is discovered to become a creator. In its highest expression it is a pursuit of truth. When scientific endeavors, knowledge, or innovations appear in a dream they will signify the dreamer's desire to know truth. Knowing is the natural evolutionary step beyond believing. To know means one has had personal experience with the truth. |
| **Scissors** *represent a means to discriminate.* | In the language of mind, scissors indicate a means for discerning or exposing the difference between two separate elements. The action of discernment is a process and it is a prerequisite for effective reasoning. For understanding |

| *Derivative Meaning* | *Thoughts to Consider* |
|---|---|
| *Dict. Anything gradu-ated, especially when applied as a measure or rule. Sanskrit* skand *meaning "to ascend".* | What kind of scale appears in your dream? A scale measuring weight will symbolize your discrimi-natory power at work. Discrimination is your abil-ity to separate and identify the qualities that make something what it is — its uniqueness. What or who is being weighed will tell you the area where discrimination is occurring or needs to take place. |
| *Dict. The mark of a wound or an ulcer remaining after healing.* | What past hurts or grievances am I holding onto? Let go of the past by becoming invested in the present and future. The past cannot be changed. Whatever occurred, has been said and done. You can come to terms with past unpleasantness by forgiving your Self or others. This means you give now, in the present, rather than holding back and causing more pain. Realize you are not the only one who has suffered unpleasantness. Con-tinuing to play the victim will not bring your peace, coming to an understanding of cause will. |
| *Dict. A place in which persons are instructed in any species of learning; an educational establish-ment.* | What have I been learning and how have I used this learning to improve my life? Am I repeating old situations that exist for my learning but ignor-ing the understanding they can bring? Change your experiences by changing your Self. True learning is not the accumulation of information but rather the incorporation of mind-expanding ideas into your way of thinking. |
| *Dict. Knowledge coordinated, arranged, and systematized; art derived from precepts or built on principles.* | What truth has become apparent to you recently? This will be a truth of a universal nature, one that applies to anyone, anywhere, and rises above mo-mentary opinion. When science appears in any form in your dream it will indicate a greater aware-ness of thought as cause. You are realizing the power of your thoughts to create your perceptions of and situations in your life. To make your life better, fill your mind with thoughts that reflect your highest ideals and aspirations. |
| *Dict. A cutting instru-ment consisting of two blades movable on a pin in the center and which* | The faculty of discrimination enables you to dis-tinguish hot from cold, male from female, good from evil. It is a precursor to realizing your power of choice. Develop your discriminatory faculty, |

| *Symbol* | *Meaning in Universal Language of Mind* |
|---|---|

to occur, the thinker must be able to separate the elements comprising a whole. Scissors in a dream indicate this means for separation or discrimination.

*Screaming indicates uncontrolled thoughts.*

In the Universal Language of Mind screaming signifies uncontrolled thoughts. If the *dream-scream* arises from fright, it will indicate the dreamer's lack of awareness of his/her desires. If the *dream-scream* arises from pain, it will indicate the dreamer's denial of an apparent need. Control of the thoughts begins with the skill of directing the mind's attention at will. Concentration is the foundation for becoming aware of the Self's needs and imaging the desires that will fill those needs.

*Sea symbolizes conscious life experiences.*

In the Universal Language of Mind, water represents conscious life experiences thus the sea or ocean signifies the conscious perception of facts and events which comprise the dreamer's reality. Being lost at sea will indicate that the dreamer is overwhelmed by experience, lacking a direction or goal in life. Crossing the sea in an ocean liner will symbolize the organization the dreamer is using in his life to accomplish goals.

*Seasons represent the stages of growth.*

Physical time is measured by the earth's rotation around the sun. This produces changes in the atmosphere and weather which man denotes as seasons. In the Universal Language of Mind, seasons indicate the thinker's cycles or stages of growth. Each stage corresponds to a season and the activity that occurs in creation during that season, thus winter signifies infancy, spring - adolescence, summer - adulthood, and autumn - wisdom. How the seasons appear in a dream will often indicate the theme of the message being conveyed.

| *Derivative Meaning* | *Thoughts to Consider* |
|---|---|
| *cut from opposite sides against an object placed between them. Latin* caedo *meaning "to cut"*. | realizing it is not the commonly misconceived idea of prejudice but rather the mental acuity for separating and identifying the uniqueness in anything. This understanding of discrimination will free your mind to remember accurately, imagine expansively, and willfully choose the best course of mental and physical action. |
| *Dict. To cry out with a shrill voice as in a fright or in extreme pain.* | Note the source of the scream in your dream. This will enable you to identify the aspect(s) of Self that are uncontrolled. By determining why the scream is arising, you will be better equipped to respond to your dream by directing your attention toward the fulfillment of the needs or desires that you have been neglecting. Once identified, cause your thoughts to be of a nature that will bring you fulfillment rather than dissatisfaction, pleasure rather than pain, peace rather than chaos. |
| *Dict. The continuous mass of salt water which covers great parts of the earth; the ocean.* | Note the way in which the sea appears in your dream. Is it tumultuous and threatening, or peaceful and awe-inspiring? The activity occurring and your response to it will give you feedback concerning how you are leading your life or running away from it. Realize your experiences are your own. No two people perceive the same experience exactly the same owing to the differences in temporary and permanent memory. However, in any experience there are facts. Seek to identify the facts in your experience, free from bias or ego motivation, then draw upon your intuitive understanding to gain the most from life experiences. |
| *Dict. One of the periods into which the year is naturally divided, as marked by its temperature, moisture, etc. Latin* sationis *meaning "a sowing"*. | Note the season and its meaning in the language of mind. This will tell you what stage of growth you are experiencing. For instance, if the dream occurs in a wintry setting it will indicate new learning you are pursuing and the stage of infancy. Infancy is a time of rapid learning, absorbing information that will be useful as maturity continues. To use this dream, cultivate receptivity to the new information and experiences occurring in your life. An autumn setting will indicate the wisdom gained from learning. To use this dream, seek to teach or pass on to others the benefits of what you have learned. |

| Symbol | Meaning in Universal Language of Mind |
|---|---|

*Seed*
*indicates origin.*

In the language of mind, a seed represents a complete blueprint for what will become a fully formed and matured idea. A seed therefore indicates the origin. The type of seed will describe what origin is being referred to in your dream; ie. a seed of a fruit or vegetable will indicate the origin of knowledge; a seed of nonedible plants indicates the origin of subconscious thought. Often "seed" is used to describe a thought — a seed idea. This indicates an imaged desire that has been or can be impressed in subconscious mind substance for reproduction.

*Sense*
*represents*
*perception*
*gleaned from*
*directing the*
*attention of the*
*mind.*

The physical body has five sensory systems: seeing, hearing, tasting, smelling, and touching. Each is a means of receiving input from the environment outside of Self. In order for the input to be acknowledged, recognized and used, the mind's attention must be directed toward what is being received from that sense. Thus in the language of mind a prominent sense will indicate perception gleaned from directing the attention of the mind. A dead man's eyes see nothing because there is no intelligence, no thinker, present to see.

*Serpent*
*symbolizes*
*compulsive use*
*of life force or*
*creative energy.*

Animals in a dream including a serpent represent compulsion or habit. Throughout man's history, the snake has enjoyed a specialized symbology and therefore meaning from the Biblical serpent in the Garden of Eden to naga of Hindu teachings. The snake is even a part of the caduceus, the physician's symbol. In the Universal Language of Mind the serpent represents the compulsive use of life force or creative energy known in Eastern philosophies as the Kundalini.

*Servant*
*is an aspect of*
*Self.*

As with all people, in the language of mind, a servant represents an aspect of Self. A servant in a dream is an aspect that serves the dreamer, one who does the dreamer's bidding. If the *dream-servant* is serving food it will symbolize an aspect that provides knowledge for the dreamer. If the *dream-servant* is cleaning the house it will indicate an aspect involved in restoring order in the mind.

*Serve*
*indicates the*
*giving of*
*energy.*

In the language of mind, the action of serving indicates the aggressive action in the cycle of giving and receiving which is giving. Noting the nature of the service gives the dreamer indications of how his energy is being used. For instance,

| Derivative Meaning | Thoughts to Consider |
|---|---|
| *Dict. The impregnated and matured ovule of a plant, containing an embryo, which may be developed and converted into an individual similar to that from which it derives its origin; first principle.* | Note what type of seed appears in your dream and its meaning in the language of mind. Knowing the point of origin or cause of anything frees you to reproduce an exact replica of your desires or in other cases gives you the power to make alterations when desired. The quality of your thought will determine the speed and accuracy of the manifestation of your visualized desires. Enjoying the fulfillment of your desires depends largely upon your understanding and command of the seed ideas you create. |
| *Dict. One of the faculties by which man and the higher animals perceive external objects by means of impressions made on certain organs of the body; sight, hearing, taste, smell, touch.* | Be attentive to your perceptions of the world around you. Look to see, hear to listen. Use your senses fully by focusing your attention. By sharpening the command of your attention you will also develop greater depths of awareness both consciously and subconsciously. Subconscious awareness is known colloquially as "extrasensory perception"; the ability to receive input from the environment within the Self. |
| *Dict. A reptile of an extremely elongated form, without feet, and moving by muscular contractions of the body. Sanskrit srip meaning "to creep".* | What is the serpent doing in your dream? If it's biting you, you need to become attentive to how you are using your creative energy, moving from habit to reasoning with awareness. If it is poisonous, your compulsive use of life force is breeding negativity which drains your life force. If you find the serpent friendly, even though in your waking state you are afraid of these reptiles, you are using your creative energy to manifest what you want in your life. |
| *Dict. One who serves; a person employed by another for menial offices or other labor, and is subject to his command.* | Servants in your dream are aspects of Self who are attentive to your needs and responsive to your desires. Identifying these aspects will aid you to accomplish what you desire in life more quickly and efficiently for they support your efforts. |
| *Dict. To perform duties in behalf of; to render spiritual obedience and worship to; to help by* | Your ability and willingness to give sets into motion Universal Laws which work on your behalf. Decide to give your time, energy, and resources toward the accomplishment of the highest ideals. |

| Symbol | Meaning in Universal Language of Mind |
|---|---|
| | serving food in a dream will symbolize giving energy to learning, public service in a dream symbolizes giving energy to all aspects of Self, religious service symbolizes giving energy to the highest Self or the Creator. |
| *Sex signifies duality; the aggressive or receptive principle.* | In the Universal Language of Mind, sex indicates duality: the male signifies the aggressive principle of action, the female signifies the receptive principle of expectancy. The sex of people in a dream is particularly helpful in determining the meaning of unknown aspects in a dream. |
| *Sexual Intercourse symbolizes the unification of the conscious and subconscious minds for the purpose of creation.* | Anytime sexual intercourse occurs between a male and female there is the possibility of procreation or conception. The man and woman will represent the conscious and subconscious minds. Intercourse symbolizes the unified effort for the purpose of creation. Those familiar with the mechanics of visualization will understand this mental process. Visualization is a science by which consciously imaged desires are subconsciously produced becoming manifested into physical reality. The conscious mind creates, the subconscious mind recreates. |
| *Ship represents an organization.* | A ship or any large vehicle in the language of mind symbolizes an organization which the dreamer is a part of. An organization is comprised of many people in the dreamer's life such as a company, a church, or a club. The dreamer must determine which organization is being referred to in the dream message. |
| *Shoes symbolize a covering of your spiritual foundation.* | Shoes are footwear designed to protect the foot from external elements. Feet in the language of mind represent the dreamer's spiritual foundation. An individual's spiritual foundation is the understandings which have become a part of soul. These understandings note the individual's point of spiritual evolution and contribute to the individual's current Self awareness and attitudes toward God and humanity. |

| *Derivative Meaning* | *Thoughts to Consider* |
|---|---|
| *good offices. Latin* servo *meaning "to preserve".* | To know prosperity, give to aid others to abundance. Whatever you desire to receive from others, be willing to give that your Self. The Laws will work in response to the quality of your giving. |
| *Dict. The distinction between male and female. Latin* sexus *meaning "a sex", from* sco *meaning "to cut."* | In addition to the wealth of information you can gain by interpreting the meaning of people in your dreams, the characters in your dream will tell you how you tend to approach life. A predominance of unknown males in your dream, in addition to revealing information concerning the division of mind, will indicate a tendency toward aggressive action; a predominance of females will indicate a tendency toward receptivity. Make sure your aggressiveness is action not forcefulness and your receptivity expectant waiting not passivity. |
| *Dict. Reciprocal dealings and communication between a male and a female of a species.* | Separate your dream state from your waking state. Dreams of sexual intercourse do not indicate the dreamer's physical, waking desire for sexual activity. Rather the dream is revealing the state of your conscious awareness in symbolic images. What are you desiring to create in your life? What have you been visualizing, imaging in your thoughts, or daydreaming? This dream is giving you feedback about those directed images or fantasies. |
| *Dict. A vessel of some size adapted to navigation.* | Is the ship sailing on smooth, clear seas or is it in stormy peril? Dreams involving large vehicles will help you to identify the associations in your life that are productive and compatible to you and those which aren't. Respond to the guidance your inner Self affords. |
| *Dict. A covering for the foot, usually of leather.* | Are you drawing upon the wealth of understandings you possess? Do you use the talents and abilities you have or do you ignore them or deny their existence. Are you protecting your spiritual foundation or hiding it? Become more aware of the understandings in your soul through the practice of daily meditation upon the Creator or your God within. |

| Symbol | Meaning in Universal Language of Mind |
|---|---|
| *Shopping* *indicates* *investigation* *and the assess-* *ment of value.* | The action of shopping is an active search for goods. In the language of mind, this symbolizes the investigation and assessment of value. What is being sought will give the dreamer further insight into his needs and desires, as well as what s/he finds of value. |
| *Shower* *represents* *conscious life* *experiences.* *(see rain)* | |
| *Shrubs* *represent* *subconscious* *existence.* | Like flowers, shrubs spring from the earth. In the language of mind, earth is subconscious mind substance; shrubs being a product of the earth represent subconscious existence. Subconscious existence includes the state of being within the dreamer's subconscious mind and it also indicates the condition of universal subconscious mind. |
| *Sister* *is a familiar* *aspect of Self.* *(see people)* | A sister in a dream will represent a well-known aspect of your own Self. Depending upon your physical sex, this will signify a conscious or subconscious aspect. |
| *Skates* *indicate a tool* *for quickened* *forward motion.* | A skate is a foot covering, a shoe, which enables quick mobility. In the language of mind, a skate symbolizes how the dreamer's spiritual foundation provides forward motion in the life. Forward motion is assured through learning, the building and using of understanding. Forward motion promotes soul growth and spiritual maturity. |
| *Skeleton* *represents* *structure of* *mind.* | In its most common usage a skeleton refers to the frame for the physical body. In the language of mind it represents the structure of mind. The mind's structure is the result of millions of years of spiritual evolution. Reason- |

| Derivative Meaning | Thoughts to Consider |
|---|---|
| *Dict. Action of seeking goods sold at retail from a building or establishment.* | What are you looking for? Is it something you need that will promote a better life for your Self and others or merely something that will temporarily satisfy your senses? The happiest life is led by one who seeks to identify the needs of the soul and earnestly works to satisfy those needs. Live in a way that will produce and bring you happiness. |
| *Dict. A low dwarf tree; a woody plant of a size less than a tree.* | Are you noticing serendipitous happenings occurring in your life? If so, this dream may give you information regarding how your subconscious mind is attempting to manifest your desires. Your subconscious mind's duty is to fulfill any imaged command given by your conscious, waking mind. To accomplish this, your subconscious mind will draw to you the people, places, and things that will assist in fulfilling your desires. Likewise, you will be drawn to them. |
| *Dict. A female born of the same parents as another person.* | After identifying the specific aspect your sister represents, determine your attitude toward your sister. Do you admire and respect her with great affection or do you find her offensive and wish you weren't related? Your attitude toward your sister will reveal how you view this aspect of your Self. |
| *Dict. A contrivance consisting of a steel runner or ridge fixed on a wooden sole or a light iron framework, fastened under the foot and used to enable a person to glide rapidly.* | Are you finding it easier to move toward what you desire in life? Your spiritual foundation, the understandings stored in your subconscious mind, will spur forward motion in your life when used as a source of inspiration, guidance, wisdom, and expanded consciousness. |
| *Dict. The bones of an animal body separated from the flesh and retained in their natural* | This symbol in a dream will direct your attention to the basic inner workings of your mind. Become familiar with the different parts of mind and their function: the conscious mind, the subconscious |

| Symbol | Meaning in Universal Language of Mind |
|--------|----------------------------------------|
| | ing man enjoys the benefits of those years of development with a fully formed structure for consciousness that affords him the capability of creating with thought. |
| *Sky represents superconscious existence.* | Heavens or sky in the Universal Language of Mind represents the highest level of consciousness in man: the superconscious existence. (See authority figures) The superconscious existence refers to what is universally true when referenced in the spiritual literature of the world as well as in dreams. |
| *Sleep indicates a loss of conscious awareness and will.* | Sleep in a dream symbolizes a loss of conscious awareness and will. The loss of conscious awareness is easily recognized by the ignorance of what transpires in the minutes and hours of sleep. This leads to a loss of conscious will as well because the thinker does not respond to what occurs during the sleeping period. The telephone may ring, a child may cry, without the sleeper's knowledge because the attention was never moved from the inner levels of consciousness to the outer, physical stimuli. |
| *Smoke brings the dreamer's attention to what expansion has caused.* | Fire in the language of mind indicates expansion. Smoke is one of the by-products of fire representing what has occurred from expansion. Smoke in a dream will bring the dreamer's attention to the effects caused by expansion. |
| *Snake symbolizes compulsive use of life force or creative energy. (see serpent)* | |
| *Snow signifies unchanging life experiences.* | Water in a dream symbolizes conscious life experiences. Snow is made of frozen water particles symbolizing stagnancy in experiences. When there is no change in life, the same experiences are repeated. When the thinker uses reasoning to alter the thoughts, the experiences are different from what has gone before. |

| *Derivative Meaning* | *Thoughts to Consider* |
|---|---|
| *position; the supporting framework of anything.* | mind, and the superconscious mind. Each are separate but interrelated divisions of consciousness required for your whole Self to function as a single, wholistic and complete entity. |
| *Dict. The apparent arch or vault of heaven.* | Is your *dream-sky* clear or obscured? This will indicate your awareness of this part of Self closest to your spiritual parent or the Creator. Knowledge of superconscious existence is revealed according to individual spiritual development and is accessed through the practice of spiritual disciplines such as meditation. |
| *Dict. To be in that well-known state in which there is a suspension of the voluntary exercise of the powers of the body and mind.* | Are you moving through experiences with little or no understanding of them? This dream can indicate a "sleeping consciousness" during your waking hours; a tendency to scatter your attention and ignore learning opportunities. Wake up! Be alert to the people, places, and things around you. Become a part of life's action, rather than being a victim of circumstances beyond your control. |
| *Dict. The exhalation or vaporous matter that escapes from a burning substance. Greek* smycho *"to burn slowly".* | Are you in control of your attention or does it wander, becoming scattered? To manifest your desires give your mind direction by causing your attention to continue to be focused toward what your thoughts have caused. |
| *Dict. Watery particles congealed into white crystals in the air and falling to the earth in flakes.* | Are you trying to maintain the status quo? Compulsive thinking or a fear of something new will produce repeated and similar life experiences. To "thaw" your frozen attitudes, think differently each day. Seek new ways to look at life. Take a risk by doing something you have never done before. |

| Symbol | Meaning in Universal Language of Mind |
|--------|----------------------------------------|
| *Soap symbolizes means for purification.* | In a dream, soap indicates the dreamer has the means to purify his existence. Purification can indicate releasing the past, eliminating detrimental factors in the present, or replacing imagined fears with desires. |
| *Song represents harmonious vibratory pattern. (see melody, music)* | |
| *Soldier is a disciplined aspect of the Self.* | Anything worth accomplishing requires discipline to overcome inertia. Until the thinker establishes Self discipline he/she will experience inner conflict arising from fear and doubt. A soldier in a dream represents an aspect of Self that is disciplined. |
| *Soup symbolizes knowledge.* | In the Universal Language of Mind food symbolizes knowledge. Knowledge is information received through the five physical senses, or the sixth sense which is the mind's attention, and aggressively placed in the brain's memory. Knowledge used in experiences can produce understanding. Understanding repeatedly applied in experience becomes a part of permanent memory stored in the soul. |
| *Sports signify the manner in which the dreamer is approaching life.* | In a dream, sports will represent how the dreamer approaches life. Individual sports, such as fishing or swimming, will indicate the dreamer's tendency for self-direction where excelling or enjoyment is a significant motive. Team sports, such as basketball or football, will indicate the dreamer's tendency to unite aspects of Self in a common endeavor where competition is a significant motive. Because of its original meaning, a sport in a dream will often reveal how the dreamer tends to distract the Self. |
| *Spouse is an aspect committed to wholeness.* | Commitment to Self means more than making your word good, although the qualities of dependability, trustworthiness, reliability, and responsibility are present in one who has established this bond. The dreamer's spouse represents |

| *Derivative Meaning* | *Thoughts to Consider* |
|---|---|
| *Dict. A chemical compound of potash and soda with fat, soluble in water, and used for detergent or cleansing purposes.* | Does your purification relate to the past, present, or future? Releasing, eliminating, or replacing that which holds you back propels you toward growth and awareness. Embrace the present, making it productive for Self and others. This will insure a bright and desirable future. |
| *Dict. A man who serves in any army; a man of military experience and skill. Brave, honorable.* | Do I lead a disciplined life? How do I understand discipline — is it something I am forced to do to get what I want or is it a refined ability to attain what I desire. Discipline is the acquired awareness and personal implementation of the Laws of creation. |
| *Dict. A kind of broth; a sort of food made generally by boiling flesh of some kind in water with various other ingredients.* | What dream action is transpiring involving the soup? Is it a nutritious meal you are enjoying or is it spoiled and untouched by the people in your dream? This will tell you how you perceive knowledge. The dream action will also indicate how you are using or failing to use the knowledge available to you. |
| *Dict. A pastime or amusement in which a person engages; a game; a diversion. Sport is an abbreviation for disport, from the French deport meaning "properly diversion resorted to in order to divert the thoughts".* | Review the *dream-action*: are you participating in the sport or an observer? Which sport is being played and what other symbols can you interpret that will lend insight into your dreams meaning? Did you win or lose? Did it matter? Answering these questions will help you assess the message. Pay particular attention to what the dream is describing as your mode of motivation; the way you approach achieving a goal or the way you distract yourself from goals. |
| *Dict. One engaged or joined in wedlock; a married person. Latin* spondeo *meaning "to promise solemnly, to* | Do I keep my promises? Realize sincere efforts made by your conscious mind are recognized by your inner Self. Each time you follow through on commitments made to your Self or others you strengthen the bond between your outer and inner |

| Symbol | Meaning in Universal Language of Mind |
|--------|----------------------------------------|
| | an established trust between the conscious mind (being the dreamer) and the subconscious mind (the spouse). Commitment to Self means the thinker recognizes that the conscious and subconscious minds are two halves of a whole; for completeness they must function reciprocally, compatibly. |
| *Square symbolizes stability and inertia.* | The geometric form of a square signifies stability in picture form. Stability is the quality of strength that produces endurance. When a square appears in a dream it will reflect this stableness, and perhaps inertia — a resistance to movement or change. |
| *Stairs indicate a means of moving to and between levels of consciousness.* | Similar to an elevator in function and in language of mind meaning, stairs indicate a means of movement from one level of consciousness to another. There is a difference however. Stairs require the locomotion of the individual; a person must climb stairs on their own power. Stairs represent the drive and/or motivation to move from one level of consciousness to another. |
| *Star signifies awareness in the conscious mind.* | In the Universal Language of Mind, light symbolizes awareness. A star is a celestial body that shines by its own light. Each individual has a unique conscious mind filled with their own awareness. In a dream, stars signify this conscious awareness. The original meaning from the Sanskrit reflects this inner meaning as "scattering light". This is particularly relevant since the awareness in the individual is most scattered or dispersed in the physical level of consciousness. |
| *Steal indicates attitude of taking from.* | To steal is to take without right. In a dream stealing indicates an attitude of taking from rather than giving and receiving. Such a dream will indicate the dreamer is taking from the Self or others what s/he has no claim to. |

| *Derivative Meaning* | *Thoughts to Consider* |
|---|---|
| *engage one's Self'.* | Self. This causes an alignment between these two parts of mind and they function as a wholistic unit. You are more centered and at peace with your Self and others. |
| *Dict. Having four equal sides and four right angles; adjusted so as to leave no balance. Latin* quatuor *meaning "four".* | Am I firm in my resolve or merely stubborn? You must determine the meaning of this symbol in your dream. If you find it indicates stubbornness, you need to use reasoning completely, particularly imagination, to power your will. This will transform irrational willfulness into the strength of endurance. |
| *Dict. A succession of steps rising one above the other arranged as way between two points at different heights in a building. From Greek* steigen *meaning "to climb".* | How Self aware am I? Am I aware of the different levels of consciousness existing within my mind, or does it all seem to run together and I do the best I can? Use your dreams to become familiar with all parts of Self. Learning about the elements that comprise the whole Self increases your awareness and effectiveness in using the potential existing within you. |
| *Dict. celestial body that shines by its own light. Sanskrit* tara *meaning "to strew", from "scattering light".* | To be apprised, cognizant, or informed is to be aware. Are you using what is available to you in your conscious mind to be aware? Become more familiar with the physical "equipment" you have to use: your body, its five sense receptors and the brain. Become more familiar with the power in your conscious mind: reasoning. The more informed you are about your Self, the more cognizant you can become. This is the foundation for greater Self awareness which includes six other levels of consciousness. |
| *Dict. To take and carry away feloniously; to take clandestinely without right or leave. Greek* stereo *meaning "to deprive"; Sanskrit* stenas *meaning "a thief".* | Remember all people in your dream are aspects of you. Therefore when a *dream-person* is stealing from you in the dream the message will be addressing an aspect that is detracting from your conscious desires. |

| Symbol | Meaning in Universal Language of Mind |
|--------|---------------------------------------|
| **Stone** *represents the will in subconscious mind.* (see rock) | |
| **Store** *indicates a place in universal mind.* | Universal mind describes the interconnectedness of all minds experienced in the inner levels of consciousness. A store represents a place in universal mind where all forms of energy (goods) can be exchanged (bought/sold). |
| **Storm** *indicates inner conflict.* | Storm in the language of mind is defined by its elements: high winds symbolize rampant thoughts, rain symbolizes conscious experiences, snow/hail symbolizes a refusal to change, thunder indicates restless thoughts, and lightning represents spontaneous, short-lived awareness. When the meaning of these symbols is united, the meaning of a storm is revealed as inner conflict. |
| **Stove** *symbolizes the means to prepare for knowledge.* | A stove is a means to contain or control fire for cooking. In the language of mind, fire represents expansion and food represents knowledge. A combination of these basic symbols, a stove in the language of mind indicates the means to prepare the mind for new knowledge. |
| **Stranger** *is an unidentified aspect of Self.* | An unfamiliar, unrecognized person in a dream symbolizes an unidentified aspect of Self. The *dream-person's* sex will indicate whether the aspect is a part of the conscious mind or the subconscious. The *dream-person's* actions in the dream will lend further insight into this unknown part of Self. |
| **Stream** *indicates the direction of the dreamer's conscious life experiences.* (see river) | |

| *Derivative Meaning* | *Thoughts to Consider* |
|---|---|
| *Dict. A warehouse where supplies of any and all kinds are collected for sale either by wholesale or retail; an abundance.* | You give and receive subconsciously each day. Some describe this as atmosphere or the "vibes" of a place or person. Your thoughts emanate a particular vibration, an aura, which can be intuitively sensed by others. Likewise others' thoughts can be received by you. Make your thoughts positive, loving, and attractive to those with like minds. |
| *Dict. A violent commotion of the atmosphere, producing or accompanied by wind, rain, snow, hail, or thunder and lightning; a tempest.* | Most inner conflict arises from indecisiveness. Laziness, procrastination, passivity, victimization, irresponsibility, and related attitudes all begin in the mind of the weak-willed. To resolve inner conflict, give your will something positive to work upon. Direct your thoughts toward what you desire, making the kind of life you want to live. Decisiveness broadens your arena of experience and increases your scope of understanding. |
| *Dict. An apparatus to contain a fire for warming a room or house, or for cooking or other purposes.* | When you are constantly open to learning it is easy to expand your consciousness. An open mind absorbs more information than a closed one. Learn to listen to others, stilling your mind and becoming mentally aggressive only after you have received the knowledge they impart. Train your mind to remain open upon your command. |
| *Dict. A foreigner; one of another place. Latin* extraneus *meaning "that is without".* | To determine the meaning of strangers in your dream, note their demeanor and action. This gives you indications of the quality within Self. Your reaction to the stranger during the dream will tell you how you react to this part of your Self; an unknown *dream-lover* will symbolize something very different from an unknown dream-thief. |

| Symbol | Meaning in Universal Language of Mind |
|--------|----------------------------------------|
| *Streets* represent the direction the dreamer is taking toward goals. | In the Universal Language of Mind, a street represents the direction the dreamer is taking toward goals. A dark street will symbolize a lack of awareness of the means to fulfill desires; a busy street indicates opportunities for achieving goals and the many aspects of Self related to those goals. |
| *Student* is an aspect of Self. | As with all people in a dream, a student represents an aspect of Self. Because of the specialized activity pursued by one described as a student, it will further indicate an aspect invested in or desiring learning. |
| *Suburb* represents a particular pattern of thinking. | A suburb in a dream, like a city, will indicate a particular pattern of thinking. Each physical suburb exists as a common living and working place for many different people. In a dream, it reveals a specific attitude the dreamer holds; a condition of mind involving many aspects of Self. |
| *Subway* symbolizes a predetermined direction of an organization. | A subway is an underground train. A train symbolizes an organization of people the dreamer is affiliated with and using to attain common goals. The fact that the train moves on a track indicates a predetermined destination symbolizing a goal for the organization to reach. A subway being an underground tunnel also indicates the vehicle and its goals involve subconscious mind as well as conscious mind. |
| *Suit* signifies how the dreamer is expressing Self. (see clothes) | |
| *Suicide* indicates a refusal to learn. | Suicide is self-murder, the end of physical life. It does not however end the existence beyond the physical, what is often termed the soul or spirit. Suicide is the willful cessation of learning from physical experience and this is its symbolic meaning in the language of mind. |

| *Derivative Meaning* | *Thoughts to Consider* |
|---|---|
| *Dict. A way or road in a city having houses on one or both sides, chiefly a main way in distinction from an alley. Latin* sterno *meaning "to pave or strew".* | Am I taking the most direct route for the fulfillment of my goals or do I become distracted easily, dropping one goal before it is attained and pursuing another? How the street appears and is being used in your dream will assist you in learning to pursue your goals in the most effective and efficient manner. |
| *Dict. A person engaged in learning something from books, or attending some educational institution, especially of the higher class. Latin* studeo *meaning "to study".* | These aspects of Self are fulfilling the purpose for your existence — to learn and grow in understanding. Become familiar with them. They are your greatest asset for soul progression. |
| *Dict. An outlying part of a city or town.* | Determine your waking attitude about the suburb. Is it the place where you live or do you just visit? The former will indicate your general attitudinal approach to life be it happy or sad, agreeable or combative, prosperous or poor. The latter will indicate a tendency to deny your own patterns of thinking by remaining aloof or separated from them; these are attitudes you do not own, they are temporary. |
| *Dict. An underground way.* | What organization do you belong to that has predetermined goals? Are your goals in alignment with that organization, company, church, or group? It is important to your well-being to affiliate your Self with others of like minds. Much can be learned by interacting with others who share common ideals. The more you interact, the more your soul progression can be accelerated. |
| *Dict. Self-murder; the act of designedly destroying one's own life. From Latin* sui *meaning "of himself"* | Identify the symbolic meaning of the *dream-person* who has committed suicide. This will tell you the aspect of Self that is refusing to learn. This is the part of you that fights life by refusing to initiate or cooperate with change. Affirm your in- |

| Symbol | Meaning in Universal Language of Mind |
|--------|---------------------------------------|
| *Sun* represents awareness in the superconscious mind. | The sun is the center of our physical universe. In the language of mind, the sun symbolizes awareness in the superconscious part of mind. Although when incarned the attention tends to become engrossed or centered on temporal, physical life, the true center of man's existence is his superconscious mind, the seat of the spirit. A *Sunrise* indicates the initiation of awareness; *Sunset* signifies the completion of awareness. |
| *Supermarket* is the act of gaining or procuring knowledge. *(see grocery)* | |
| *Surgeon* is an aspect of Self. | In the Universal Language of Mind, a surgeon represents an aspect of Self invested in the elimination of destructive mental attitudes. It can also signify an aspect skilled in reorganizing attitudes to produce full functioning and wholeness. |
| *Surgery* symbolizes the elimination of destructive mental attitudes or the reorganization of mental attitudes to cause wholeness. | Surgery attempts to relieve the body of the burden of disease by removing the poisoned tissue or repairing damaged tissue. Through innovative research over the past three decades, the School of Metaphysics has researched the cause for bodily malfunctions. As a result, specific attitudes or ways of thinking have been linked to specific bodily diseases or disorders. Thus surgery in a dream represents the elimination of destructive mental attitudes or the reorganization of mental attitudes to cause wholeness. |

| *Derivative Meaning* | *Thoughts to Consider* |
|---|---|
| and caedo *meaning "to kill"*. | herent ability of free will. Take control of this aspect by facing life's challenges and moving toward understanding. All things of the physical are temporary, they do not last. The understandings gained become a permanent part of your soul. |
| *Dict. The self-luminous orb which, being in or near the center of our system of worlds, gives light and heat to the earth and other planets. Latin* sol *from a root meaning "to shine"*. | To know Self as spirit, expand your consciousness by seeking Truth that is universally applicable to anyone, anytime, anywhere. Move beyond transient opinions, they are of the physical only. What is true today is disproved tomorrow and another viewpoint arises. Seek transcendental Truth that opens the mind, warms the heart, and feeds the soul. To exist within superconsciousness meditate daily. |
| *Dict. A medical person whose profession is to cure diseases or injuries of the body by manual operation or by medical appliances employed externally or internally. Greek* cheirourgos *meaning "the hand work"*. | Since the activity of a surgeon is to eliminate disease from the physical body, a surgeon in your dream will reflect your willingness to cease negative patterns of thought that undermine and destroy your desires. Use this aspect to cause the changes in thinking that will bring about mental health and wholeness. |
| *Dict. The operative branch of medicine; that branch of medical science and practice which involves the performance of operations on the human subject.* | Which attitudes do I need to release? These will be attitudes which keep you chained to the past, draining your energies and depleting your zest for living. Replace these with attitudes that seize the moment with a joy and lust for life. Reorganize your thinking patterns to consciously look for answers to problems, to meet challenges instead of holding onto obstacles, to strive toward excellence in thought and deed. |

| Symbol | Meaning in Universal Language of Mind |
|--------|---------------------------------------|
| **Swimming** *indicates how the dreamer is moving through life experiences.* | Water in the Universal Language of Mind is conscious life experiences. The act of swimming indicates how the dreamer is moving through those experiences. Agility indicates mental dexterity and will power in daily experiences; drowning signifies being overwhelmed by experiences. |
| **Sword** *is a tool for change.* | As with other tools used to kill, a sword represents a tool for change. In spiritual literature, the universal meaning is even more specific: a sword represents karma. Karma is the manifestation of the Universal Law of Cause of Effect. It is a tool used by the soul to facilitate learning and growth in the physical. Karma is indebtedness to Self, enabling the individual to understand what s/he causes to occur. |
| **Symphony** *represents the unified effort to produce harmony.* | A symphony is comprised of a wide variety of musicians and their instruments working together under the direction of a conductor. In the language of mind, a symphony symbolizes a unified effort to produce harmony. This can be the result of a common goal, being in love, the anticipation of receiving something long desired. |

## T

| Symbol | Meaning in Universal Language of Mind |
|--------|---------------------------------------|
| **Table** *is a means of support.* | A table in a dream represents a means of support. To the thinker, this means of support can take several forms: endurance and forbearance, upholding by aid or assistance, providing for or maintaining, or substantiating. The way the table is used will assist in discerning its meaning. |
| **Tape Recorder** *represents memory.* | In the Universal Language of Mind a tape recorder signifies the dreamer's memory. Memory is a temporary record of what has been experienced that is impressed and stored in the brain. Recall is the mental faculty for accessing this memory at will. |

| *Derivative Meaning* | *Thoughts to Consider* |
|---|---|
| *Dict. The act or art of sustaining and propelling the body in water.* | Do I respond to life or look for someone to credit or blame? By employing the success equation you can direct your life as you desire. Formulate your ideal Self, condition, world; then create a purpose for that ideal. Now keep this ideal and purpose in mind as you encounter life. Make your ideal and purpose the guide for your choices. |
| *Dict. An offensive weapon having a long metal blade with a sharp point for thrusting.* | Are you aware of the workings of Karma in your life? Become familiar with this concept for it is more than an idea or philosophy, it is a manifestation of Universal Law and the means for your soul progression. Karma is the law of balance. It is not punishment, rather it is a means whereby you can come to know the power of your thoughts and understand the importance of your intention. |
| *Dict. A consonance or harmony of sounds agreeable to the ear; harmony. Greek* symphonia *meaning "with voice".* | This or related symbols in a dream indicate a working together of many aspects of Self to produce accord, integration, or unity. The oneness experienced when many aspects work toward the same ideal gives insight into the full potential of the whole Self. Seek to continue the frame of mind reflected in this dream and the experience of wholeness will become more than a brief glimpse of what can be. |
| *Dict. An article of furniture consisting of a horizontal frame with a flat upper surface supported by legs.* | What kind of table appears in your dream — a kitchen table, a computer table, an operating table? Identifying the type of table and its symbology will help you determine what kind of support is present in your attitude. This symbol indicates attitudes of assisting, maintaining, or vindicating. |
| *Dict. An appliance for preserving the memory of sounds or the replaying of them.* | Am I using my past experiences productively? The past is over. What has been thought, said, and done cannot be erased. Learn how to use your memory to stimulate reasoning in the present. You cannot change the past but you can change your present attitude toward the past and create the future you desire. |

| Symbol | Meaning in Universal Language of Mind |
|---|---|
| **Target**<br>*is a goal.* | In the Universal Language of Mind a target represents a goal. A goal is a mentally conceived physical objective. A goal gives the mind a direction, the attention a focus, and the will power. |
| **Teacher**<br>*is the*<br>*superconscious*<br>*mind.* | A teacher is one more knowledgeable than the Self. In the language of mind a teacher represents the dreamer's superconscious mind. The superconscious mind holds the complete plan for maturity as spirit, and the previous progress made toward that maturity. Dream interaction with a teacher indicates a desire and need for communication and rapport with the deepest part of mind. |
| **Teenager**<br>*is an aspect of*<br>*Self experienc-*<br>*ing adoles-*<br>*cence.* | All people represent aspects of Self in the Universal Language of Mind. When a *dream-person* is between the ages of thirteen and nineteen this signifies an adolescent aspect of Self. Adolescence is characterized by experimentation and the building of reasoning skill. It is a time of accelerated growth and learning in preparation for the productivity of adulthood. |
| **Teeth**<br>*represent a*<br>*means of*<br>*assimilating*<br>*knowledge so it*<br>*can be used.* | Teeth are the first instruments of the digestive system. In a dream, teeth symbolize a means of assimilating knowledge. Losing teeth is a common symbol in a dream indicating a change in the way the dreamer assimilates what is learned. |
| **Telephone**<br>*is a means for*<br>*communication,*<br>*particularly*<br>*telepathy.* | Because of the nature of how a telephone operates and the distant communication it affords, a telephone is a symbol for communication from one mind to another. Telepathy is the subconscious mind's capacity to receive and send thought. |

| *Derivative Meaning* | *Thoughts to Consider* |
|---|---|
| *Dict. The mark set up to be aimed at in archery, artillery practice, and the like. Greek* zarge *meaning "a frame or border".* | Are your goals physical only? Think about what the car represents to you; the freedom to go where you want to go, when you want. Think about what the marriage represents to you; friendship, love, companionship throughout the years of your life. For a fulfilled life, extend your thinking to create ideals from your goals. |
| *Dict. One who instructs or guides the studies of another. Latin* dico *meaning "to say"; Sanskrit* dic *meaning "to point out".* | As you become more familiar with the parts of Self beyond the physical body and conscious mind, you will have access to great understanding. A teacher in a dream signifies your attitude toward your own inner wisdom and guidance. A strong conscious mind and an honest ego will always be prepared to heed the inner teacher. |
| *Dict. The years of one's age having the termination -teen beginning with thirteen and ending with nineteen.* | Be sure to keep your ideal in mind. Without an ideal, adolescence can be a mentally distressing and painful experience of rebellion. Battling with your Self or others prolongs this stage of growth. Imaging what you desire to become stimulates reasoning and accelerates the gleaning of understanding needed for productivity. |
| *Dict. The projecting bony growths in the jaws of vertebrate animals, serving as the instrument of mastication. Sanskrit* danta *meaning "to divide".* | Am I assimilating the knowledge available to me? Some people collect information without ever applying it to themselves or their lives. This is wasted energy. "Chew" on new ideas, assimilating their meaning and import to your Self and your life. |
| *Dict. Any instrument which transmits sound beyond its natural limits of audibility; transmitting sound and words uttered by the human voice by means of electricity and conducting wires by means of vibration.* | By knowing your own thoughts you can more quickly identify the thoughts of others as they are received by your consciousness. Strengthen your command of your own mind through concentration exercises. Build your skill in sending thought by practicing thought-projection with a friend. |

| Symbol | Meaning in Universal Language of Mind |
|---|---|
| *Television represents the use of imagination for visualizing.* | For visualization to be effective, an image must be created in the conscious mind. This sets into motion the reproduction of this image by the subconscious mind. Television, in the language of mind, symbolizes this process. Television also implies the element of broadcasting. Broadcasting visualized desires indicates the power of the subconscious mind to reach out to other subconscious minds when it lacks what is needed to fulfill conscious desires. |
| *Temple symbolizes the mind, specifically spirituality.* | As with any building structure, a temple in a dream will represent the mind of the dreamer. Because a temple is used in physical life for the specific purpose of religious worship, it signifies the dreamer's intention toward spirituality. |
| *Tennis signifies the manner in which the dreamer is approaching life. (see sports, games)* | |
| *Test signifies the need to access what has been learned.* | In the language of mind a test symbolizes the need to draw upon what has been made a part of Self; a need to access what has been learned. A missed test indicates neglect of what has been learned. A common dream is going to class to discover a test, for which the dreamer is unprepared, is being given. This dream symbolizes procrastination of learning. Aceing a test indicates command of accessing what has been learned. |
| *Theater signifies an imaginative frame of mind.* | In the Universal Language of Mind, theater represents the imagination in action. Imagination is the inventive faculty of the mind. It enables the thinker to progress, advance, develop, and enlighten. Imaginative attitudes cause all aspects of the dreamer's life to be what they are. |

| *Derivative Meaning* | *Thoughts to Consider* |
|---|---|
| *Dict. The transmission of scenes or moving pictures by conversion of light rays to electrical waves, which are reconverted to reproduce the original image.* | Realize your subconscious mind will seek to manifest the visualized images you create. Your subconscious mind can be the best friend you ever had. It constantly seeks the resources within your Self or by using the Universal Laws of creation that will manifest what you desire. Also realize your visualized images have an impact not only on your subconscious mind but on the subconscious mind of others. For this reason you must think positively and with love for the betterment of Self and others. |
| *Dict. An edifice dedicated to the service of some deity or deities. Latin* templum *meaning "a place marked" or "cut off".* | Do you live a spiritual life? How often do you think about your existence beyond the physical? Do you contemplate the origin and nature of the universe, seeking to understand creation and your place within it? A sense of spirituality is necessary for a sound mind and a strong body, for this is the quest for Self knowledge and wholeness. |
| *Dict. An examination by the cupel, hence any critical trial. Means of discrimination. Latin* testum, *"an earthen vessel".* | Do I view the tests of my life as challenges or obstacles? Your mental attitude will determine the rate of learning in life. Make life a joy, an opportunity for discovery and enlightenment. This will create an attitude conducive to meeting the tests of life and open the door to greater understanding. It is interesting to note the Latin word origin of test means "earthen vessel". In the language of mind this would indicate accessing the permanent memory of the subconscious mind or soul, the storehouse of all understandings. |
| *Dict. A building for the representation of dramatic spectacles. Greek* theatron *meaning "to see, a view".* | In *As You Like It*, William Shakespeare wrote, "All the world's a stage, And all the men and women merely players. They have their exits and their entrances, And one man in his time plays many parts." Use your imagination to create all aspects of your life — as you like it! |

| Symbol | Meaning in Universal Language of Mind |
|--------|----------------------------------------|
| *Theft* *symbolizes* *foregoing and* *therefore losing* *opportunities.* | Thievery is taking without right. In a dream thieving indicates an attitude of taking from rather than giving and receiving. Such a dream will indicate the dreamer is taking from the Self or others what s/he has no claim to. It can also signify the attitude of taking for granted what is already in the dreamer's possession. |
| *Thunder* *indicates* *restlessness in* *thoughts.* | When a thinker allows himself to be bombarded with external stimuli, when his thoughts are scattered, when he is out of touch with the inner Self, he finds his mind restless and his body tense. Thunder in a dream represents restlessness in thoughts. |
| *Ticket* *represents a* *means for* *identification.* | There are a wide variety of tickets: movie or theater tickets, parking tickets, sales receipt tickets. What they have in common, and what they symbolize in the language of mind, is a means for identification. To further understand the ticket's meaning in a dream, reference entries related to the type of ticket; ie. movie, sports. |
| *Tiger* *represent habits.* *(see animals)* | |
| *Toaster* *is a tool for* *knowledge.* | An appliance created primarily to dry and heat bread, a toaster represents a tool for knowledge. |
| *Tools* *signify the* *mechanics that* *cause or assist* | There are a wide variety of mental mechanisms available to man. Each causes a particular ability to be accessed and used. Each can be honed into a skill. Examples of these mental tools include: undivided attention, the ability to fo- |

| Derivative Meaning | Thoughts to Consider |
|---|---|
| *Dict. The wrongfully taking away the goods of another with intent to deprive him of them; act of stealing.* | Remember all people in your dream are aspects of you. When a *dream-person* is stealing, the message involves an part of Self that is detracting from your conscious desires. If your theft is taking for granted what you have, you probably find it difficult to receive. To help change this attitude, practice receiving compliments from others. |
| *Dict. The sound which follows a flash of lightning.* Greek stohnen *meaning "to groan".* | Do you know how to calm your mind and relax your body? Practicing some method to accomplish this state of mind will ease the restlessness and free you to concentrate your energies at will. Try sitting in a comfortable position, eyes closed, and listen to your breath. Do this for fifteen minutes each day. In time you will notice a leisurely rhythm to your breathing that produces a mental and physical calmness. This is the state of mind you want to maintain throughout your day. |
| *Dict. A label stuck on the outside of anything to give notice of something concerning it; a piece of paper with something written on it serving as a notice or acknowledgement.* Greek stecken *meaning "to stick".* | Note the type of ticket appearing in your dream and research the full meaning of the symbol to receive the message being relayed by your subconscious mind. Being able to put the meaning of symbols together is the art of dream interpretation. It will move you beyond being a translator only to being an interpreter of the mind's energies. |
| *Dict. An instrument for drying or scorching by heat of a fire.* | To fully use the knowledge available to you, prepare your mind to absorb what is at hand by stilling your mind, focusing your attention, and receiving impressions. |
| *Dict. Any implement used by a craftsman or laborer at his work; an instrument employed in* | Are the tools in your dream in good repair, are they well used? How the tool appears, what it is used for, and who is using it will help you to understand the message of your dream. Learning |

| *Symbol* | *Meaning in Universal Language of Mind* |
|---|---|
| *the mind to fulfill its function.* | cus the mind on one point; recall, the ability to retrieve information gained in the past by accessing the brain's memory; and listening, the ability to receive projected thoughts and words. |
| **Tornado** *symbolizes inner turmoil and confusion.* | Wind in the Universal Language of Mind represents the dreamer's thoughts. When that wind is formed into a tornado it indicates the dreamer's inner turmoil and confusion. |
| **Town** *represents a condition of mind where many aspects are connected.* | A town in a dream will indicate a particular pattern of thinking. Each physical town exists as a common living and working place for many different people. In a dream, it will give insight into a common attitude that dreamer holds. |
| **Toys** *symbolize ways to use the imagination.* | To understand the full meaning of toys in a dream, the dreamer must realize a toy is a plaything for a child. A child in the language of mind represents an immature aspect of Self; an infant would be a new idea. Therefore, a toy symbolizes the imagination applied toward the maturing of a new idea. |
| **Train** *symbolizes an organization.* | As with any large transportation vehicle, a train symbolizes an organization in the language of mind. An organization is a group of people with whom the dreamer associates and affiliates. A unique part of this symbol is the railroad or train tracks which predetermine the course of the train. Similar to a road, the railroad tracks symbolize a direction or goal. This indicates a predetermined goal for the organization. |
| **Transport** *signifies movement.* | Movement in mind occurs as a result of will. Will is the mental muscle that empowers the faculties, functions, and abilities of the mind. Will, hence movement, is set into motion by desire or fear, whether conscious or unconscious. |

| *Derivative Meaning* | *Thoughts to Consider* |
|---|---|
| *the manual arts for facilitating mechanical operations. A. Saxon* tawian *meaning "to make, to prepare".* | the skills of the mind gives you freedom to use its power and manifest your potential as a creator. |
| *Dict. A violent whirling wind; a tempest. Sp.* tornado *meaning "to return".* | To ease turmoil and confusion, still your mind. This will calm your thoughts and relax your body, enabling you to think more clearly or to rest and turn the problem over to your subconscious mind. |
| *Dict. Originally a walled or fortified place; a large assemblage of adjacent houses intersected by streets.* | Is the town familiar to me?  The town where you grew up will indicate a long-standing attitude. An unidentified town will signify a predominant attitude you have yet to consciously identify.  A mythical town will signify fanciful attitudes. Determine your waking attitude about the town for this will help reveal the attitude highlighted in the dream message. |
| *Dict. A plaything for children; a thing for amusement and of no real value. A trifling object.* | How are you nurturing your new ideas?  Are you giving them instruction through what you are learning in life so they mature and are useful to your Self and others?  Almost everyone has innovative and bright ideas during their life.  Only a few cause those ideas to grow and mature.  Such people are remembered, admired, and respected. Seek to be one of them. |
| *Dict. That which is drawn along behind; a retinue; a connected line of cars on a railroad together with the locomotive. Latin* trahere, *"to draw".* | Which organization is your dream referring to — your job, a club, a religious group, or perhaps a political affiliation. Do your goals align with those of that organization?  If so, seek further involvement or leadership in the group as a field of greater learning and contribution.  If not, find a group of people who do share your ideals. |
| *Dict. To carry or convey from one place to another.* | Where am I going?  Do you know what you want in life?  Have you learned how to obtain your desire?  Each thought you create will cause movement.  Create your ideas from desire.  If you have fears admit them, bring them to light.  Once what was unknown becomes known, fear no longer exists. |

| Symbol | Meaning in Universal Language of Mind |
|---|---|
| *Trash* *indicates what is of no value.* | "One man's refuse is another man's treasure." Trash in a dream indicates what is deemed as having no value, revealing the dreamer's attitude. The thinker deems something as having little or no value because it is not understood, it is not seen as furthering the accomplishment of desire, or there is a lack of knowledge of what it is and how to use it. It is worth-less than something the thinker finds familiar. |
| *Treasure* *represents past understood experiences.* | What is stored in permanent memory as part of the soul are the understood experiences gained by the individual. These understandings are the individual's treasure gleaned from years of invested experience. |
| *Trees* *represent subconscious existence.* | Similar to a forest in a dream, trees represent subconscious existence. Subconscious existence includes the state of being within the dreamer's subconscious mind; the recreative part of mind. Subconscious existence also indicates the condition of universal subconscious mind; the fact that all subconscious minds are connected. |
| *Triangle* *represents the expansiveness of creation.* | The geometric form of a triangle signifies creation in picture form. When a triangle appears in a dream it will reflect the expansiveness creation brings. |
| *Trombone/ trumpet* *are the means by which harmony is produced within Self. (see musical instruments)* | |
| *Truck* *is the physical body.* | As with all small vehicles, a truck in a dream indicates the dreamer's physical body. A tractor trailer will represent a vehicle for learning, probably your career or job. |

| Derivative Meaning | Thoughts to Consider |
|---|---|
| *Dict. Loppings of trees; waste or worthless matter; rubbish.* | One of the greatest challenges facing mankind is the waste he produces. What are you wasting — money, time, energy, your potential? Seek to use everything to its fullest. Learn by observing nature. In nature there is no waste, everything has a use. Be use-ful. |
| *Dict. Wealth accumulated; particularly a stock or store of money in reserve, a great quantity of anything collected for future use. Greek* thesauros *meaning "a store", from root* tithemi, *"to put" or "place".* | The greatest value you possess is not material, it is spiritual and is revealed to you in the form of talents or abilities that you did not learn in the present lifetime. These talents are the beginning of accessing your past understood experiences. Be attentive to them, and add new understandings to your soul through your present experiences. |
| *Dict. A perennial plant having a woody trunk of considerable size from which spring branches.* | Am I aware of how my conscious thinking affects my inner Self? How are my conscious thoughts related to what I experience on deeper levels? Daily meditation will aid you to expand your conscious awareness beyond the confines of the physical level of consciousness. |
| *Dict. A figure bounded by three lines and containing three angles. Latin* triangulum *meaning "three, an angle".* | Which recent experiences have brought you new ways of thinking and acting? Be aware of the expansive quality in your life as a means toward greater Self awareness. |
| *Dict. A heavy motor vehicle used for transport.* | Be attentive to the health and well-being of your body. It is the vehicle your mind will use throughout this lifetime. Take care of it, and it will serve you long and well. |

| Symbol | Meaning in Universal Language of Mind |
|---|---|
| **Tunnel** *represents a means of moving from one inner level of mind to another.* | In order for the thinker to receive the manifestation of his/her desires, the visualized desire undergoes a recreative process in the subconscious mind. Owing to the universal function of subconscious mind, the imaged thought is produced in each inner level of subconscious mind, growing and maturing, until it is sufficiently developed to manifest. A tunnel represents a means of moving from one inner level of mind to another. |
| **Typewriter** *symbolizes a means for communication.* | Physical communication requires knowledge of a common language. Communication is the exchange of ideas through use of words which symbolize the meaning of those ideas. It requires aggressively forming ideas to convey thoughts and receptively stilling the mind to receive thoughts. A typewriter represents the means by which this exchange takes place. |

## U

| Symbol | Meaning in Universal Language of Mind |
|---|---|
| **Unidentified Flying Object** *symbolizes an inner level body.* | Just as the thinker resides in a physical body for experiencing in the physical level of consciousness, there exist inner level vehicles or bodies corresponding to each of the inner levels of consciousness. These inner level bodies are used for experiencing the inner realms of mind. In a dream unidentified flying objects will symbolize these inner level vehicles. |
| **Umbrella** *indicates a barrier in conscious life experiences.* | Used for protection, the umbrella in the language of mind symbolizes a barrier in conscious life experiences. It will indicate something the dreamer is trying to thwart or avoid in life. |

| *Derivative Meaning* | *Thoughts to Consider* |
|---|---|
| *Dict. A subterranean passage cut through a hill, a rock, or any eminence to carry a road in an advantageous course.* | During a sleeping period, your subconscious attention will move into and through each inner level, re-energizing the mind and assimilating what has transpired during the previous waking experiences. The tunnel in your dream is symbolic of the way or route your consciousness takes to move between levels of consciousness. In out-of-body experiences or near-death experiences this symbol often appears. |
| *Dict. A keyboard machine for producing writing resembling type impressions. Greek* typto *meaning "to strike".* | To increase your command of communication, practice describing in detail the ideas you hold in mind. Read classical literature to learn how to describe thoughts with all of the senses. Make your words paint a picture. For increased receptivity in communication, practice holding your mind still with your will through concentration. Listen with your mind as well as your ears. |
| *Dict. identify: to make to be the same, fly: to move through the air or rise, object: that toward which the mind is directed in any of its states or activities.* | Have you experienced astral projection or out-of-body experiences? Dreams of this nature will indicate your ability to experience in the inner planes of existence. You are dual in nature, experiencing in both spiritual and physical realms. Your waking experiences are often centered around your physical body and physical activities. Your dream experiences, however, are centered around your inner consciousness and inner level bodies. The you in action in your dream is not your physical body, rather it is your inner level vehicle that exists in the level of consciousness where the dream is taking place. |
| *Dict. A portable shade, screen, or canopy of material extended on an expanding frame, carried in the hand for sheltering the person* | What do I need to face up to? Am I avoiding taking risks, or saying what I need to say, or revealing more of my Self? Whatever it is, conquer it by 1] admitting the limitation, 2] determining you want to be free of it, 3] imagining what you can do to be free, 4] imaging the new you this will |

| Symbol | Meaning in Universal Language of Mind |
|--------|----------------------------------------|

*Unicorn symbolizes the compulsive use of reasoning.*

Unicorns are imaginary creatures described in literature throughout the world. In the Universal Language of Mind, the unicorn symbolizes the habitual use of reasoning. This becomes evident when the different elements that create the unicorn are interpreted; ie. the horse symbolizing the will, the deer and lion symbolizing habit, and the horn symbolizing means for harmony. Imagination is signified by the unifying of these separate elements into a created whole — the unicorn. When memory (habit), will, and imagination work together harmonious reasoning is the result.

*Universe signifies all of creation.*

In the language of mind the universe symbolizes all of creation. Spiritually, man recognizes a Supreme Being or Creator of the universe. Scientifically, everything in the universe is made of the same substance, from planets to people to gases. The differences are determined by the consciousness that dictates the form through utilizing energy.

*University represents a place in mind for learning.*

In a dream, a university will indicate the dreamer's thoughts are centered on his or her learning. Because of the wide variety of curricula available at universities, in the language of mind a university represents a place in mind for expansive learning.

| Derivative Meaning | Thoughts to Consider |
|---|---|
| *from the rays of the sun or from rain or snow.* | produce, 5] determining how you will accomplish your ideal and purpose (a plan or the steps), 6] bringing your desires into activity, becoming the new you. |
| *Dict. A fabulous animal having the head, neck, and body of a horse, the legs of a deer, the tail of a lion, and a long horn growing out of the forehead. Latin* unicornis *meaning "one horn".* | Become conscious of how you employ reasoning in your life. Draw upon memory intentionally rather than as a habitual act. Becoming aware of previous experiences will then become a spring-board for an improved future produced by imagination. You will no longer rely upon magic, luck, or fate for your destiny. The power of reasoning will put you in control of your life. |
| *Dict. All created things viewed as constituting one system or whole; the world; pervading all or the whole; comprising all the particulars.* | When this type of dream occurs it is time for you to investigate wholistic education for the mind. Acquaint your Self with meditation practices, astral projection, intuitive skills, mystical experience. Do more than read, seek a teacher wise in these areas who has attained a degree of mastery greater than your own. Learn from that teacher, and apply what you learn in your life. |
| *Dict. An establishment or corporation for the purposes of instruction in all or some of the most important branches of science and literature, and having the power of conferring certain honorary dignities, termed degrees, in several faculties, as arts, medicine, law, and theology.* | What have I been learning and how have I used this learning to improve my life? Am I repeating old situations that exist for my learning but ignoring the understanding they can bring? Change your experiences by changing your Self. True learning is not the accumulation of information but rather the incorporation of mind-expanding ideas into your way of thinking. |

| Symbol | Meaning in Universal Language of Mind |
|--------|----------------------------------------|

## V

**Vacation**
*signifies a*
*temporary*
*suspension of*
*thoughts.*

To vacate means to leave. Most people take vacations from their pattern of life to break the routine thus escaping from what they find unpleasant. In the Universal Language of Mind, a vacation symbolizes the thinker's giving up of what does not bring fulfillment; a temporary suspension of thoughts. When the thoughts return, the thinker returns to the same old patterns of thinking and action.

**Vacuum**
**Cleaner**
*is a tool for*
*separating needs*
*or desires.*

Physically a vacuum cleaner or sweeper is an appliance that removes dirt from floors or furniture. In the language of mind it symbolizes a mental tool for separating what is wanted from what is not wanted. This mental tool is known as discrimination and is an element of reasoning.

**Veda**
*and any other*
*Holy work*
*represents*
*information of*
*creation, its*
*construction and*
*reason to exist.*

A Holy work is a text written to convey the spiritual nature of man and all of creation. What makes such a book Holy is the intention of the author(s) and its wholistic content. Holy works are penned in the Universal Language of Mind. When interpreted in this language, each reveals to man his origin, his purpose, and his destiny.

**Vegetables**
*symbolize*
*knowledge.*
*(see food)*

**Vehicles**
*represent the*
*physical body.*

All vehicles symbolize in the language of mind a means for giving and receiving experience. Small vehicles represent the dreamer's physical body. Large vehicles symbolize the dreamer's choice of vehicles (such as an organization, company, church) for experiencing what life in the physical affords. The use of the vehicle will give indications of the type of experience being related in the dream message. For instance, an *Ambulance* will indicate a need for healing in the giving and receiving of experience, a *Bulldozer* will signify means to move mind substance, *Fire Engine* will indicate a means to control expansion in

| *Derivative Meaning* | *Thoughts to Consider* |
|---|---|
| *Dict. The act of leaving without an occupant; having no contents, unfilled.* | What do I find undesirable in my life? Instead of trying to escape from unpleasant situations in your life by leaving them, examine the thinking that promotes these conditions in your life. Seek the cause for them, not through blaming others but through identifying your own thinking patterns that perpetuate their existence. Remove your ignorance by birthing new awarenesses. |
| *Dict. A mechanical appliance which removes dirt by means of the suction of air. From Latin* vacuus *meaning "empty".* | Notice how you determine what is desired and what is not desired in your life. Know what standards you use for making these determinations for it will give you insight into how you make choices. Making correct choices builds will power. |
| *Dict. The general name for the body of ancient Sanskrit hymns and comments believed by the Hindus to have been revealed by Brahma.* | What am I seeking to understand about creation? Respond to your yearning for spiritual awareness by pursuing information of a spiritual nature. Cultivate your desire for understanding by applying the learning you gain in your own thoughts and actions. Strive toward compatibility with your Creator through daily meditation and service to others. |
| *Dict. Any kind of carriage moving on land, a conveyance.* | How do I understand giving and receiving? When I want something do I look for what I can give that will bring what I desire closer to me, or do I take what I want? Giving and receiving is a cycle which functions according to Universal Law. The key to setting this cycle into motion is to give. As taught in all Holy Scriptures, give and you will receive. By determining what you will give, you set into motion what will return to you. Always give your best. |

| Symbol | Meaning in Universal Language of Mind |
|---|---|
| | experience, a *Garbage Truck* will indicate what is wasted in experiences, a *Police Car* will signify the need for discipline in experiences, a *Space vehicle* will signify a means to experience the inner levels of consciousness, a *Tractor Trailer* will indicate a means for productivity. |
| *Violence represents destructive thoughts.* | External violence arises in and from the mind of its perpetrator. When thoughts that promote harm are transformed into productive and beneficent thoughts, the subsequent actions are also changed. In the language of mind violence symbolizes these types of destructive thoughts that cause injury. The specific characters and action in the dream will reveal the specific thoughts which are causing the dreamer pain and turmoil. |
| *Violin is a tool for producing harmony. (see musical instruments)* | |
| *Volcano represents an opportunity bearing potential for mind expansion.* | A volcano is a mountain which potentially spews forth fiery gases and lava. Mountains in the Universal Language of Mind represent challenges or obstacles. Which one will depend upon the dreamer's own attitude. A volcano in a dream adds the dimension of fire which symbolizes expansion. Therefore a volcano in a dream symbolizes an opportunity bearing potential for expansion of the dreamer's thinking. |
| *Vote indicates a decision.* | In the language of mind, voting symbolizes the dreamer's willingness to express what s/he desires. A wish is a helpless desire; will power is the result of predetermined actions that bring about an imaged desire. Will power is always enacted toward the fulfillment of something. A decision is a commitment in thought toward an action. |

| *Derivative Meaning* | *Thoughts to Consider* |
|---|---|
| *Dict. Vehemence, intensity of action or motion; injury done to anything which is entitled to respect or reverence.* | It is much easier to think positively and with love than to think negativity and with hate. Violence in a dream is the result of denying the true nature of Self and Self's relationship with the Creator and all of creation. To end inner turmoil, spend time daily in deep meditation, reaching for a mental state of calmness. With sincere devotion, in time, this calmness will lend itself to contentment, and ultimately the bliss of communion with your Maker. |
| *Dict. A hill or mountain more or less cone shaped with a circular cuplike basin at its summit from which are sent out clouds or vapo, gases, showers of ashes, hot fragments of rocks and streams of lava. Latin Vulcanus, "the god of fire"; Sanskrit ulka meaning "fire".* | Control your attitude toward the unexpected. Purposefully see opportunities as challenges rather than barriers to what you desire. Embrace each experience for what it offers you, rather than what you might lose. By actively seeking the manifestation of your desires you will unlock the potential for expansion and new awarenesses will become yours. |
| *Dict. The expression of a preference or choice in regard to any measure proposed in which the person has an interest in common with others.* | How are you acting on your desires? Do you wait for an invitation to express what you want, or are you actively involved in the direction of your life? Be assertive. When your desires are important to you, when you know they will aid others as well as your Self, you will be willing to share them with others. And you will find others are ever ready to assist you in manifesting those desires. |

| Symbol | Meaning in Universal Language of Mind |
|--------|----------------------------------------|

# W

**Waiter/Waitress** *symbolizes an aspect of Self.*

As with all people, in the language of mind, a waiter represents an aspect of Self. A waiter in a dream is an aspect that serves the dreamer, one who does the dreamer's bidding. If the *dream-waiter* is serving food it will symbolizes an aspect that provides knowledge for the dreamer.

**Wall** *indicates a limit in thinking.*

Similar to a fence, a wall in the Universal Language of Mind symbolizes a limit in thinking. This can indicate a physical goal, an obstacle in the dreamer's life, or a barrier to what the dreamer desires.

**Wallet** *symbolizes place for storing valuables.*

A wallet in a dream symbolizes a place for storing what is highly prized by the dreamer. A stolen wallet signifies a loss of value, buying a new wallet indicates reassessing value.

**War** *represents inner conflict destructive to Self.*

War is a violent contest fought for many purposes from territorial to religious but always with an economical undercurrent. In the Universal Language of Mind it symbolizes inner conflict that is destructive to the dreamer. Conflict is destructive to the thinker because the lack of resolve drains the will, disperses the attention, and scatters mental energy away from positive, productive ends. Individual conflict embodies the opposing viewpoints of good and evil.

**Washing Machine** *symbolizes a means for reorganizing thoughts.*

A washing machine in a dream is a tool for reorganizing thoughts and attitudes. The articles being cleansed will lend further insight into the areas requiring the dreamer's attention. For instance, washing clothes will indicate a reorganization of how the dreamer is presenting Self to others.

| *Derivative Meaning* | *Thoughts to Consider* |
|---|---|
| *Dict. One who waits; an attendant on the guests in a hotel or similar place.* | Waiters in your dream are aspects of Self who are attentive to your needs and responsive to your desires. Identifying these aspects will aid you to accomplish what you desire in life more quickly and efficiently for they support your efforts. |
| *Dict. A structure of stone, brick, or other materials of some height and breadth serving to enclose a space, for a division, support weights, etc. Latin* vallum *meaning "a fence of stakes".* | What function does the wall serve in your dream? This will give you clues for identifying what type of limit you are facing. If the *dream-wall* is keeping you in a restricted area in your dream, it is time to use your imagination to extend your thinking beyond what you have previously settled for or accepted. If it is a support for a house, it will symbolize the boundary of your mind which separates you from all other minds. |
| *Dict. A bag or sack for containing articles which a person carries with him.* | Examine what has recently occurred in your life. Did these events make you feel worthy or worthless? Realize you determine your sense of Self worth; the situations in your life are merely a stimulus for you to evaluate your Self. Valuable people undertake valuable activities. Fill your life with worthwhile activities that aid others. |
| *Dict. A contest between nations or states carried on by force of arms. Greek* wirren *meaning "to embroil, confuse".* | Review your standards of life and your sense of morality. How do you determine what is right? Does your sense of right guide your thoughts and actions or is it merely a means to pass judgement on others while you remain undisciplined? Resolve inner conflicts by employing your power of reasoning. Envision the outcome of your present thinking and action. Choose that which will bring peace and understanding to your Self and others. |
| *Dict. A machine used for cleansing clothing or other materials.* | Is your mind clear and focused or cluttered and scattered? Eliminating extraneous, unrelated thoughts clears the mind to discern truth. When you find your mind wandering, becoming distracted away from your desire, use your will to redirect your attention toward your desire. |

| Symbol | Meaning in Universal Language of Mind |
|---|---|
| **Waste** *indicates the elimination of what is no longer desired or needed.* | In a dream, waste indicates the elimination of what is no longer desired or needed. In the way man uses his creativity, he is prone to producing unwanted or unusable waste products. Landfills attest to this. However there is another facet to waste. Waste such as the final products resulting from food consumption are natural and actually have a productive use as fertilizing agents. |
| **Water** *represents conscious life experiences.* | Physical water is essential to life on this planet. In the language of mind, water symbolizes the experience in the physical level of consciousness. These are the everyday, waking interactions, situations, and circumstances that arise bringing opportunities for conscious enrichment. How well the conscious mind of the thinker is directed towards its inherent purpose of learning from experiences determines the quality and rate of individual growth and evolution. |
| **Weapons** *represent tools intended to cause change.* | In the Universal Language of Mind, weapons are a means to cause change. When used offensively in a dream, change is being initiated by the dreamer. When used defensively, change is being forced upon the dreamer. |
| **Weeds** *represent undesirable thoughts imaged by the conscious mind and developing in the subconscious existence of the thinker.* | Every gardener or farmer knows well the nemesis of weeds. They steal nourishment from viable plants that have been intentionally planted. In the Universal Language of Mind plants are subconscious knowledge; weeds represent the undesirable thoughts imaged by the conscious mind and developing in the subconscious existence of the thinker. |
| **Well** *symbolizes the cause or source.* | Anything existing in the physical first existed in the inner levels of mind. The painting of the artist or the spaceship of the scientist, thrive in the minds of their creators long before they ever become a physically manifested reality |

| *Derivative Meaning* | *Thoughts to Consider* |
|---|---|
| *Dict.* To bring to desolation; to ravage; to wear away gradually. | Waste in a dream can indicate releasing what is no longer purposeful or spending uselessly, vainly or foolishly. You must determine the meaning of your dream message. Strive to use any and every thing to its fullest, wasting nothing. |
| *Dict. A compound substance consisting of hydrogen and oxygen; a fluid covering about three-fifths of the earth and forming an essential constituent of vegetable and animal organisms.* | How am I using the experiences in my life? Do I wait for life to happen to me, then determine my good fortune or bad luck? Such an attitude creates a victim of life. Do I initiate experiences based upon my desires for a productive, harmonious, and exciting existence? Such an attitude creates an enlightened individual. |
| *Dict. Any instrument of offense or defense; an instrument for contest or for combating enemies.* | Although they have the power to fashion their lives, most people wait for others to cause change. They wait for ultimatums from an employer, a spouse, the government. Don't be like these people. Decide what you want to change, determine how you can make a difference, then initiate the thinking and action that will bring this about. What you think and do does make a difference to your Self and the world. |
| *Dict. That general name of any plant that is useless or troublesome; a plant such as grows where it is not wanted. From Danish* wiede *akin to "doubtful".* | Keep you attention on your desires. Nourish them, giving them your attention and time. Cultivate your thoughts, removing those which are unrelated or detrimental to your ideals. Separating the "wheat from the chaff" frees your mind substance to be used in the fulfillment of desires, accelerating their manifestation in your outer life. |
| *Dict. A spring; a fountain. Greek* wallen *meaning "to boil". Latin* volvo *meaning* | Being able to identify cause in your life is a skill well worth the effort of developing. Most people blame something outside of themselves for the conditions of their lives. They do not realize the |

| Symbol | Meaning in Universal Language of Mind |
|--------|---------------------------------------|
| | that others can experience. Thought is cause. A well in a dream indicates the cause or source. A water well symbolizes the cause or source of conscious life experiences, an oil well is the source of energy. |
| *Widow/Widower symbolizes a commitment between the conscious and subconscious mind that has changed.*<br><br>*Wife is an aspect committed to wholeness. (see spouse)* | When marriage ends because of the death of a partner, it symbolizes a change in the dreamer's commitment to Self. As with many dreams, often the dream teleplay makes no physical sense and has nothing to do with the existing physical condition or facts. This is owing to the symbolic nature of the communication from the inner levels of mind. Dreaming of the death of a spouse does not means that person is physically in danger or will die. It does universally symbolize an inner change that has occurred in the dreamer's consciousness. |
| *Wild signifies something untamed, uncivilized.* | Nature untamed functions according to instinct. For man, this is animalistic because he has the capacity to rise above instinct into reasoning. Reasoning frees intelligence to excel, to cooperate with others, to learn, and to advance evolution. In the language of mind, when something is wild it is in its untamed state, yet to be understood and educated. For instance, a wild child will symbolize an undisciplined new idea; wild animals represent uncontrolled habits. |
| *Wind represents the movement of thoughts.* | In the language of mind, wind represents thoughts. Whether as a dream symbol or as an image used in spiritual literature, wind signifies the movement of intelligence acting upon mind substance by use of prana or energy. Tumultuous winds, storms or tornadoes, indicate restless thoughts in conflict. A gentle breeze indicates calming thoughts that bring peace. |
| *Windmill symbolizes a way to channel the movement of thoughts, an energy transformer.* | There are seven major energy transformers which enable the thinker to continue to exist and to fulfill desires. In Eastern literature, these transformers are known as chakras. Each chakra is a mental recycling center, taking energy used in manifesting desires and returning it back into mind for future creations. A windmill in a dream symbolizes the activity of an energy transformer. |

| *Derivative Meaning* | *Thoughts to Consider* |
|---|---|
| *"to roll"*. | Universal Truth that thought is cause. Understanding this truth and living by it frees you to be Self reliant and enables you to attain excellence in everything you do. |
| *Dict. A person who has lost their spouse by death and who remains still unmarried. Latin* vidua *meaning "deprived, void"*. | What has recently occurred in your life that affects the way you perceive your Self and life? A dream of this nature can indicate a change in your awareness of what is most important to you, or how you want to dedicate your time and energy. It will also indicate the closing of one chapter of your life and the potential initiation of another. Remember death in a dream indicates change. This is a transition period in your life. |
| *Dict. Living in a state of nature; raving at will; growing or produced without culture.* Gothic wiltheis *meaning "an animal that is wild, wandering at its will"*. | Note what is wild in your dream, and research its meaning in the language of mind. This will give you the full meaning of the symbol in your dream. Realize there is a distinct difference between instinct and intuition. Instinct is compulsive learning without the benefit of reasoning. Intuition is the direct grasp of truth, the result of reasoning. |
| *Dict. Air naturally in motion with any degree of velocity.* | What have I been thinking? The kind and quality of your thoughts will directly and immediately affect your perception of your Self and your circumstances. Your attitude is important for it embodies every thought you create. |
| *Dict. A mill driven by the force of the wind and used for grinding corn, pumping water, etc.* | The best way to insure that the energy you have used to fulfill your desires is replenished so you can continue to manifest what you want is to learn from your experiences, to build understandings that replenish the soul. Living for sensory stimulation only drains the mind of energy. Living for soul progression restores the mind's energy. |

| Symbol | Meaning in Universal Language of Mind |
|---|---|
| *Window* *is a means for awareness.* | A window enables light to enter a building and provides viewing of what is outside the structure. In the language of mind a window symbolizes the means for greater awareness of Self. |
| *Wings* *indicate a tool for compulsive subconscious thoughts.* | In the language of mind birds, as with all animals, represent compulsive thoughts. Unlike other animals, birds also represent thoughts from a specific part of mind, the subconscious mind. Wings afford birds the means for mobility. Thus in the language of mind wings signify the motion of compulsive subconscious thoughts. Most often this will indicate instinct. |
| *Woman* *an aspect of Self.* *(see female)* | |
| *Work* *represents how you are choosing to be productive in life to promote your growth and learning.* | Work is effort directed to some purpose or end. Work is a means to provide for the rudimentary needs of Self and others — food, shelter, clothing — and to fulfill the desires of Self. An individual's work is the place for adult learning. When work transcends being just an activity to fulfill physical needs and becoming a means for productivity and creative endeavor, it becomes a place for service and soul progression. In the language of mind, work represents how you are choosing to be productive in life to promote your growth and learning. |
| *World* *symbolizes all aspects of Self and creation.* | The world is the scene of human existence. It is a place of creating which the dreamer experiences and uses for evolutionary development. In the language of mind the world symbolizes creation and all aspects of Self. |

| *Derivative Meaning* | *Thoughts to Consider* |
|---|---|
| *Dict. An opening in the wall of a building for the admission of light or of light and air when necessary. Icelandic* vindauga *meaning "a wind-eye".* | Seek to "see the light" in your experiences. Transform your consciousness by initiating thoughts and actions that will produce an enlightened frame of mind. |
| *Dict. One of the anterior limbs in birds in most cases serving as organs of flight.* | Many people, because they lack education in the nature and workings of inner consciousness, react to life instinctively. They make choices on what they describe as "feelings", without conscious awareness of their own motivation and without reasoning. This symbol indicates a reliance on instinct. Sometimes beneficial, sometimes misinterpreted, instinct has limitations for one capable of reasoning. Instead of relying on this lazy access to subconscious mind, use reasoning to produce intuition which is the direct grasp of truth. |
| *Dict. Exertion of energy, physical or mental; toil, labor; matter upon which one is employed or engaged.* | Do you approach the responsibilities of life with a sense of excitement and joy or one of dread and drudgery? When work appears in your dream it will indicate your general attitude about life. Realize any activity in life can be hard, boring, and undesirable, although necessary. Give meaning to your life by thinking about the purpose of the activities you pursue. A willingness for productivity enriches your learning experiences and accelerates your growth. |
| *Dict. The earth and all created things thereon. Greek* welt *meaning "man-age, the age of man, course of time".* | Note what has been transpiring recently. The events and your attitude toward them are having a profound and significant effect upon every part of your Self. Be sure to attend to the entire dream message for greater insight and suggestion from your subconscious mind. |

| Symbol | Meaning in Universal Language of Mind |
|---|---|
| **Wreck**<br>*signifies ruining*<br>*of constitution.* | A wreck symbolizes the destruction or ruining of constitution. The most common use in a dream involves vehicles. When they are small, such as an automobile, this will symbolize potential dis-ease or disorder of the physical body. The wreck represents the ruining of the constitution of the body which is symbolized by the car. |
| $\mathbb{X}$ | |
| **X-ray**<br>*symbolizes the*<br>*ability to*<br>*perceive the*<br>*essence.* | In the language of mind, x-rays signify the dreamer's capacity to perceive beyond physical appearances. What is beyond the physical is thought; the cause. X-rays in a dream highlight how the dreamer is reaching to determine the origin or essence of what is transpiring in his/her life. |
| $\mathbb{Y}$ | |
| **Yard**<br>*symbolizes*<br>*subconscious*<br>*existence.* | Yards are the planned cultivation of substances that spring from the earth. In the language of mind, earth is subconscious mind substance; yards being a product of the earth represent subconscious existence. In a dream, a yard will indicate the receptive and readied mind substance of the subconscious mind. |

| *Derivative Meaning* | *Thoughts to Consider* |
|---|---|
| *Dict. The destruction of a vessel by being driven ashore; destruction or ruin generally.* | Dreams are messages originating in the inner levels of consciousness, therefore this kind of "health" dream occurs some time before the disease is manifested in the body. Therefore understand the dream message, heed it, and respond accordingly to insure your good health, mentally, emotionally, physically, and spiritually. |
| *Dict. rays generated by the impact of high-speed electrons on metal target; electromagnetic waves of high frequency, very penetrating and able to affect a photographic plate so that they are of great value in medical diagnosis.* | What is the underlying meaning of your experiences? What values and standards do you uphold in your daily activities? These are what you stand upon for they are your under-standings of the nature of life and existence. Think deeply about your choices in life, revealing your true essence and knowing your purpose for being here now. |
| *Dict. A small piece of enclosed ground adjoining a house. Latin hortus meaning "a garden".* | How aware am I of the thoughts I hold toward Self and others? The thoughts you create are re-created in the substance of your subconscious mind. Once "planted" in the subconscious mind they begin a developing process that will culminate in the manifestation of your thoughts. This creative process occurs according to Universal Law and works for desire-thoughts and fear-thoughts alike. Give care to the quality of your thoughts. Make them ideas that you look forward to living. |

| Symbol | Meaning in Universal Language of Mind |
|--------|----------------------------------------|

**Yen**
*represents
exchange of
value. (see
money)*

**Young**
*indicates early
stage of
growth,
immature.*

There are four stages of man: infancy, adolescence, adulthood, and old age or wisdom. When someone in the dream is considered young, this will symbolize the early stages of infancy or adolescence. Characteristic of infancy is the ability to absorb information from the environment; characteristic of adolescence is the ability to experiment in experiencing. These stages transcend physical age. They are indicative of the thinker's progress in learning anything; from the first moment of encounter to the passing on of wisdom gained. In a dream, when an object is deemed young, such as a young animal or young nation, interpret the object's meaning in the language of mind to gain insight into the dream's message.

ℤ

**Zoo**
*represents a
condition of
mind where
habitual
attitudes are
maintained.*

A zoo is a place where animals are removed from their natural habitat, put into a confined area, and cared for and often raised by humans. Animals in a dream represent compulsive ways of thinking. When the thinker has repeated the same thought over and over it becomes a pattern of thinking etched in the neuron pathways of the brain. A zoo in the language of mind will signify the dreamer's tendency to be controlled by habitual patterns of thinking.

| *Derivative Meaning* | *Thoughts to Consider* |
|---|---|

*Dict. Being in the first or early stage of life; not yet arrived at maturity, fresh or vigorous, having little experience.*

Learn to embrace the early stages of growth in any endeavor. When you begin something new be willing to absorb as much as possible from those more adept, those who know what you desire to know. When you have absorbed enough information to be able to use reasoning, begin to imagine the kinds of results you desire and follow through with the activity that will manifest those results. View each conceived experience as an experiment where you can accelerate your learning of what produces your desire. Knowing the four stages of man frees you to learn anything at any time regardless of your physical age.

*Dict. resembling or pertaining to an animal.*

Do you go to work by the same route everyday? Are your conversations with your spouse the same day after day? Free your thinking from compulsive patterns by intentionally pursuing new activities, new relationships, new ways of expressing your Self. Dare to be different than you've ever been before.

# The Dreamer's Dictionary
# Section III

*"Men have conceived a twofold use of sleep:*
*that it is refreshing of the body in this life;*
*that it is preparing the soul for the next."*

John Donne (1573-1631)
*Meditation XV*

## *The Art of Dream Interpretation*
## *Thinking in the Language of Mind*

When I was in the seventh grade of school I took a course in French. After the first ten minutes of class the very first day, we were not allowed to speak English, only French. Our learning of the foreign language was stimulated by filmstrips and physical actions that produced pictures for us to identify and describe with our new vocabulary. Although I didn't know it at the time, I've since learned that this way of teaching a foreign language produces the ability *to think in that language.* Far beyond rote memorization, this type of thinking gives the communicator the freedom to understand physical language more readily and quickly. The result is mental dexterity in producing thought images, the language of the inner mind, and fluency in describing those images with the verbalized sounds representing the words of a physical language. Those who are familiar with several languages in this manner can often recall using them in the dream state. Those who learn a language by rote rarely if ever communicate in that foreign language in their dreams. Their dreams are only in the mother tongue.

As you learn to interpret your dreams, you develop the art of thinking in images. This stimulates the use of both your conscious and subconscious minds. Most people rely solely on the physical part of Self for thinking. In this way they become creatures of habit, clinging to past experiences, and predestining themselves to repeat those past experiences over and over again. Instead of using memory as a component of reasoning, these individuals become dependent on the recall of their own or others' experiences thereby eliminating an essential ingredient for reasoning -- imagination. When the conscious mind uses the will to draw on memory and create with imagination, reasoning is produced. This unlocks the power of the conscious mind and sets the reproductive power of the subconscious mind into motion. You've heard the saying, *"Two heads are better than one."* The same is true for parts of mind.

Since the time that we were created as spirit in the likeness and image of God, our Creator or Spiritual Parent, we have grown in maturity. In discovering what it means to be made in the likeness, with similar attributes, we have formed many facets of ourselves. These facets are revealed to us by the people who appear in our dreams. Each symbolically represents an aspect of a specific part of our Self. As we interpret what each aspect signifies, we find that our *dream-people* relate valuable information concerning the divisions of our mind and the levels of consciousness. As we deepen our understanding of these aspects, we begin to realize what being made in the image means. Now it is time to learn the basics of the language of mind.

The first step in understanding what aspect of Self your dream is revealing to you is to identify the sex of the *dream-person* and their relative position to you. *Dream-people* of the same sex as you are presently experiencing will indicate aspects of your conscious, waking mind. *Dream-people* of the opposite sex will be aspects of your subconscious mind.

Remember our gentleman caller who was concerned about his dreams of infidelity? In his dream he was making love with a female coworker. Because our gentleman is experiencing the male expression in his physical existence, his subconscious mind chose a familiar female and the action of making love to indicate how he is in harmony with this particular subconscious aspect. Remember we have discussed how the conscious and subconscious minds are two halves of a whole. Each has a duty and purpose to fulfill toward each other. When the people in a dream are of the opposite sex and are engaged in sexual activity, it will indicate to the dreamer that those aspects of Self are working together toward a common goal. This dream was telling our gentleman *how* he was manifesting his desires.

As you learn to identify what an aspect symbolizes to you personally, you will discover new doorways to greater Self awareness. Conscious aspects will reflect the ways you think when you are consciously awake *(see Glossary)*. These will tell you how you tend to approach life on a day-to-day basis. The actions that your *dream-people* are performing will tell you if these aspects are productively moving you toward being a whole functioning Self or destructively stagnating your growth and awareness.

When people of the opposite sex appear in your dream, they will represent aspects of your subconscious mind. These aspects serve to inform your conscious mind about the directing intelligence in the subconscious mind. Subconscious aspects and their actions can tell you about understandings you possess that are being used or misused in creating your desires. They will tell you what you have consciously set into motion that is now a part of your subconsciousness. Even more, these *dream-people* will represent the stage of development your manifesting thoughts are in as they seek to make themselves known in your conscious physical life. Learn how to identify the aspects in your dreams and you unlock the creative power of your mind so you can have anything you desire.

As you consider the sex of your *dream-people*, you will also want to consider another factor -- their relative position to you. When a person appears in your dreams who you would recognize as an authority figure in your everyday conscious life, this *dream-person* will be telling you about the part of your mind that is closest to your origin as a thinker, your superconscious mind.

Beyond a definite separation in the inner levels of your consciousness your superconscious mind exists. Beyond the reasoning power of the conscious mind and the intuitive abilities of the subconscious mind lies the part of you that knows where you came from, why you are here, and where you are going. It is your superconscious mind that holds the perfect seed idea, a blueprint, for your maturation as a thinker. Here the idea of what it means to be made in the likeness and image of God has been, is and will remain stored until that idea is manifested and understood. Your superconscious mind houses the Christ Consciousness, the Buddha Consciousness, the Cosmic Consciousness in you. This enlightened part of Self is the inner authority of man.

When a male authority figure appears in your dreams, your subconscious mind is telling you about your conscious awareness of the aggressive action of your superconscious mind. A female authority figure represents the receptive action of your superconscious mind. The action that these dream figures take will give you insight into your soul progression. When interpreted, these dreams will tell you when you are consciously creating experiences with the intent of using and gaining understandings thus fulfilling the duty and purpose of your conscious mind, and when you are causing yourself to be a prisoner of experiences produced by habitual, victim thoughts.

Because the conscious mind holds the responsibility of learning the language of mind to develop inner communication, it is up to you to be honest in your assessment of why particular symbols are used by your subconscious mind. At least part of Sigmund Freud's idea was based in truth. If you have had a "falling out" with your mother, thereby producing anger, resentment or distress in your waking relationship with her, you will be tempted to deny that your *dream-mother* appears as an aspect of your superconscious mind. Be alert to this temptation! Your subconscious mind will use the language of mind to convey to you the state of your conscious awareness, so whether you love or hate your mother when you're awake, she will still represent your superconscious mind in your dreams. Others who will represent your superconscious mind are your father, your employer or supervisor, a teacher, a minister, a doctor, the president of your country, anyone who holds a position of authority relative to your chosen position in life.

Once you have admitted that your *dream-mother* represents your superconscious mind, observe the action of the dream -- the places and things that appear to make the dream move -- *then* begin analyzing in order to comprehend the dream's message.

In our everyday life, we may pass a school building on our way to work day after day, month after month. We can identify the building by a sign denoting that the structure is used as a school. We have learned to associate the word *school* with a place to learn and teach. Until we stop, enter the building, and communicate with someone, we remain oblivious to what in truth is learned and taught at this school. When we become aware of this, and take part in the action of learning and teaching we then have an opportunity for Self growth.

Learning the language of mind and using it in your life is a similar process. We dream many dreams during a lifetime. When we stop to enter into the dream by faithfully recording each detail, then learn to translate the symbols used, communication occurs. Our next step is taking part in the learning available in this communication. Then action can be taken by teaching ourselves to act on or respond to the inner guidance the dream has given us.

It has been said many times that the world is our schoolroom. Because the physical is the farthest level of consciousness from our origin where we have free will, it is up to our conscious minds to respond to the inner mind's urge toward maturity by producing actions that will fulfill that urge. When this is accomplished peace, security, and contentment are achieved.

## The Male Who Became Pregnant
## Interpreting Dream Messages

Because our subconscious mind has at its disposal all the information we have stored in our brains from birth, our dreams are varied in form and content. Imagine the growing command you could possess of a physical language with a daily increase of vocabulary! As we add the images of new people, places and things to our computer-like brain, our subconscious mind's "vocabulary" increases proportionately.

Armed with the cornerstone of understanding *dream-people*, knowing what their sex and relative position to us symbolizes, we are now free to understand more elements of the language of mind. As we recall dreams, we can readily see that the aspects appearing in our dreams come in many shapes, sizes, colors, and likenesses. Made of our own subconscious mind substance, our *dream-people* are formed precisely by our subconscious mind to convey very truthful and precise messages.

It took several years of teaching people to interpret dreams for me to meet the first male who would admit that he dreamed he was pregnant. Yes, in the dream this male was pregnant and giving birth! As he told his classmates the dream, there were giggles, gasps, and a host of reactions from his listeners. I was overjoyed for I knew what his subconscious mind was telling him.

We can all recall dream experiences that would not or do not happen in "real" life. At this stage of development the carrying and birthing of a child remains a feminine ability, so to most this uninterpreted dream experience would be immediately linked to the physical impossibility of a male bearing a child. The result of this kind of physical thinking is to label dreams as strange, weird, crazy, or ridiculous. This is true for those who do not "read" the language of mind.

A child in a dream symbolizes a new idea. The sex of the child will tell you where this new idea is being birthed, in the conscious or subconscious mind. The subconscious mind of my male student was telling him about an important new idea he was consciously creating. This was a most encouraging dream for the student. As he interpreted the rest of the action in his dream, he began to see its meaning in his life. He realized his subconscious mind was letting him know that indeed he was becoming an independent, mature thinker.

This was a young man who had allowed his conscious thinking to be harnessed by his thoughts of pleasing and fearing his father. He had actively been creating and pursuing in his life only those things that he believed would bring praise from his physical parent. As a result, he was attending a college he did not enjoy, engrossed in a course of study that did not interest him so he produced mediocre grades, engaged to a woman he did not want to spend his life with but who was socially acceptable, and a practicing hypocrite when it came to religion. The week before his "pregnant" dream, he had started action on changing colleges according to the course of study he wanted to pursue, he had broken the engagement to the woman and begun to evaluate his religious beliefs taking them much more seriously. This student was birthing new ideas that indeed were his own. His dream was a well-earned compliment.

Since people in our dreams represent aspects of ourselves, our *dream-people* will tell us how we are consciously guiding the action that affects our conscious, subconscious, and superconscious minds. In this way, *dream-people* often seem to have a life of their own. As you begin to take a more serious look at what your dreams have to offer, you will probably begin to remember dreams that include many people you do not know. As this occurs, pay close attention to the role they play and their actions in the dream. Also note your reaction to them *during* the dream. Was this unknown *dream-person* a lawyer, a doctor, a policeman? This will tell you the role of the aspect. In these examples the aspect would deal with understanding Universal Law, healing or discipline respectively. What action did they take in the dream? If the doctor was operating on your best friend, who is of the opposite sex, this would symbolize healing in the subconscious mind under the direction of the superconscious mind. Once you determined which aspect of you your best friend symbolizes you would identify the quality of self needing and receiving healing. When consciously aware of the message in your dream you would be able to cooperate and show more conscious initiative in aiding this healing process within your mind.

Many times people will report a dream where some unknown assailant has attacked or stolen something valuable from them. These dreams can be frightening when left uninterpreted. If the assailant is the same sex as you are experiencing, the dream will be talking about an unfamiliar conscious aspect. These unfamiliar conscious aspects are keys to unlock the chain that restricts our ability to fully use the power in the conscious mind. Admit their existence and you have the key. Identify which aspect of Self it is and you use the key to remove limitations in your awareness.

We have identified a *dream-thief* as an unfamiliar aspect who is taking from the rest of Self causing us to miss valuable opportunities. This kind of dream activity usually indicates that we are taking an important part of Self for granted. Of all the sins man is capable of committing, taking the Self for granted ranks among the greatest for it destroys Self awareness. To further discover what we are taking for granted in ourself, look to see how the *dream-thief* expressed him or her self. Was he abrasive, sly, apologetic? This will give you insight into the aspect of you that is taking from the Self. If he was abrasive, look to see how you are unconsciously abrasive. Perhaps you adamantly reject compliments, thereby stealing from your own awareness the talents and skills unique to you that could be put to use for attaining your desires. If he was sly, look to see how you are unconsciously clever in your thoughts and actions. Perhaps you manipulate others into doing things for you because you fear the challenge, thereby promoting weakness in you and stealing your own awareness of abilities toward Self reliance. If he was apologetic, begin to admit the times you apologize out of habit thereby denying truth as you see it.

As you become aware of these previously unfamiliar aspects of Self you will begin to determine an action of conscious thinking that is productive toward what you want in life. By paying attention to unfamiliar dream aspects, you will endow your conscious mind with newfound awarenesses daily. Life will cease to be a burdened drudgery of endless battles. It will become an exciting purposeful adventure as you learn to use the wisdom from the inner levels of your own mind. Indications that you are accomplishing this will appear in your dreams. When you appear in a dream with other aspects and you are controlling the action in the dream, this conveys to your conscious mind that you, as you see your Self, are taking charge of these parts of Self.

Remember the woman from Kansas City who feared her dream was precognitive? For fifteen years the meaning of her dream was misunderstood in her conscious mind. The comprehension of how she could understand and productively use her dream was foreign to her. When anything is foreign to our pattern of conscious thinking, the line of least resistance is to try to deny its existence. Denial requires time, energy and great amounts of effort with very little intelligent direction. Denial's benefits are poverty, disease, pestilence, and famine in our inner and outer worlds. For our KC lady, these manifested in fearing that the dream would come true, doubting her ability to consciously control herself and her car, and so deciding she just wouldn't drive. As she became aware of the meaning of her dream, she realized she no longer needed to be a slave to her fear. Her first step was conquering denial by admitting that her dream experience was about her state of consciousness rather than a forecast of impending physical doom. Identifying each reaction -- the fear, doubt, and refusal to act -- produced awareness of her self-imposed limitations that had literally ruled her life for fifteen years. With the responsibility in her own hands, she could then begin to use her newfound information to rebuild her confidence and discipline to be able to drive an automobile again.

Discipline is a key to Self awareness. Self discipline produces security, character, integrity, dependability, determination, and a host of positive attributes. Although most would agree that childhood discipline is an important part of the maturing process from infancy to adolescence and from adolescence into adulthood, we can also probably remember times when we failed to see the need for discipline. Perhaps this was when, as a child, we wanted to go to a neighbor's by ourselves or eat cookies instead of supper, or when in adolescence we wanted to borrow the family car or hitchhike across the country. Discipline is the training that develops Self control or what your father might have told you was character. The word is derived from the word *disciple*, meaning a pupil or follower of any teacher or school of thought. As we strengthen our thinking ability we approach life experiences as lessons in the physical world. As we endeavor to master our Self, we discover more and more inner disciples. This is accomplished by using the aspects of Self we are familiar with and identifying those that at one time eluded our awareness.

Your growing mastery will be indicated when you, as you see your Self, appear in the dream and you are determining the *dream-action*, much like a parent instructs a child or a boss sets the direction for his employees. This type of dream will signify your growing command of discipline. When you are fighting discipline in your waking conscious mind, you will have dreams of being a victim of other aspects of Self. This indicates your need to take control of these aspects of Self, putting them to use toward what you desire rather than being a slave to them.

During a question and answer period at a lecture I gave at a university in Texas, a woman described a type of dream I have heard many times. In the dream, she was riding in the backseat of the family car. Her husband was driving and she was telling him where she wanted to go. She was also telling him to go faster or slower. He wasn't listening to her. The lady thought the dream strange since in her everyday life her husband drives his own car and rarely drives the family car. As she began to discover what you already know, that the dream was about her, it began to make more sense. This subconscious message revolved around her reliance upon the subconscious mind to give direction and control to her physical body. We have already discussed that the subconscious mind does control autonomic functions of the body until the conscious mind understands how to regulate the breathing, heartbeat, and function of each system. A key element in this dream was the woman telling her husband how to drive and his refusal to listen to her. This indicates the lady's conscious desire to take control of the body without the full responsibility.

As it turned out, this woman had been in and out of the hospital several times in the months preceding this dream. She could see that she would become very motivated to produce physical health, care for her body, and *"do the things I should do"* several days or weeks after her hospital stays. She had even been taught ways to cause relaxation during her hospital stays which she would immediately practice. However, this desire waned in a short period of time and she was back to relying on her subconscious mind to do what she thought her conscious mind was too undisciplined and weak to accomplish. Thus to her conscious mind she would perceive her subconscious mind as paying her informed and fitful efforts no attention. I assured her that as she developed purpose for her conscious use of what she had learned to improve her physical health, she would be able to sustain her motivation. Her subconscious mind would heed and support her conscious efforts. Then she would find herself driving the car in her dreams.

This dream brings up another manifestation of aspects that is worthy of noting. Marriage in a dream represents the conscious union of your outer Self with your inner Self. When you are experiencing marriage in the physical, you have chosen to enter the course of study in life's schoolroom that can be simply described as commitment to Self. The physical situation of a male and female living, working, playing, sharing, and cooperating together is an excellent place to gain understanding of your relationship with your own subconscious mind. In fact, the marriage made in heaven as spoken of in the beginning of the Bible is between the man, symbolizing subconscious mind, and woman, symbolizing conscious mind. If you recall, the man leaves his mother and father, symbolizing the superconscious mind, and clings to his wife and the two become one flesh. This is why there is a separation between the superconscious mind, and the subconscious and conscious minds. When we cause our conscious and subconscious minds to function in harmony, with one ideal and purpose, we experience the discovery of our true soulmate. Therefore for those of us who are married in our physical lives, when our spouse appears in a dream this will relate information to our conscious minds about our commitment to our subconscious mind. Your *dream-spouse* will tell you much more about the inner workings of your subconscious mind than any other subconscious aspect. Your *dream-spouse* and his/her activities will tell you how you consciously view your relationship with your inner Self.

Consider the following dream: You find yourself in a meadow with your beloved, enjoying a clear, warm spring day. Suddenly the scene is transformed and you are in a church about to take your wedding vows. You turn, expecting to see the shining face of your beloved, and find yourself holding hands with a stranger, someone you have never seen before! How would you interpret this dream and what would it indicate about your state of awareness? To understand your dreams, you must go beyond merely looking up the symbols in this dictionary. You must be willing to learn how to communicate in the language your subconscious mind speaks. Giving attention to your dreams, seeing them as a valuable asset available to you for greater insight, and using the meaning you derive from your nightly communication, are acts of commitment to Self that culminate in greater and greater strides in Self awareness.

Some people dream about former loves — ex-husbands, ex-girlfriends — long past the time of their physical association. They wonder why these people who no longer hold an important place in their lives suddenly reappear. Dreaming of a person from your past brings your attention to the need to use and express particular qualities that you specifically associate with that person. Relationships with others throughout our lives provide us with the oppotunity to learn by realizing and developing particular qualities. Sometimes the full benefit of what was gained from earlier experiences is left behind with the physical part of the relationship. When there is no one presently in the dreamer's life who reflects this quality, the subconscious mind will draw upon information stored in the brain during an earlier time period in order to get its message across. Thus you may dream about a former love, your first employer, or a grade school teacher.

The people in your dream reveal the qualities of Self; the action in your dream reveals the manner of thinking. For instance, a common dream revolves around taking a test in school and realizing you are unprepared. The school represents a place where learning can occur. Opportunities for learning are available every day as a result of your chosen experiences. It is your responsiblity to learn from these experiences, adding to your soul's understanding of creation. To dream of being unprepared for a test indicates the need to assimilate and use the information received from daily experiences. A test is a means of drawing forth what has been learned; an evaluation. To have an experience without producing understanding from it perpetuates ignorance of the purpose for existence. This dream brings attention to the dreamer's need to use what has been received from life's experiences for greater Self awareness.

Sometimes the *dream-action* can be unsettling such as dreaming of drowning in water. The earth is 75% water. The physical body is over 70% water. As physical beings we exist and live in water. In our dreams, water represents conscious life experiences. Your dreams of water reflect back to you how you exist on a day-to-day basis. These dreams provide an image of being deluged by water in various ways indicating the dreamer's thought pattern of being overwhelmed by life and daily experiences. How can the dreamer use this message to improve his life? By setting ideals for Self and acting upon them, the dreamer can begin taking control of Self in everyday experiences. If you have these kinds of dreams, whenever you feel overwhelmed or like you are struggling, bring your ideals to the forefront of your mind and act upon them. You will no longer feel a need to escape from life. Your dreams will change to a more pleasant scene; perhaps you are paddling down a river or sailing on the ocean, very much in control of your existence.

Another common *dream-action* involves losing teeth. Teeth are used to chew food so it can be transformed into usable energy for the body. In a dream, food represents knowlege which can be transformed into usable energy for the mind. In this dream, the attention is being drawn to the need to use the knowledge received for enriching the mind. It is difficult to accomplish this when the proper equipment, as symbolized by the teeth, is lacking. A productive response to this dream would be to imagine purposes for the goals in life. Receiving knowledge with an intention of putting it into practice for the betterment of Self and others, insures the productive use of the knowledge available.

Dreams will reveal how we think, what we think about, and why we think as we do. Your thoughts and attitudes are the most important elements in your life. Your attitude determines your success or failure, your pleasure or pain, your health or disability. Your attitude determines the quality of your life regardless of the physical situations surrounding you. Being rich does not bring happiness; being poor does not bring sorrow. To believe that the physical situations dictate your worth, security, and peace is to confine your soul to the wheel of rebirth. Your dreams are opportunities to learn, opportunities to experience beyond the limitations of the physical Self. Heeding the messages sent by your subconscious mind expands your consciousness bringing the awareness that thought is indeed cause. Your attitude about your Self and your life makes you more than just a winner or loser, it can make you a master of spiritual Enlightenment.

## *Accessing Subconscious Capabilities*

Eventually, just as a great writer can achieve command of a physical language to express his ideas in a way we might view as genius, you can become proficient in your use of the language of mind producing clairvoyance. Clairvoyance is the result of using the five physical senses to produce the sixth sense. This sixth sense is the sense of the mind, used spontaneously by most, used purposefully by great Masters. To be clairvoyant is to free your self from the bonds of sense-slavery by producing the knowing that comes with understanding the inner workings of your mind.

To be clairvoyant is to consciously possess that incredible sense of freedom at one time achieved only sporadically in experiences like flying dreams.

Not long ago, a woman told me a story about her best friend. The woman was pregnant and her best friend called to tell her she had had a dream that the woman would have twins, a male child and one female. The woman was surprised and amazed when several months later she did indeed give birth to twins, a boy and a girl.

"How did my friend know?" she asked.

Clairvoyance is a French word translated into English as *clear seeing*. It denotes the ability to use the inner subconscious mind to honestly perceive the past, present and probable future. In this case, the woman's friend had remembered a dream experience that conveyed the probable future based on the present situation and circumstances. When this type of experience occurs during conscious sleep, we say we had a precognitive dream. Precognitive dreams bring our conscious waking attention to the supernatural and supernormal abilities we each possess but rarely develop and fully use.

To understand this and other abilities of the whole mind that lie dormant and latent, we begin by identifying and understanding the parts that comprise the unit. The part of mind that demonstrates the ability of clairvoyance is the subconscious mind. This is the same part of mind that creates what we consciously remember as dreams.

When we go to sleep at night, our conscious attention is drawn away from the five physical senses and the activity of our day. Our mental attention goes into the inner levels of consciousness within the subconscious levels of existence. Most of the time, we are unaware that we knocked the covers off the bed, or a siren passed by, or we disturbed our bed partner. We experience what is known as sleep, a temporary state of consciousness characterized by lack of awareness of the outer world around us and many times ignorance of the inner world within us as well. When we do have awareness of what is occurring in our inner world, we awake with the memory of a dream.

As we build the rapport between our inner and outer minds, we begin developing awareness of the vast abilities natural to the subconscious mind. Precognition is one of these abilities. There are many ways that precognition is used with little attention in our physical everyday lives. Think of the times you have planned vacations and have produced the expected experience weeks or months later. Think of marriage plans that were made and did culminate in the wedding day, or acting on a desire to receive excellent grades in a course of study. These are just some examples of how we use this ability of precognition in our everyday waking state. These are examples so common that we take them for granted, losing sight of the precognitive ability of our minds. For this reason, most people only recognize the precognitive workings of their minds when they involve someone else. Rather than desire to gain new awarenesses being the impetus for realization, fear of what we do not want to occur becomes the motivating force for remembering. Thus we note pre-knowledge of someone's death, a plane crash, losing a career promotion, or other foretold disasters, ignoring the many times the precognitive ability was giving us pre-sight of desired events.

Once we begin to appreciate and understand how precognition works in our lives, we strengthen our ability to use precognition in ways like the woman who predicted twins. When we fail to use fully what we already experience in our lives, we often react with fear, which makes us a slave to the mind's potential rather than a Master of it.

I have seen many people enter the course of study in the School of Metaphysics because they experience precognitive dreams that have never been explained. Having so few answers to their questions, most of these people have self-described negative attitudes toward this ability. Having no understanding or control of their precognition, it is viewed more often as a curse than a blessing.

I remember a student who first experienced his own precognition when he dreamed that his wife drowned in an unexpected boating accident. Several months later during a gathering of friends at a nearby lake, the event actually occurred. He remembered having the dream and thought little more about it until a similar event took place.

This time he dreamed of his mother dying in her home. When this dream came to pass in the physical, he dismissed it as "it was time, after all she was in her eighties." When the same type of experience occurred a third time, this one involving the heart attack of a close coworker in his forties, he began to think something was seriously wrong. Why did he have this pre-knowledge of events when others did not? He began to attempt to repress the memory of his dreams from fear that they might be previews of coming events. Possessing this type of knowledge was so far removed from what is habitually ordinary, he believed there must be something wrong or evil about it. To him, denying dreams was a matter of self preservation because he had begun to believe in some way he must be responsible for these physical happenings since he knew they would happen beforehand.

This type of thinking is frequently present in people who experience precognitive dreams and have yet to learn how and why they occur. After a time, the idea of informed responsibility causes such a burden of guilt that they cease talking about their dreams to anyone and attempt to deny the experiences altogether. Because there is still the desire to understand how and why this occurs, their attempts at denial become relentless memories that consume their waking thoughts as if they were possessed by a demon that will not let go.

Since denial only adds power to what we do not understand, the answer lies in conscious enlightenment of what is taking place and why. The duty of the subconscious mind is fulfill any conscious command when allowed. Denial does interferes with the true nature of the Self for it does not allow the inner mind to perform its function. The many ways the subconscious mind can offer assistance can only be restricted by the conscious limitations we imagine and place upon it.

When the inner and outer minds enjoy communion, they can work in accord for the fulfillment of any conscious desire. Working with your dreams strengthens this communion and both minds are free to perform their duties unimpaired. Gathering experiences in the physical plane of existence, not denying them, is the duty of our conscious minds. The conscious mind also has a purpose to fulfill. As we consciously create our desires -- the experience of owning a home, enjoying a family, achieving a position in our career -- we are responsible in our conscious minds for *understanding* the nature of that experience.

For instance, let's say you desire a new car. You can consciously imagine the kind, make, model and year of car you desire. You can even create in your mind's eye the color and type of upholstery. With your mind in directed action, you have set a goal for an experience that you consciously desire. When you begin to extend your thinking to include how owning the car will benefit you as an individual, you add to this goal your purposes for fulfilling your desire. This means you begin to imagine what you will be like when you possess the car. What will be the difference *in you* when you derive a 1973 Chevrolet that needs painting and when you drive a new 1995 Mercedes? Will you have more confidence, carry yourself with greater pride, respond differently to the attention you may receive? How will you use attaining that physical thing to make *you* different?

This is purpose. And this kind of thinking builds understandings. As your thinking is extended to include purpose for your goals, your consciousness expands and you begin to transform goals for physical acquisition into imaged ideals for greater Self awareness, for learning and growth. When this occurs, you become aware of your purpose for existing in the physical plane. Whatever physical attainment is achieved -- money, possessions, position, associations, friendships, children, fame -- they will all be left behind when you complete your sojourn of this lifetime. They are temporal and therefore do not hold lasting value to your Real Self. How you acquire these physical conditions and how you respond to them once you have them in your life, opens the doors for greater understanding that will become a permanent part of your soul. With ever-deepening thinking, you realize it is the freedom you experience by making and using money that is important. It is the creativity stimulated in and expressed by acquiring and using possessions that adds to your Self. It is the intelligence and determination utilized in your life's work which enriches the soul. It is the love, respect, discipline, and cooperation gained through relationships with others which builds understandings. It is the authority and wisdom born from fame that is important to the Self. These qualities that increase the Self are permanently stored in your subconscious mind. Their pursuit by the conscious mind enables the subconscious mind to fulfill its purpose -- retaining your understandings in permanent memory.

Because human man has progressed in his use of reasoning, when we incarn into a physical body we bring with us this storehouse of understandings previously gained. These understandings are at our disposal to be put to use, rather than consciously misinterpreted by remaining in ignorance, fear, and doubt. Individuals who *remember* precognitive dreams have progressed in their soul's evolution to a point that it is important to develop and use their minds more fully. It becomes that person's responsibility to his or her Self to explore the how's and why's causing this experience. Because there is free will in the conscious waking existence of human man, we each have this opportunity to explore, learn and understand, or to fight, deny and remain a victim of our own potential.

In our physical existence, we measure time by the amount of activity we can perform from the time the sun rises to the time it sets. In the subconscious mind time is measured not by experiences, rather by understandings. This gives our subconscious mind the ability to move freely into what the conscious mind recognizes as the past, present, and probable future. What is perceived in the subconscious mind sometimes catches the attention of the conscious mind in the dream state. When this occurs and physical time finally catches up, we say we have had a precognitive dream.

In the case of the gentleman who experienced precognitive dreams of friend and family members dying, these were consciously remembered subconscious experiences that could be used to aid him in preparing for what would probably occur. As long as these messages remained misunderstood in his conscious mind, they served as a seed for fear, guilt, and anger. This is why he became ambivalent toward his ability seeing it as a curse rather than a blessing. The responsibility of pre-knowledge of probabilities was not in causing those physical occurrences, rather the responsibility was in consciously determining what action would be taken based on the information received.

When I was directing a SOM center in Wichita, Kansas, some years ago, I read a front page headline story in the local paper about a man who had a precognitive dream nine days earlier about a Boeing 727 crashing, resulting in the loss of many lives. When the man awoke he had sketchy pieces of information: numbers on the plane but no airline denotation, description of the airport but no city. He did have recognition of the faulty part that caused the plane to be out of control. The dream was so profoundly real to him that he contacted the local authorities, who referred him to the Federal Aviation Agency. Because he did not have every detail required by the FAA, and because human man habitually tends to doubt the awesome power of his mind, his information was recorded and largely ignored. Until the actual physical event transpired.

When the information from his phone calls was reviewed, the details he had reported were verified and after much research and money spent, the physical reason for the crash was reported by the investigation team. This, too, was the same as the man had described several days before the actual crash occurred. These types of experiences happen daily for thousands of people around the world. This individual showed great courage in sharing his precognitive dream. As reported, he though it was his responsibility to share what he knew with people in a position to use the information.

It is true that each of us isresponsible for the use and development of our minds. How much we master our minds by understanding how and why the mind functions will produce greater control and responsibility in the use of our mental capacities.

With each of these instances of precognitive dreams, we are aware that we do have the ability to change what may initially appear as fate. We can realize that we always have the availability to change and control our own mental attitude about our physical experiences. This brings us to the importance of knowing the language of mind. As we sharpen our conscious ability to receive and retain the messages given by our subconscious minds in dreams, we give ourselves the key to identifying with our souls. As we become more proficient in communicating in the language of mind we also gain the awareness we need to know about what action we are willing to take and be responsible for in what we perceive with mind.

When we know the language of mind, we also know that even when a dream proves to be precognitive, it is still a message for us and about us as individuals. This is why interpreting dreams is important in our lives.

## Steps for Using the Language of Mind

With practice you will gain confidence in using your dreams for the wealth of inner guidance they provide. Identifying the details will give you the basic text for study and application in your everyday life. Learning how to put the elements of your subconscious mind's messages together will take time and practice. Responding to the meaning in your dreams will free you to expand your awareness of your whole Self.

Keep in mind the nine steps to using the language of mind:

*1. Have a dream.* Remember dreams are real. Recurring throughout each sleep cycle, all you need to do is become aware of their presence. If you have difficulty remembering your dreams, try this. Before going to sleep, write down in your dream journal "It is my conscious desire to remember my dreams for my soul progression." Read this aloud, then put the next day's date on your steno pad in expectation of the morning's memory. This conveys your sincere desire to listen to what your inner Self has to say, and gives a conscious command to your subconscious mind which will work on your behalf for the fulfillment of your desire.

*2. Develop conscious concentration skills to experience the dream fully.* The more details you consciously remember, the more detailed the information for you to use will be. In this way, you will receive clearer and more complete messages. Practice focusing your attention on one object or thought at a time *during your waking state.* Too many people pride themselves on dividing their attention. They do not realize they are scattering the mind's intelligence and energy. By employing mental concentration, you will readily access the information being placed into or retrieved from your computer-brain.

*3. Place the information in your brain so you can draw upon it at will.* To improve dream recall, practice using memory in your waking life. The memory you want to build is in your conscious, waking existence. By directing your undivided attention to what is at hand you add the full reception of this experience to the information stored in your brain. How you store information determines what will be available for later use. With focused attention you will store *all* information available to you, thus recall becomes much easier.

*4. Recall the dream experience.* Immediately upon awakening, be ready with pen and pad. Record your dream. All the details will be fresh in your mind, and each part of the dream is significant. With practice, you'll discover that the memory of one dream will stimulate the memory of other dreams which occurred earlier in the sleep cycle.

*5. Decipher the symbols.* Use your a, b, c's to identify the universal elements in your dream. Refer to the dictionary section of this book for assistance. A teacher fluent in the Universal Language of Mind will aid you in mastering the language.

*6. Combine the symbols.* Form thought-words and thought-sentences by using reasoning so you understand the complete meaning of the message. Keep in mind, dreams are a spiritual-mental phenomenon; in order to understand their message think spiritually and mentally! Also, remember to cause your conscious mind to be honest.

*7. Determine how the dream relates to your life now.* Analyze your conscious thinking and action in relationship to the new insight you have gained from interpreting your dream. In this way you are fulfilling the purpose of dreaming in your life. Be open minded using the power in your conscious mind -- reasoning.

*8. Determine the action you will take with your newfound insight.* Choose how you will add to your whole Self by using the information given in your dream. Avail your Self of knowledge and application that will produce understanding and wisdom in how the mind functions and why.

*9. Be receptive to feedback from your subconscious mind.* Your subconscious mind will supply you with feedback to the change you are making in your thinking. Be alert to this inner truth, for it will aid you in fulfilling your desires.

As you use these nine steps repeatedly, you will become adept at communicating in the language of mind. Your dreams will still entertain you. Now they will also serve as keys to greater and greater Self awareness. After many nights of recording dreams, eventually you will have a mental novel recounting the history of your inner life and your soul progression.

As your curiosity and awareness of your dream grows, so will your temptation to tamper with the scene, theme, characters, and script of your dreams. Many times I have talked with people who have discovered they can cause the action in their dreams to stop or change at will. This is a capability we all possess and it can be refined into a productive skill that will further your soul progression. What is often missing in the awareness of the curious is the understanding of the language of mind and how the inner levels of consciousness function. For this reason I advocate learning to control your dream under the guidance of a teacher who is skilled in this art. In this way, you will fully understand the changes you are causing by making your dreams do what you want.

Remember how you learned to drive a car? By riding in a car from a young age you became familiar with the motion of the vehicle. As you grew older and began to set goals for driving, you watched the driver more closely. You noticed things you'd never noticed before, where the key was placed, what made the car stop and go, what you would need to do to signal a turn or to make the car go in reverse. With these pieces of information gained from someone who knew how to use an automobile, it was still helpful to have an experienced driver giving you instruction at the time you were first behind the wheel of a car.

This is true of using the inner levels of consciousness. Instruction in how and why the whole mind and its parts operate as they do is intrinsic in gaining the mastery of mind you desire. For when you change something in your dream state, you change something in the inner levels of your consciousness that will eventually manifest in your physical life.

A young man attending a lecture on dreams told of a dream where a tiger was about to attack him. He became aware that he was dreaming and chose to create a *dream-gun* so he could kill the tiger, which he did. He was amazed and pleased at this newfound ability and most insistent about his ability to control his dream. I discussed the meaning of his dream, affirming his ability to control the action in the dream. Then I asked a simple question, "Do you know what habit you have changed and are you ready for the manifestation of that change in your life?" The man stopped his thoughts. He had not considered that his action in his dream would have any repercussions other than the immediate thrill of being able to manipulate his dream state.

When we fail to interpret the dream so we know the content and subject matter, we are tampering with the inner level manifestation of thoughts we have already set into motion. When we change the structure, quality and element of these thoughts to something different, the original thoughts cease to exist. The new thought structure will continue to manifest through the inner levels until it becomes visible to the physical eye in our lives.

Upon further discussion, the young man realized that the animal in his dream represented his habit of running five miles each morning. The original subconscious message had been telling him that he was losing control of a habit. Since he had changed the dream by killing the tiger, he had changed the habit in the inner levels of his own consciousness. The habit no longer existed in its previous form. Since the time of the dream, the man had begun to notice that he could not run as far as before without becoming tired, winded, and experiencing pain in his muscles. He had indeed taken control of the habit but without conscious awareness of what inner transformation he had caused, therefore he experienced the pain and discomfort that occurs when change is forced upon outer consciousness. Had he allowed the dream message to run its course, he would have received the full message his subconscious mind was offering which might have included insights into how the habit was controlling him and what actions he could take as a response for greater conscious productivity. Because he interfered, in effect interrupting the subconscious mind while it was speaking, he discarded the message by refusing to fully receive it.

As we avail ourselves of those who have gained mastery of the language of mind, we can learn to approach controlling the dream state with confidence and knowing. Our dreams become a step in speeding our spiritual growth as well as enhancing the quality of our daily lives. We can learn to control our dreams with awareness of what will manifest, thus preparing ourselves consciously to respond rather than react to the changes.

This ability is produced with study, application, and skill of using the conscious mind first, then expanding the awareness to include the inner levels of consciousness. We train our conscious minds with Self discipline which produces the ability to use the inner levels of mind at will. As this talent is built we further our objective of enlightenment -- the ability to function in all levels of consciousness simultaneously. This ability has been demonstrated time and again by all the great Spiritual Masters of the world. It is this enlightenment that gave Jesus the ability to heal, Gautama the ability to drink poison without harm, Zarathustra the ability to expel demons, and Quetzlcoatl the ability to control the rain. In fact all holy scriptures of the world were penned in the Universal Language of Mind, the same language your subconscious mind uses for communication. Once you become fluent you will be able to read and interpret the inner Truths of all holy scriptures and you will realize they are all describing the same Universal Laws and Principles that guide mankind's evolving awareness as a spiritual being.

The desire for mastery is part of the inner urge within each of us. This inner urge is present at any age, in any incarnation. The key to responding to your inner urge is ever present within you when you understand the Universal Language of Mind.

# The Dreamer's Dictionary
# Glossary & Index

# Glossary of Frequently Used Terms

## Activity
is motion, the mobilization and use of energy. Can describe mental action or physical action. All activity begins with a thought. Walking is a response to a conscious thought, the desire to move; the heart beating is a response to subconscious thought. Activity is the third element of the equation for success: *Ideal + Purpose + Activity = Success.*

## Aspect
is an identifiable and descriptive quality of the individual. Described as characteristics, an aspect could be a schoolgirl/boy, a peacemaker, a devil's advocate, a loner, a cheater. As qualities, an aspect is defined by the manner of expression. These qualities can be positive, producing harmony, or negative, producing discord. The quality of thought will motivate the action. A list of possible qualities that will define an aspect include:

| Positive Aspects | Negative Aspects |
|---|---|
| trustworthy | suspicious |
| compassionate | indifferent |
| disciplined | lazy |
| creative | unimaginative |
| responsible | unreliable |
| courageous | cowardly |
| patient | anxious |
| determined | hesitant |
| humorous | depressing |
| loyal | uncommitted |
| obedient | headstrong |
| perceptive | ignorant |
| innovative | sterile |
| intuitive | assumptive |
| generous | selfish |
| supportive | critical |
| gregarious | reticent |
| courteous | rude |
| honorable | unethical |
| frugal | miserly |
| peaceful | violent |
| concentrated | scattered |
| resourceful | inept |
| respectful | insolent |
| purposeful | aimless |
| charismatic | repulsive |
| intelligent | dull |
| cooperative | cutthroat |
| committed | vacillatory |
| idealistic | uninventive |
| adaptable | stubborn |
| confident | insecure |
| practical | useless |
| helpful | detrimental |
| integrity | deceit |

## Assimilation

is the mental process of incorporating information, knowledge, experience, or understanding as a part of the thinking. Accomplished through reflection, discrimination, reasoning, and integration. Mental calmness and peace is required for full assimilation of what is being learned through experiences. This state of mind begins with mental relaxation, a stilling of the thoughts through focused attention and will power.

## Attention

is the application of the mind to objects presented to its contemplation. Attention is the only sense of the mind. The physical body has five senses for the receiving of stimuli. The mind has only one. Attention enables the mind to receive impressions from both the inner and outer environment. Undivided attention requires the employment of the will to focus the mind on a single object or thought. Undivided attention sustained for a prolonged period of time is known as concentration.

## Attitude

is a mental posture or position which produces a specific result reflective of its quality. An attitude is a particular arrangement of thoughts, either generally or specifically. A positive attitude is descriptive of the former; a compassionate attitude or an arrogant attitude are examples of the latter. Attitudes are thoughts in motion that will seek to manifest themselves through action or, as a last resort, the physical body of their creator.

## Awareness

is the ability to be cognizant. Man is the only life form on earth that demonstrates the capacity for sentience. This facility to be self-conscious gives man the aptitude for Self realization, ultimately leading to full awareness known as a state of Enlightenment and exhibited by all great master teachers throughout history.

## Condition of Mind

describes a state of consciousness presently existing. The condition of the mind is the result of the quality and kind of thoughts the individual creates, holds, or allows to exist. Related thoughts create patterns of thinking in the mind. Thoughts which comprise the individual's general outlook on self and life produce a frame of mind. The condition of the mind changes according to the calibre and frequency of thoughts. A natural condition of the mind is stillness although most find the condition of their minds to be characterized by scatteredness or turmoil owing to conflicting, restless thoughts.

## Conscious Existence

is the state of being as experienced by the physical mind. It is comprised of the day-to-day waking experiences we call life. Conscious existence includes all parts of physically manifested creation — from people to places to things.

## Conscious Experience

is the background, experience, or training acquired by the conscious mind through the use of the physical body and senses. Experiencing in the physical world is the function of the conscious part of the mind. Experience is gained by putting the mind into directive action through conscious reasoning.

## Conscious Mind

is intelligence as it expresses in the physical level of consciousness. This is the part of mind capable of Self awareness. The conscious mind works directly with the brain and physical body, using them to experience the external world. This enables the thinker to gather experience for the purpose of gaining understanding. The power in the conscious mind is reasoning.

## Consciousness

is immediate knowledge as given in sensation and perception. It is the faculty of knowing the causes and effects of what goes on in one's own mind. Man's consciousness originates as spirit. From its source, consciousness extends outward, slowing in vibratory rate, and enabling the thinker to produce with and by thought. The extension of consciousness is comprised of seven major transformations described as the seven levels of consciousness. (See mind diagram)

## Destructive Attitude

is a mental posture undermining the individual's quest for understanding and wholeness. An attitude is a particular arrangement of thoughts. Thoughts of worthlessness, ignorance, condemnation, hatred, restlessness, restrictiveness, passivity, dominance, selfishness, are examples of attitudes which are destructive to the Self and others. Such ideas reflect a lack of understanding which produces an incomplete use of the Universal Laws of Creation resulting in disharmony, discord, violence, and ultimately death.

## Dream

is a communication from the subconscious mind to the waking mind occurring during sleep and concerning the conscious state of awareness. This communication is needed to insure the mental, emotional, and physical well-being of the dreamer. Dreams are relayed in the native language of the inner, subconscious mind, called the Universal Language of Mind. The conscious mind must learn this language in order for messages to be received, understood, and a response made. Dreams occur within ninety-minute cycles throughout each sleeping period. Physical evidence that a dream is transpiring can be measured by brain wave activity or noted by rapid eye movements of the body, as if the dreamer is "seeing" action not physically present.

## Existence

is the state of being. For something to exist is must have being whether in form of matter or of spirit. From the mind of man to the cells of his body to atoms, all find existence in their capacity to be, to live, to continue to have life. Existence is one of the two principles found in every expression of creation.

## Habit

is mental or physical action accomplished without the benefit of conscious thought. Habits are patterns of thought established through repetition which create neuron pathways in the brain. Most often habits are patterns meant to increase mental and physical efficiency, such as walking. As a child learns to walk a considerable amount of attention and time is invested in mastering the mental and physical actions required. Once learned, the ability to walk seems automatic because it requires little thought to accomplish. Although such habits are time savers, they are not a replacement for conscious reasoning and response. For instance, when walking is taken for granted an individual may stumble causing injury to the body due to the lack of mental attention given. In this way, the individual realizes the value of habit does not lie in an escape from thinking but rather in the acceleration of command of thinking.

## Ideal

is an imaged idea of a desire. An ideal is an active goal or objective that the thinker produces in his mind as thought. Beyond the idea of acquiring something, such as a house or job, an ideal transcends the physical limitations of desire in the thinker's contemplation of its meaning. An ideal for acquiring a house thus becomes a place to make a home; an ideal for a job becomes a vehicle for creativity, productivity, learning, and maturity. Ideals give the individual a reason to excel and promotes a sense of purpose in his or her activities.

## Ignorance

is a lack of awareness produced by the refusal to admit what is available in experiences at hand. The root word for ignorance is ignore. Disregarding facts is a form of ignorance. This leads to pretense, loneliness, deceit, and other forms of negativity which blind the individual to his or her potential. Neglect is also a form of ignorance which undermines the individual's capacity to respond with authority and understanding.

## Imagination

is the inventive quality of the conscious mind enabling innovation and spurring creativity. Imagination is the ability to conceive with thought what can be. It moves the individual beyond what has existed before, resulting in rapid growth and expanding consciousness toward wisdom. Imagination is a key to unlocking the creative genius in man.

## Information

is knowledge available through experience. Such knowledge is received primarily through the five physical senses, feeding the conscious mind, and is stored in the brain for future use. In order for the information acquired to remain useful during and beyond the lifetime it must be put into use, otherwise recall fades due to lack of attention or is dispelled when the brain no longer exists.

## Intuition

is the direct grasp of truth. Intuition is produced through the application of reasoning in the acquiring of understanding. When something is understood the individual's awareness embraces Universal Truth. For instance each individual sooner or later realizes that his thoughts are real; they have substance and energy and are the causal agent for the Self and the quality of the life. As understanding of this deepens, the individual makes the truth, "you are as you think" a part of Self. All subsequent thoughts include the awareness of this truth, reflecting in the individual's quality, direction, and calibre of thinking. He or she now demonstrates intuition, or the direct grasp of truth.

### Knowledge

is information applied to experience. Information must be made to be useful. This occurs through the action of reasoning. Information is drawn from the storehouse of the brain as memory. When the will is employed to use the information in the life, it becomes knowledge that can be of benefit. For instance, you can memorize the interpretation of dream symbols but for this to become knowledge it must be applied to your own dream experiences.

### Learning

is education and instruction afforded through experience. Learning is an extension of knowledge produced when the imagination is employed to move the awareness of Self beyond that existing presently. Learning adds to the resources available to the mind. Learning can take place in each division of mind. In the conscious mind learning increases the awareness by expanding the consciousness beyond previous limitations. In the subconscious mind learning takes on the form of adding understandings to the soul. In the superconscious mind learning is the fulfillment of the maturity of Self toward Enlightenment and compatibility with the Source of Creation.

### Levels of Consciousness

describe the unique combination of intelligence, energy, and substance which causes the development of thought and leads to its expression into a different form. There are seven distinct levels of consciousness available to man. Each level is defined by unique qualities in the expression of energy, and is interrelated with all other levels for the creation and ultimately the manifestation of thought. (See mind diagram)

### Life Force

describes the utilization of cosmic energy by a particular life form. Everything in creation is made of energy which pervades our universe, hence the term cosmic energy. When cosmic energy enters a physical life form, such as the human body, it becomes the energizing power that sustains life. Usually functioning according to Universal Law, energizing life force can be understood and harnessed, replenished and directed at will.

### Lucid Dreaming

describes the ability to become consciously aware during the dream state. With refined concentration, an individual can actively observe the dream as it is transpiring. Holding the conscious mind still enables the message to continue without interference, whether it be in the form of changing what is occurring in the dream or terminating the dream.

### Memory

is a temporary record of what has been consciously experienced that is impressed and stored in the brain. Memory provides a temporary storehouse of information, knowledge, experiences, and understandings that have transpired in the physical life of the thinker. Recall is the mental faculty for accessing this memory at will. The thinker identifies the nature and quality of a current experience by using will to draw upon information previously stored in the brain as memory.

### Mental Tools

are the mental mechanisms available to man. Each mental tool causes a particular ability to be accessed and used. Each can be honed into a skill. Examples of mental tools include: undivided attention, the ability to focus the mind on one point; recall, the ability to retrieve information gained in the past by accessing the brain's memory; and listening, the ability to receive projected thoughts and words.

### Mind

describes the structure and function of consciousness from its point of origin to its final expression in the physical. The mind is individualized intelligence expressing man's inner urge to become a creator. The three divisions of mind derive their distinctiveness from function, duty and purpose. The seven levels of mind are the result of successive transformations in the development of thought and its effects upon energy and substance. This diagram illustrates the form and structure of mind:

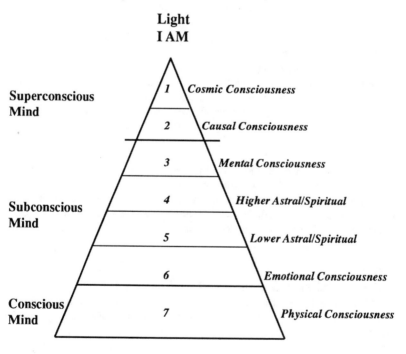

Light
I AM

Superconscious Mind

1  Cosmic Consciousness

2  Causal Consciousness

3  Mental Consciousness

Subconscious Mind

4  Higher Astral/Spiritual

5  Lower Astral/Spiritual

6  Emotional Consciousness

Conscious Mind

7  Physical Consciousness

## Nightmares

are repeated messages from the subconscious mind that have gone unheeded. A nightmare elicits an emotional reaction in the conscious mind causing the message or dream to be retained. Once the message is received and understood, the nightmares cease because there is no longer a need for subsequent messages to relay the old message.

## Perception

is the mind's capacity to receive, realize, and divine meaning of what is within and around Self. In order for input to be acknowledged, recognized and used, the mind must be directed toward what is being received either from the physical senses or the mental sense, attention. For perception to be accurate and truthful, it must be employed by command of conscious objectivity. Extrasensory perception is commonly used to describe the exceptional abilities beyond those tendered by physical senses. These are in the realm of telepathy or mind to mind communication, precognition, telekinesis, and so forth. All are abilities natural to the subconscious mind.

## Permanent Memory

is the lasting record of what has been understood that is impressed and stored in the soul. These understandings are relative to the ability to create with and by thought. Permanent memory provides a lasting storehouse of the wisdom necessary to become a mental creator.

## Physical

signifies the material, finite existence. It is the final expression and manifestation of creation, including all corporeal forms. The physical expression of man includes the conscious mind and conscious ego, the assertion of identity in the physical. The physical body is the vehicle temporarily used by man during a lifetime for the purpose of experiencing and gaining understandings of how to become a mental creator.

## Precognition

is the subconscious ability for foreknowledge of the probable future. Unlike the conscious mind, the subconscious mind is not subject to physical limitations of distance or time. The subconscious mind can clearly perceive the past, the present, and the probabilities of the future. What is perceived in the future is only a probability owing to one of the two principles found in every expression of creation — free will. With free will or volition, the anticipated outcome seen today can be changed before tomorrow.

## Productive Attitudes

are mental postures which further the quest for understanding and wholeness. An attitude is a particular arrangement of thoughts. Thoughts of worthiness, resourcefulness, compassion, love, peace, freedom, receptivity, aggressiveness, generosity, are examples of attitudes which are productive to the Self and others. Such ideas reflect understanding which produces a complete use of the Universal Laws of Creation resulting in harmony, cooperation, health, soul progression, and spiritual growth.

## Purpose

is the ability to conceive thought intentionally and deliberately. It is more than a reason for an idea; it is the mental impetus that fuels the idea into action. Ideals give the individual a reason to excel and promote a sense of purpose in his or her activities. Purpose makes any ideal uniquely significant to its creator. Purpose promotes the growth and evolution of the Self through the accomplishment of ideals.

## Reasoning

is the power in the conscious mind which fosters inventiveness through the full use of memory, attention, and imagination. When reasoning produces an image of what is consciously desired, the subconscious mind will work to reproduce that desire. This mental process of creation is known as visualization and is man's ability to create with and by thought for the maturing of his awareness.

## Repetitive Dreams

occur when the same dream message is pertinent to the dreamer. These dreams may occur successively over several sleep periods or may occur at intervals of time. Once the dream is interpreted and a response is made which changes the dreamer's awareness, the repetitive dream will cease and new messages will arise.

## Self

describes the individual as a whole being: spiritually, mentally, emotionally, and physically. When the word is capitalized it denotes the full scope of man's consciousness, when it is lowercase it denotes the conscious, physical part of man only.

## Sleep

is that well-known state in which there is a suspension of the voluntary exercise of the powers of the body and conscious mind. Sleep is a time for rejuvenation of the mind and physical body. Characterized by the cessation of reception of incoming stimuli from external objects, sleep is a time for receiving stimuli from the inner, subconscious mind in the form of dreams.

## Sleep Walking

indicates the dreamer's attention is partially held on the physical body while the consciousness remains in the inner levels. Thus the dreamer remains inwardly alert and outwardly unaware of the movement of the physical body. Somnambulate: The act or practice of walking in sleep, resulting from a peculiar perversion of the mental functions during sleep. The same is true for *Sleep Talking.*

## Soul

is the vehicle for the subconscious mind. A storehouse of permanent understandings gained in the present lifetime or gleaned from prior physical existences. To the unaware, connection with the soul often comes in the form of conscience, the inner sense of what is right, or intuition, the direct grasp of truth. The soul is where the thinker exists before physical incarnation and after physical incarnation.

## Spirit

in its broadest definition is breath or life; the intelligence or mind of man. Spirit is the immaterial and immortal part of man. Being the vital and essential essence spirit also describes the vehicle for the superconscious mind.

## Subconscious Existence
is the state of being as experienced by the soul. Subconscious existence includes the state of being within the dreamer's subconscious mind; the recreative part of mind. Subconscious existence also indicates the condition of universal subconscious mind; the fact that all subconscious minds are connected.

## Subconscious Mind
is intelligence as it expresses in the inner levels of consciousness collectively known as the soul. The function of the subconscious mind is to recreate the conscious mind's imaged desires thus furthering experiences for learning. Its purpose is to permanently store understandings gleaned from conscious experiences. The power of the subconscious mind is intuition or the direct grasp of truth. The subconscious mind is the source of dreams. Other abilities natural to this part of mind include telepathy or mind to mind communication, precognition, telekinesis, and so forth.

## Superconscious Existence
is the state of being as experienced by the spirit. Here is the origin of man as a thinking being, made in the likeness and image of his Maker. Superconscious existence is the state of omnipresence, omniscience, and immortality.

## Superconscious Mind
is intelligence as it expresses in the innermost levels of consciousness collectively known as the spirit. The superconscious mind is the part of mind that is closest to the source, the Creator. Here rests the individual's inner authority and divinity. The function or duty of the superconscious mind is to supply the spark of life which animates the outer parts of mind. The purpose of the superconscious mind is to hold the seed idea for the thinker's maturity as a creator.

## Structure
indicates arrangement, design, or organization. Structure is the form or pattern which makes up the composition of anything. The structure of the human body is made of atoms, molecules, cells, tissues, and systems. Together these individual components comprise the human form in response to a genetic code found in the chromosomes which exist in every cell. The structure of the mind includes seven levels of consciousness, three divisions of mind, and the expression of individuality or ego, which reflect the organization of mind substance and the utilization of energy throughout consciousness. Together these individual components comprise the mind's form in response to the blueprint for maturity, a kind of spiritual genetic code, present in each individual.

## Unconscious
is the state of being unaware arising most often from ignorance. Information stored in the brain which is unused promotes a lack of awareness. Except in the case of remembered dreams, the state of sleep produces a lack of awareness in the conscious mind. Inattentiveness promotes unconsciousness in the waking life. What an individual re-

mains unaware of — whether thoughts, motivations, facts, or perceptions — reveals what, how, and why s/he is unconscious. Functioning from habit promotes this limited frame of mind.

## Understanding

is comprehension gained by direct perception. The perception is honed by experiencing what causes creation. Understanding is permanent knowledge which is stored by the soul. Where there is understanding of cause there is awareness, compassion, love, service, and enlightenment.

## Universal Laws

are the active principles which govern creation. They apply to anyone, anywhere, at anytime in our universe.

## Universal Mind

Universal mind describes the interconnectedness of all minds experienced in the inner levels of consciousness. The subconscious, intuitive ability for telepathy is an example of this interconnectedness which transcends physical limitations of time and space. The power of influence has its origin in the ability to send and receive thoughts through the energy and substance of universal mind.

## Universal Truths

are omnipresent facts relative to transcendent reality. Universal Truths describe the workings of Universal Laws. For example the Universal Truth "as above, so below" describes the Universal Law of Cause and Effect.

## Visualization

Visualization describes the mental process of creation. Visualization is a skill employing the conscious and subconscious minds which enables the individual to conceive a desired image and experience its manifestation. Visualization begins with the formation of "seed" ideas in the conscious mind. These ideas are then "planted" in the receptive, subconscious mind substance where they grow and mature to fruition or manifestation in the physical life of their creator.

## Will

A wish is a helpless desire; will power is the result of predetermined actions that bring about an imaged desire. Will power is always enacted toward the fulfillment of something. Will power is the ability to engage the will toward an imaged desire. It is a positive action of the mind that promotes growth and always leads to the fulfillment of a desire.

## Wisdom

is insight gained by the application of understandings. As a communication and rapport is built between the conscious mind and the subconscious mind, the individual aligns these minds thus gaining access to understandings stored in the soul. Consciously drawing upon these understandings in the waking life produces wisdom.

## Index of Images/Symbols appearing in Dreams

## About the Author

Born in New Orleans and reared in Missouri, Barbara Condron has served as an educator throughout her adult life. After earning a Bachelors of Journalism degree from the University of Missouri, she pursued her urge for spiritual knowledge through applied studies in metaphysics with the School of Metaphysics. Since earning all degrees offered by that not-for-profit educational institute, Dr. Condron has continued her association with the School in a wide range of positions and responsibilities as a way to serve the growing needs of humanity for spiritual enlightenment. In recognition of her varied accomplishments she is a biographee in Who's Who Among Outstanding Americans and the World's Who's Who of Women. A minister in the Interfaith Church of Metaphysics, Dr. Condron presented a seminar on *Spiritual Initiation: Gateways to Transcendent Consciousness* during the 1993 Centennial Parliament of the World's Religions held in Chicago. Whether teaching, lecturing, or writing about the development of man's potential as a creator, Dr. Condron has stimulated thousands to open their minds and hearts to greater Self awareness. She is international coordinator for the annual *National Dream Hotline*, an educational service consisting of fifty-six continuous hours of sharing dream research. When she is not traveling, Dr. Condron teaches on the campus of the College of Metaphysics, where she lives with her husband, Daniel, who is also a teacher, author, and administrator for the School of Metaphysics.

*Additional titles*
*available from SOM Publishing include:*

**The Universal Language of Mind:**
**The Book of Matthew Interpreted**
Dr. Daniel R. Condron   ISBN 0944386-15-6   $13.00

**Permanent Healing**
Dr. Daniel R. Condron   ISBN 0944386-12-1   $9.95

**Dreams of the Soul**
**The Yogi Sutras of Patanjali**
Dr. Daniel R. Condron   ISBN 0944386-11-3   $9.95

**Kundalini Rising**
**Mastering Your Creative Energies**
Dr. Barbara Condron   ISBN 0944386-13-X   $9.95

**Shaping Your Life**
**The Power of Creative Imagery**
Laurel Fuller Clark   ISBN 0944386-14-8   $9.95

**Total Recall**
**An Introduction to Past Life & Health Readings**
Dr. Barbara Condron, ed.   ISBN 0944386-10-5   $9.95

**Going in Circles**
**Our Search for a Satisfying Relationship**
Dr. Barbara Condron   ISBN 0944386-00-8   $9.95

**What Will I Do Tomorrow?  Probing Depression**
Dr. Barbara Condron   ISBN 0944386-02-4   $4.95

**Who Were Those Strangers in My Dream?**
Dr. Barbara Condron   ISBN 0944386-08-3   $4.95

**Meditation: Answer to Your Prayers**
Dr. Jerry L. Rothermel   ISBN 0944386-01-6   $4.95

**HuMan, a novel**
Dr. Jerry L. Rothermel   ISBN 0944386-05-9   $5.95

**Discovering the Kingdom of Heaven**
Dr. Gayle B. Matthes   ISBN 0944386-07-5   $5.95

**Autobiography of a Skeptic**
Frank Farmer   ISBN 0944386-06-7   $7.95

To order write:

**School of Metaphysics**
**National Headquarters**
**HCR 1, Box 15**
**Windyville, Missouri  65783**

Enclose a check or money order payable to SOM with any order.  Please include $2.00 for postage and handling of books, $5 for international orders.

A complete catalogue of all book titles, audio lectures and courses, and videos is available upon request.

## About the School of Metaphysics

*We invite you to become a special part of our efforts to aid in enhancing and quickening the process of spiritual growth and mental evolution of the people of the world. The School of Metaphysics, a not-for-profit educational and service organization, has been in existence for more than two decades. During that time, we have taught tens of thousands directly through our course of study in applied metaphysics. We have elevated the awareness of millions through the many services we offer. If you would like to pursue the study of mind and the transformation of Self to a higher level of being and consciousness, you are invited to write to us at the School of Metaphysics National Headquarters in Windyville, Missouri 65783.*

*The heart of the School of Metaphysics is a three-tiered program of study. Lessons introduce you to the Universal Laws and Truths which guide spiritual and physical evolution. Consciousness is explored and developed through mental and spiritual disciplines which enhance your physical life and enrich your soul progression. We teach concentration, visualization (focused imagery), meditation, and control of life force and creative energies. As a student, you will develop an understanding of the purpose of life and your purpose for this lifetime.*

*Experts in the language of mind, we teach how to remember and understand the inner communication received through dreams. We are the spon-*

*sors of the National Dream Hotline, an annual educational service offered the last weekend in April. Study centers are located throughout the Midwestern United States. If there is not a center near you, you can receive the first series of lessons through correspondence with a teacher at our headquarters.*

**There is the opportunity to aid** *in the growth and fulfillment of our work. Donations are accepted and are a valuable way for you to aid humanity by supporting the expansion of the School of Metaphysics' efforts. Currently, donations are being received for Project Octagon, the first educational building on the College of Metaphysics campus. The land for the proposed campus is located in the beautiful Ozark Mountains of Missouri, less than four hours from St. Louis and Kansas City, and one hour north of Springfield. The four-story octagon design will enable us to increase headquarters staff and enrollment in our College workstudy program. This proposed multipurpose structure will include an auditorium, classrooms, library and study areas, a cafeteria, and potential living quarters for up to 100 people. We expect to finance this structure through corporate grants and personal endowments. Gifts may be named for the donor or be designated as an ongoing memorial fund to a family member or special friend. Donations to the School of Metaphysics are tax-exempt under 501 (c) (3) of the Internal Revenue Code. We appreciate any contribution you are free to make. With the help of people like you, our dream of a place where anyone desiring Self awareness can receive wholistic education will become a reality.*

**We send you our Circle of Love.**